CW01583882

Expressions From Yorkshire

Edited by Claire Tupholme

YoungWriters
First published in Great Britain in 2007 by:
Young Writers
Remus House
Coltsfoot Drive
Peterborough
PE2 9JX
Telephone: 01733 890066
Website: www.youngwriters.co.uk

SB ISBN 978-1 84431 279 5

Foreword

Young Writers was established in 1991 and has been passionately devoted to the promotion of reading and writing in children and young adults ever since. The quest continues today. Young Writers remains as committed to the nurturing of poetic and literary talent as ever.

This year's Young Writers competition has proven as vibrant and dynamic as ever and we are delighted to present a showcase of the best poetry from across the UK and in some cases overseas. Each poem has been selected from a wealth of *Little Laureates* entries before ultimately being published in this, our sixteenth primary school poetry series.

Once again, we have been supremely impressed by the overall quality of the entries we have received. The imagination, energy and creativity which has gone into each young writer's entry made choosing the poems a challenging and often difficult but ultimately hugely rewarding task - the general high standard of the work submitted ensured this opportunity to bring their poetry to a larger appreciative audience.

We sincerely hope you are pleased with this final collection and that you will enjoy *Little Laureates Expressions From Yorkshire* for many years to come.

Contents

The Poems

The Cat And The Dog

I took my pet to the vet.
He said my cat was too fat.
We sold the cat because it was too fat.
We got the dog sat on the log.
We took the dog for a walk.
On the way we taught him to talk.
We take him to the park.
When the full moon has appeared it's dark.
Then the dog starts to bark.
I think I'll call him Mark.

Sophia Kauser & Kimberley Hammill (11)
Abbey School

The Fish

The fish is dead.
I lost the fish.
I'm sad.
I liked it swimming about.
It was very nervous.
It swam away.
I'm sad about the fish.

Katie Hill (9)
Abbey School

My Fat Dog

The dog was fat.
He sat on the cat.
The cat was flat
and that was that.

Reece Duke, James Alderson (11)
& Georgia Mills (10)
Abbey School

The Bird

We found a bird.
It had a poorly tail.
We kept it in our house.
We used to give it bread.
We didn't have a cage.
It lived in a box.
The old printer's box
In the living room.
It flew away.
I was at my cousin's house.
When I got home I felt sad.

Ehteshaam Razaq (10)
Abbey School

Precious Pets

My best friend has a little dog
and her name is Tilly,
she jumps up and round and round
acting rather silly.

My friend's grandad has a cat
and her name is Gillian,
and even though she's rather fat
he thinks she's worth a million.

My little cousin has a pet
and his name is Peter,
she didn't really want a fish
but her mum said it was neater.

I have a dog and a cat
I have a fish as well,
I'd like to get a little mouse
but Grandma says they smell.

Amy Williams (7)
Ackton Pastures Primary School

Animals

The elephant stomps through the jungle . . .
Stomp, stomp, stomp!

The mouse tiptoes through the jungle . . .
Squeak, squeak, squeak!

The lion is the king of the jungle . . .
Beware, beware, beware!

The cheetah's on her hunt . . .
Run, run, run!

Gazelles are grazing . . .
Hush, hush, hush!

Crocs are in the river . . .
Snap, snap, snap!

Monkeys behind you . . .
Watch your lunch!

Keep an eye out for our animal bunch!

Melissa White (11)
Ackton Pastures Primary School

Brother Or Sister?

My mum is having a baby, my mum is having a baby.
I wonder what it will be? A boy? A girl?
It really doesn't matter to me.

Pink, blue, red, white, what colour will it like?
Will it like me or will it cry?

Now what will we call it? Chris, Phoebe, Zoë,
Kieran, Hannah, Matthew, Crystal.
My mum is going crazy just looking for a name!

I hope it's not called Owen because it will be a real shame.

Ben Boothroyd (11)
All Saints Harworth CE Primary School

The Dog's Barking

The dog's barking,
Mum's marking,
Dad's gone away,
I won't see him again today,
I can't wait until Sunday,
For my really fun day,
I go out to play,
The sun shines all day,
I had to come in,
It really was a sin,
When the moon comes out,
I never have a doubt,
The moon shines bright,
Floating in its own pool of light,
After that I go to bed
And I snuggle up to my ted.

Josh Waterhouse (10)
All Saints Harworth CE Primary School

The Girl With One Eye

The girl with one eye
Oh my, oh my.

It got so bad
She soon got mad.

She got so stressed
But now she's the best.

She now has two eyes
The shape of two beautiful pics.

Now she's so glad
She will now never be mad.

Maisie Clarke (10)
All Saints Harworth CE Primary School

The Monster Under My Bed

There's a monster under my bed
And I call him Fred
He's big and scary
And really, really hairy
His big yellow eyes
Are as big as pies
And two orange tongues
He must have big lungs
Because he breathes heavily all night
He sounds like he's trying to put up a fight.

One night I dared myself
To go under the bed
And see Fred
But you will never guess
When I got there he was . . . *dead!*
Oh no!
I mean *yes!*

Emma Wainer (11)
All Saints Harworth CE Primary School

My Pet Dog

I named my dog because he chased a lot of frogs,
All day long he ran and ran until he bumped into a tin can.
He plays and plays every day, never stops anyway.
He loves to play in the garden with his friends,
Twisting and turning around the bends.

Kimberley Goodlad (10)
All Saints Harworth CE Primary School

Bramall Lane

Bramall Lane,
Bramall Lane,
The very place to watch a football game.
Bramall Lane,
Bramall Lane,
Where the walls of Sheff United's stadium stands with fame.

Man Friday,
Man Friday,
It's where you eat on a footie day.
Man Friday,
Man Friday,
The place to buy chips and gravy,
But beware, do not wear navy.

Blades United,
Blades United,
Footie camp.
Where you can become a footie champ.
Blades United,
Blades United,
The team in which perfection is played.

So come on down to Sheff United's ground.
Where ennui (boredom) is never found!

Laura Walker (11)
All Saints Harworth CE Primary School

The Deserted Beach

As I wander through the rockpools, my thoughts turn to the sea,
That's the place, I thought, *where I really want to be.*
I keep on walking.

I can hear distant music, from a nightclub maybe, or a pub,
The odd shouts of laughter ring in my ears,
Probably old men laughing over their beers.
I keep on walking.

I am so close now; I can hear the water rushing
against the jagged rocks,
I can see the last boat arriving at the docks.
I am there, I stop walking.

The sun obviously set long ago.
I close my eyes and picture the ball of fire sat on the
smooth horizon.
I open my eyes, it's not really there, I know.
I sit down.

Sand crawls up my legs and sticks to them -
Why does it seem to get everywhere?
The smell of seaweed is hanging strangely in the thick air.

I turn around, heading for home.
Mum would be waiting.
But I wish I could stay here all night - all alone.

Zoë Firth (11)
All Saints Harworth CE Primary School

It's An Irish Dancing Thing!

Cross your legs,
Jump up high.
Why?
It's an Irish dancing thing!

Kick your bottom,
Don't be lazy.
Why?
It's an Irish dancing thing!

Lock your legs,
Do the splits.
Why?
It's an Irish dancing thing!

Hold your thumbs,
Don't go numb.
Why?
It's an Irish dancing thing!

Straighten those arms,
Don't go flying with your arms.
Why?
It's an Irish dancing thing!

Sit down,
Do what you're told.
Why?
It's an Irish dancing thing!
But why?
Because I said so.

Collette Eloise Patricia Ward (11)
All Saints Harworth CE Primary School

Pussy

My sweet, fluffy pussycat,
Enjoys sleeping on her light blue mat,
She's creamy coloured, like the cat queen,
This way, that way, what have you seen?
Purring calmly, rolling over,
Relaxing and looking at a four-leafed clover,
Comfy and cosy, lying in the sun,
Licking up my biscuits, last crumb.

When it was dark, I took her for a journey in the car,
My pussy sat there and looked at the biggest star,
I turned my radio on,
On our favourite song,
My pussy climbed up her seat,
And danced to the funky beat,
When we arrived at our little hotel,
We went to the counter and my pussy rang the bell.

The man came and gave us the keys,
My pussycat was so pleased,
Number 20, our favourite room,
It's time to give my pussy a groom,
We went upstairs, my cat jumped on the bed,
Then I gave her a stroke on her head,
My pussy is so wonderful,
I know that she will always rule!

Emily Howard (10)
All Saints Harworth CE Primary School

My Puppy

My little puppy so cute and small,
When you're older you will be tall.

My puppy is called Bliss
And everyday we have a kiss.

My puppy stares into my eyes,
Like an eagle searching the skies.

My puppy Bliss wags his tail fast,
Making a noise like a big blast.

My little puppy is so great,
If I ever lose him I will be in a big state.

Bliss's best mate, who is named Kate,
Plays all day with her garden rake.

Kate, Kate is white and brown,
She's always happy and never frowns!

Kate Beamish (10)
All Saints Harworth CE Primary School

Football Is My Favourite Thing

Football is my favourite thing,
I play it every single day.
I'm a striker.
I score loads of goals.

Tanner, Tanner, Tanner, you're so good at striking,
Striking, striking loads of goals.
Brad, Brad, Brad, you're so good all around,
Striking the most goals.
Keeper, keeper, keeper, you're so cool,
You never let any goal in, you're not a fool.

Tanner Scott (10)
All Saints Harworth CE Primary School

Leeds United

Leeds United to me are the best,
In a few years they'll beat all the rest,
When I go to Elland Road,
The fans are cheering a load,
When Leeds open up the score,
Letting out a huge roar.

The other fans are upset,
When none of their shots go in the net,
As the Leeds keeper saves them all,
The manager gets a call.

Then the second half gets underway,
And Leeds really start to play,
Leeds get a second goal
And opposition fans at home bang their heads on a pole.

Then the ref finally blows his whistle for full time
And some fans at home have a lime,
The fans are cheering for their favourite club,
Whilst having a drink at the pub.

Sam Dexter (11)
All Saints Harworth CE Primary School

Fat Cat

Cat, cat you are so fat,
I think you ate too much,
You eat all day
And you never play,
You really need to stop!

Lewis Hutchinson (10)
All Saints Harworth CE Primary School

That Dirty Little Lady

That dirty little lady,
Standing over there,

Picking her nose
And wiping it in her hair,

She thinks she's really pretty,
Miss, what's the problem?

You're not from New York City,
You're from Rotherham,

Well I don't really agree with that,
Miss, you're as ugly as a rat,

You pick it, lick it, roll it, flick it,
You make people really sad,

I am going to have to say,
Woman, your reputation is really bad.

Kieran Siddall (11)
All Saints Harworth CE Primary School

Headteacher Kennings

Chocolate lover,
Supply cover,

Loud talker,
Corridor stalker,

Fancy dresser,
Quick guesser,

Detention giver,
Makes me shiver,

Staff bosser,
Penny tosser.

Libby Hodgkiss (9)
Altofts Junior School

My First Time On The Beach

I got in the car, I knew we'd be driving far,
I couldn't wait to get there,
I stepped out of the car when we got there,
I walked on the sand holding my mum's hand,
I was excited, the sea was amazing,
I ran down to the sea, running with glee,
I took my clothes off, my top and shorts,
I whipped my swimming cossie on,
I walked in,
It was cold but I still loved it,
I was in there for ages,
I was having so much fun,
Then my dad came,
It was time to go home,
I didn't want to go home
But I knew it had been the best day ever.

Laura Jackson (10)
Altofts Junior School

Springtime

S pring is when all the flowers come out.
P rancing grasshoppers in the fields.
R acing children doing sports day.
I ce lollies to cool us down.
N ew lives, baby lambs being born.
G round covered in fresh grass.

Samantha Bailey (9)
Altofts Junior School

Headteacher Kennings

Work marker
Nosey parker

Teller offer
Bully stopper

Housepoint cheater
Chocolate eater

Posh talker
Corridor stalker

Detention giver
Makes me quiver.

Niamh Walton (9)
Altofts Junior School

Lambs

L ambs come out, frisky play
A ll the sheep are waiting
M arch is the month to be born
B aa go the newborn fleeces.

Lucy Bennett (8)
Altofts Junior School

A Dream

A dream can be joyous,
angry or sad.

A dream can be happy,
a rage or mad.

A dream can be
someone's life.

A dream can be a battle
or maybe a fantasy.

James Morton (9)
Altofts Junior School

A Volcano Is Like . . .

A volcano
is like an erupting mountain.
A volcano
is like an angry god.
A volcano
is like a rocky hill.
A volcano
is like a sea of molten lava.
A volcano
is like a pump of lava.
A volcano
is like God's heater.

Nathan Sawyer (9)
Altofts Junior School

Mack And His Sack

There once was a man called Mack,
He always slept in a sack,
The other day,
He ran away
And swore he'd never come back.

Harry Broadhead (8)
Altofts Junior School

Snow

Snow, snow, snow,
Oh so wonderful snow.
Snow, white and fluffy,
Oh snow, snow, snow.

Samuel Edwards (10)
Altofts Junior School

A Day At The Park

I can hear children laughing,
Adults chatting as the sun beats down,
Animals barking the day away.
I can see the bright yellow sun,
Families having picnics in the shade,
Children playing sports together,
I can feel the atmosphere on this hot day,
The soft, dry, warm ground,
The trees and climbing frames.
I can smell hot food stands
And the blossom on the trees,
My tastebuds awaken with the various foods.
Frosted canned drinks seem so refreshing.
Quick, lick your ice cream
It's melting with the warmth of the sun.
These are the days where memories are born.

Rhys Pedder (10)
Altofts Junior School

Dreams

D ay ones and night ones
R un away to magical lands
E xplore the world by horse and carriage
A world where everything seems possible
M agical unicorns with twirly horns
S kimming the waves on dolphins.

Now I awake, my dream is finished.

Eleasha Bell (9)
Altofts Junior School

Autumn Time

Autumn time is very true - every time I see you.
As autumn time was passing by the wind blew away.
When I heard that terrible news then I ran away.

I was very sad sitting on the bench
Then I looked away, staring at the little fence.
Suddenly I felt much better, now the wind is back again.

Autumn time is very good but in autumn when I feel down . . .
I stare down at the ground
Then I look at the bottom of the world.

Megan Leary (8)
Altofts Junior School

In The Spring

The rabbit is good at eating
In the spring.

The rabbit is good at drinking
In the spring.

The rabbit is good at running
In the spring.

The rabbit is good at hopping
In the spring.

The rabbit is good
At *everything!*

Kennedy Nuttall (9)
Altofts Junior School

Wedding Whoo

I got in the car,
we would go far,
far for the wedding.
My hair all done, my dress all nice.
What will happen at the wedding?
With jewel-white shoes and fancy flowers,
what will happen at the wedding?
Walking down the aisle,
I see familiar faces,
all smiling at me.
What will happen at the wedding?
I sit there uncomfortable,
while they say their vows
And exchange their rings.
This is what happened at the wedding.

Olivia Ellis (9)
Altofts Junior School

The Sun Shines

The sun shines
like a torch in the black room.

It shows you the way
when you're lost or afraid.

It shines to show you
the way to safety.

It's the light of your life
so don't insult it or you will regret it.

Jodie Mae Brown (9)
Altofts Junior School

The Seaside In Summertime

At the seaside I can see all the golden sand,
the different coloured parasols.
I see the deep, dark sea.
There is an ice cream van that has stopped next to a beach.

I can feel all the scalding hot sand,
the cold salty seawater as it touches my feet.
I can feel the warm sun beating on me.

I can hear the children splashing about in the deep sea,
I hear children screaming for ice cream,
I hear the seagulls squawking for food.

I can smell the ice cream and all the different flavours,
I smell the salty seawater on the sandy shore,
I can smell a rubber beach ball.

I can taste the horrible salty water splash into my mouth,
I can taste sweet, sugary ice cream,
I also taste lovely, bubbly Coca-Cola.

Charlotte Brookes (10)
Altofts Junior School

On The Beach

On the beach the sun shines bright,
all day long, all day and night.

Lovely bright fish in the sea,
swimming as fast as can be.

Glittering shells on the shore,
I keep collecting more and more.

I wish I could stay all day,
but soon it's time to go home again.

Megan Owen (8)
Altofts Junior School

Raspberry Sharing

Raspberries are healthy,
lovely and sweet,
go and pick one,
it's such a treat.
Eat one, two, three and four,
can't stop, got to pop
and give one to next door.

Caitlin Madeley
Altofts Junior School

Grandad

Grandad gives a great big cheer
While he drinks his pint of beer.
He plays with you
And tickles you too.
He loves to watch the telly,
Which is making him have a rather fat belly!
He gives you such a lovely greeting,
You just can't wait for your next meeting.

Olivia Blankley
Altofts Junior School

My Big Sister Becki

She's a boyfriend dumper.
She's a computer queen.
She's a cruel champion.
She's 12 o'clock.
She's poison ivy.
A glass of flat Coke.
She's snow.

William Wedgwood (10)
Altofts Junior School

My Grandad

He's a volcano waiting to erupt,
A bouncing rabbit,
He's a jolly Christmas Day,
He's a jumping chair,
He's the sound of singing at dawn,
He's a happy clown,
He's an artist.

Leah Watts (9)
Altofts Junior School

My Goldfish

He's as quick as a flash, it's really ridiculous.
He circles around, it's really obvious.
Sometimes he splashes water, it's notorious.
Every day he eats, you could say it's continuous
But at night he's very marvellous.
He looks around his bowl, he's very curious.
When he doesn't get fed he gets very furious.

Regan Crawshaw (10)
Altofts Junior School

Snow, Snow

Snow, snow, jump in the snow.
Snow, snow, why doesn't it stop?
Throwing snowballs to each other.
Snow, snow, please don't stop!

James Matthews (10)
Altofts Junior School

The Playground

At the sound of a bell
all the children yell.

They scream and shout
as they all run out.

Football and toys
amuse the boys.

Dances and twirls
amuse the girls.

Round the playground the dinner ladies walk
watching the children as they talk.

When the bell rings again
all the children wane.

Alexandra Callaghan (8)
Altofts Junior School

Cheetah

Meat eater,
Game cheater,

Jungle hater,
Animal slater,

People shocker,
Meat stocker,

Prey pouncer,
River bouncer,

Black dotted,
Never spotted.

Charlotte Fountain (9)
Altofts Junior School

My Day

My great day,
My great day,
The day I would hate to start again.

Man U lose,
We're on a cruise,
Singing a song,
Nothing goes wrong.

My great day,
My great day,
The day I would hate to start again.

Then on the cruise,
The comfort we lose,
Chelsea win,
Title in the bin.

My bad day,
My bad day,
The day I want to start again.

The day gets worse,
Arsenal give a curse,
The curse won't go away,
It's gonna be a long day.

My bad day,
My bad day,
The day I want to start again.

Liverpool lose,
Now there's no cruise,
I got a letter, the day never got better
And that's my day.

Michael Hill (9)
Altofts Junior School

School Alphabet Poem

A is for art we do every day.
B is for board, we write what we say.
C is for chalk we use on the board.
D is for display, we never get ignored.
E is for extra work, naughty kids do.
F is for friends that we talk to.
G is for guests, they come as they please.
H is for hilarious children that sneeze.
I is igloo we made in art.
J is for Jack who's friends with Bart.
K is for kajumps we do in PE.
L is for lipstick all the teachers wear.
M is for Mum who picks me up from school.
N is for naughty children (kids rule!).
O is for, 'Oh no!' said that kid.
P is for pencil which has no lid.
Q is for quarrelling, everyone does.
R is for reception, includes every one of us.
S is for security, on all day and night.
T is for teacher who gives us a fright.
U is for you and me, we play all day.
V is for violet flowers at play.
W is for water in the cloakroom.
X is for x-ercise we do in the room.
Y is for yell that Zak always does.
Z is for zoo that Year 5 go to.

Astrid Tate (8)
Altofts Junior School

Cross Country

Nine o'clock on the dot,
Right, you miserable lot,
Silence! Tie your running shoes,
I have a muddy field waiting for you.

There's the door, out you go!
Yes, I know there's a storm
But I'm staying here,
All nice and warm.

After a while,
Where's Kyle?
He has gone for a walk,
Instead of a talk.

What's this? A note?
You've broken your leg?
I'm not falling for this,
So you can hop instead!

Jessica-Mae Field (9)
Altofts Junior School

Monster Kennings

Mega muncher,
Bone cruncher,

Children eater,
Flesh seeker,

Body beater,
Man cheater,

Extremely mean,
Ultra green,

Animal stalker,
Strange walker.

Dylan Holmes (9)
Altofts Junior School

On The Plane

At the airport you always
See people talking.
While my brother watches planes
I play PSP games.

When we get the ticket,
On the big screens I watch cricket,
On the planes there are no fun games.

I looked down at the ground
And I looked all around.
I see litter in the bins
While my dad sits drinking bitter in tins.

While we're over the sea
I'm drinking a cup of tea.

I fall asleep.

I woke up and saw everything and didn't care
I looked out a minute again and realised . . .

We were there!

Ian Nuttall (10)
Altofts Junior School

The Odd Classroom

I went in for a pen or two
and out jumped a kangaroo.
I didn't expect such a sight,
I nearly died of fright.
I only went in for a pen
then he gave me a big fat hen.
He turned out to be a nice chap
and pulled two pens from his hat!
Then he placed them in my hand
and jumped off playing his one man band.

Joe Stanley (10)
Altofts Junior School

Football Fever

Sound of studs on rock-hard ground,
Screaming chants from the crowd.

A ball goes high into the air,
The defenders have a look of despair.

A bounce and a bump too many,
The ball, it skips along fast and merry.

Our goalie reaches across his arm,
Gloves stretched out as if to charm.

The ball back into his safe hands,
The supporters clap and raise the stands!

Joseph Chawner (10)
Altofts Junior School

Dragons

Enormous wings
swooping high in the sky,
scaly tail
stamping down on the ground.

Piercing eyes
within a dark damp cave,
fiery breath
to warn slaying knights.

Smoke bellowing out
as a knight swings his sword,
stabbing its body
through its scales of a greeny-brown colour.

Long-lost creature,
mystical times,
legends dying
along with the knights.

Luke Humphries (9)
Altofts Junior School

Summer At The Seaside

People sunbathing and putting suncream on.
Children splashing in the water excitedly.
Hear waves clashing against each other.
People talking, children laughing and screaming.
Smell the mouth-watering fish and chips.
The smell of suncream flowing through the air.
Feel the soft sand sliding through your fingers.
Soft feel of towels as you unfold them.
The taste of fatty foods and the awful taste of sea saltwater.

Amy Goldfinch (10)
Altofts Junior School

Summer In The City

Large tall buildings block out the sun.
Children playing in the park.
Stood in the traffic in the burning heat.
Wish I was somewhere else.
People rushing about in lunch
Trying to grab a few rays.
I wish I was on a beach on hot summer days.
No fun summer in the city
Shame, I hear . . . oh what a pity.

Brandon Batty (9)
Altofts Junior School

Happiness

Happiness is bright and light like the sun.
It smells like melted stringy cheese from a pizza.
Happiness tastes like a fully cooked warm English breakfast.
Happiness sounds like children having fun on a trampoline.
Happiness lives in a fairy castle far, far away.

Rachel Proctor (10)
Altofts Junior School

The Air Show

The first thing you hear is the extreme noise of the jet engine.
You can see it zooming past you at 1800mph.
You can smell the sweet, sugary smell of candyfloss.
You can hear the buzzing of the toy aeroplane's propeller.
When you stop moving you feel the heat from the sun.
On the Tornado F3 you can smell and taste smoke coming
out of the back.
When you go home you can feel the freezing cold air conditioning
on your face as you drive off.

Gregory Betts (9)
Altofts Junior School

Days In A Week

Monday, I wore tights and gave my friends a fright.
Tuesday, I wore green and I certainly could be seen.
Wednesday, I wore pink and made my fishes sink.
Thursday, I wore black and took Santa's sack.
Friday, I wore blue and helped my friends too.
Saturday, I wore red and then I wet my bed.
Sunday, I wore gold then I felt old.

Leah Williams (9)
Altofts Junior School

Betty

There once was a girl called Betty,
That ate a bowl of spaghetti,
She exploded like a bomb,
And in a flash she was gone,
And that was the end of Betty.

Amy Martin (8)
Altofts Junior School

Summertime

Summertime is so much fun,
lying in the sun and helping your mum.
You can go to the seaside and eat ice cream,
get hit by a ball and maybe even scream!

Swim in the sea and splash around,
drop your purse and lose a pound!
Go on holiday and get pampered in your room
or go to the pub and play a bit of pool.

Go out on a night and get drunk,
or go to the zoo and see some chipmunks.
You can enjoy the summer at home in your house,
you might get a new pet or hear a new sound.

Enjoy your summer as much as you can,
and make sure you get a lovely suntan!

Laura Sambrook (10)
Altofts Junior School

The Lion

I look around,
Something's changed,
What's happened to me?
Why is my habitat different?
I want to be free,
I'm the king,
They should be scared.
I stand here,
I don't even know them,
I roar loudly,
People laugh.
I don't find it funny.

Samantha Watts (9)
Altofts Junior School

Toby

Four short legs and a wagging tail,
to make me smile he could never fail.

A ball or a bone he wouldn't play,
show him a teddy he was sure to stay.

Digging a hole turned his white fur black,
chewing up shoes nearly got him a smack.

Offer a doggie bone he wouldn't eat,
show him a biscuit he was at your feet.

Out in the park he didn't chase sticks,
he didn't dance, he couldn't do tricks.

But he was the best friend with four legs that I've ever had,
he's gone now and that makes me very sad.

Daniel Bletcher (10)
Altofts Junior School

I'm As . . .

I'm as happy as a hippo,
Dancing in the sea.

I'm as graceful as a butterfly,
As beautiful as can be.

I'm as playful as a lion cub,
Running through the trees.

I'm as cute as a puppy dog,
Without the itchy fleas.

I'm as fiery as a fire,
Going up and down.

I'm as nice as my grandad,
Who does not like to frown.

Chelsey Mitchell (10)
Altofts Junior School

The Sun

I love to play in summertime,
Staying out all day in the sunshine,
Wearing only shorts and a vest,
Forget coats, wellies and all the rest.

Playing all day in the swimming pool,
Having ice cream and drinks to keep us cool,
Winter nights seem so long and drab,
Summertime makes everyone feel so fab.

Sam Matthews (10)
Altofts Junior School

Bluebird

Bluebird, bluebird in the sky
Bluebird, bluebird flying so high
Bluebird, bluebird why are you so shy?
Why don't you fly to me, why oh why?

Charlotte Gibbens (9)
Altofts Junior School

Skateboarding

Boards, boards
everywhere,
on the ground,
in the air,
on the wall,
on the floor.

Skateboarding goes high,
Skateboarding goes low,
Skateboards do this for show.

Liam Winn (9)
Altofts Junior School

When I Grow Up

When I grow up I want to be
a racing driver, fast and keen.

When I grow up I want to be
the greatest cricketer there's ever been.

When I grow up I want to be
a boxer, strong and mean.

When I grow up I want to be
a footballer on a field of green.

Adam Hoyle (10)
Altofts Junior School

Simpsons

My name is Bart,
I'm quite mischievous,
You could say I'm really ridiculous.
People might think I'm quite spontaneous,
Then I get strangled by Homer,
Which is really ridiculous.

Bradley Collinson (10)
Altofts Junior School

Summer At The Beach

The sun shines down as I turn brown,
as I eat my sandy sandwich spitting sand out.
I hear screaming children getting a chill
but the best thing is playing with my friends
on a hot summer's day.

Morgan Murphy (9)
Altofts Junior School

Alphabet Sports

A is for athletics, you begin to gasp.
B is for badminton, you've got to get there fast.
C is for croquet, it is very posh.
D is for diving, you get a lot of dosh.
E is for elephant polo, don't fall off.
F is for football, don't catch a cough.
G is for golf, try and get a hole-in-one.
H is for hockey, on the ground stay on.
I is for ice hockey, slippy and slidy.
J is for javelin, don't get it too widey.
K is for kick-boxing, kicking a lot.
L is for long jump, oh no my PE kit I forgot.
M is for monkey bars, straining your arms.
N is for netball, a ball in your palms.
O is for ocelot training, very scary.
P is for polo, don't do it if you're wary.
Q is for quail catching, yum-yum.
R is for racing, 'I'm so fast,' say some.
S is for sumo wrestling, they're very fat.
T is for tennis, no good for a cat.
U is for unicycle racing, very wobbly.
V is for volleyball, don't play on ground which is cobbley.
W is for white-water rafting, a bumpy ride.
X is for x-ray fish fishing, catch one in pride.
Y is for yak riding, they're very fast.
Z is for zebra racing, make the moment last.

Alice Paylor (10)
Archbishop of York's Junior School

Tsunami Disaster

Screaming floods the air,
Sun beating down, white hot,
Benign blue water rippling on the sand,
A fine line of breeze.

Born to swim, the sea chuckles softly,
It is a lifelong comrade,
Children splashing joyfully, enjoying their holiday,
The sky, a crystal clear diamond, sparkling brightly.

Then, all at once, it happened,
Crashing waves and screaming people,
Running for their lives.

Waves flooding 20 feet high,
Pounding on the shore,
Trees and vehicles swept away,
Innocent people made to pay.

Grieving people searching sorrowfully,
Children buried under mounds of rubble,
Dead bodies float ashore,
Over 250,000 dead.

On December 26th 2004,
People gave pity to the earth,
A heartfelt cry goes out to all,
To those that still suffer today.

Rhys Hargreaves (11)
Armthorpe Southfield Primary School

The Gorilla

The mighty gorilla is like the four seasons,
One minute it is calm and quiet,
The next it is fearsome and strong.

When the gorilla is separated from its family,
It screams
Like a little girl having a nightmare.

The gorilla's black eye
Is the starry dead of night.

It swings from branch to branch
With its face held high
Like a roaring lion.

It's an animal proud of its hairy chest
And its silver back.

The gorilla's life slowly and painfully
Comes to an end,
It leaves its loved ones behind.

Jennifer Griffiths (11)
Armthorpe Southfield Primary School

Tsunami's Victory

The air, the sea a lifelong comrade.
Benign blue water rippling on the sand.

But then there was a big shock,
A twenty-foot wave came over
And nothing could be seen.

The wave destroyed everything that got in its path.
At the start people laughing then screaming
And fighting for their dear lives.
Loving families turn into helpless families
And pray to the sea;
Born to swim, the sea chuckled lightly,
A fine line of breeze hits.

Before they knew it the tsunami was over
But left scattered bodies on the beach.
Parents holding their dead children.
The tsunami was a day that left
Sri Lanka and the entire world in shock.

Tsunami had hit Sri Lanka.

Jacob Hallas (10)
Armthorpe Southfield Primary School

The Tsunami Disaster

The warm breeze whooshing in your face,
The bright light gazing in your eyes,
The sound of laughter
Of the children playing in the sea.

But all of a sudden the sky went grey,
The waves started getting stronger and stronger,
There were people running
And screaming for their lives!

The waves were getting closer and closer
And there was panic everywhere.

When the waves started to calm down
The town was left empty,
Only a few people survived.

Molly Stevenson (10)
Armthorpe Southfield Primary School

Tsunami

A soft stream of water came gushing in gently
The next swipe - a wave of slaughter and chaos
It left our world empty.

It left us buried in our sandy graves.

The palm trees sighed in the air
As the waves crushed anything in despair!

It was a war we could not fight
It left us all in a lot of fright.

Mother Nature turned from a friend to foe
Comrade to enemy, when the tsunami hit.

It left us in despair
It took away all that was there.

Josh Jipson (11)
Armthorpe Southfield Primary School

Tsunami Poem

A lifelong fear, barely heard,
A silent, dead, ancient word,
Has rewritten its name into the dictionary,
A name, an icon of misery . . .

People laughed, played, they even cheered,
But lay dead in the ocean's grisly beard . . .
A wall of destruction, chaos, hell,
Women, children, people fell . . .

The whirling wave,
Upon that day,
Wiped clean men's lives,
Many gone astray . . .

That sunny day, how bright it shone,
A perfect paradise,
Was silenced in an instant,
A scene of evil demise . . .

The powerful flood broke many hearts,
Parents and children fell apart,
But we'll live on; our hearts will stay strong,
We'll keep on singing through hope and song . . .

On 26th December, Boxing Day, people of the world gave pity,
To the destruction and death of many lives,
Upon Banda Ache, our great city . . .

Adam Thornton (11)
Armthorpe Southfield Primary School

My Cousin Jack

He giggles like a hyena
As lovely as a lion
Always hungry as an elephant
Likes playing games
He's as fast as a cheetah
Most of all he loves chips.

Harry Betson (10)
Charnock Hall Primary School

My Friend Harry Dixon

He's always as funny as a monkey,
As bright as the sun,
He's a fizzy drink,
Always on the run,
He's like a mini army troop,
As daft as a dog,
Most of all he's a rampaging rhino.

Ryan Lee (10)
Charnock Hall Primary School

Mum

She smells as fresh as a rose
As healthy as a tomato
Her eyes are as green as grass
As fit as a cheetah
She can be a grumpy dog
As helpful as a nurse
As sweet as candy.

Amy Dale (10)
Charnock Hall Primary School

My Best Friend Grace

Her smile is as bright as the sun
She laughs like a mad hyena
Eyes like the sea
Her hair is like a pig's tail
She's clumsy like Bambi
Crazy like a mad scientist
Most of all cheerful as a jack-in-the-box.

Florence Harrison (9)
Charnock Hall Primary School

My Friend Fraz

He's a fast cheetah
Hair like a hedgehog
A carrot lover
A funny entertainer
He's the next James Bond
As tall as an oak tree
A mini Cristiano Ronaldo
Most of all, a hard rock.

Daniel Kay (10)
Charnock Hall Primary School

My Brother Elliot

He's a mini mouse
As giddy as my dog
He's clean like a windscreen
He's a flexy ruler
As sweet as candy
A wobbly jelly
A sneaky fox
As cheerful as Santa
But most of all
He's a rapid rhino, rampaging.

Frasier Hill (10)
Charnock Hall Primary School

My Dad

He's fit as a fiddle
He's tall as a coconut tree
Playful as a dog
His eyes are like the blue sky
Bright as the sun
Mad about football.

Joseph Greene (10)
Charnock Hall Primary School

My Friend Bessie

She's an athlete
Hair like an orange
A comedian
The smell of strawberries
As small as a baby giraffe
As sweet as a piece of cake
She's a pale piece of paper
Most of all, she's a bouncy trampoline.

Fern Hitchen (10)
Charnock Hall Primary School

My Best Friend

He's as happy as a hyena
He's always on the go
As cool as a cucumber
A rampaging buffalo
As tough as a wall
As happy as can be
He's as long as a crocodile
And he's as bouncy as a ball.

Alex Evans (10)
Charnock Hall Primary School

My Mum

She's as sweet as an angel
A kind parent
Not a wicked witch
A fizzy drink
A chocolate lover
She is my mum and I love her so
But she can be as shy as a mole.

Tekisha Winstanley (10)
Charnock Hall Primary School

Holiday

H olidays are great if you've got a hot date.
O n the beach is a bit of a treat.
L ooking at your tan, you will probably need a fan.
I ce lollies in the breeze make you wobble your knees.
D ays out are fun if you have a lot of sun.
A long the sand families walk hand in hand.
Y esterday I was in Spain, today I am on the plane.

Gemma Austin (11)
Charnock Hall Primary School

Chocolate

My favourite food is chocolate
the sweet scent I adore
and when I have a little bit
I just want more and more!
My favourite food is chocolate
I take one bite and just can't stop
out of all the food varieties
chocolate is top!

Joe Potts (11)
Charnock Hall Primary School

Fraz

He's as fast as a cheetah
As funny as a monkey
Bright as the sun
He's as fit as a fiddle
Strong as a lion
Most of all, he's a sharp eagle.

Marc Gray (10)
Charnock Hall Primary School

Orange

Orange is a fire on Bonfire Night.
Orange is an ice lolly fresh from the freezer.
Orange is a sunset in the night sky.
Orange is a peach, all juicy and sweet.
Orange swims around the tank like a goldfish.
Orange is a bright flower growing in the grass.
Orange can be anything you imagine!

Hannah Sargent (11)
Charnock Hall Primary School

Ode To A Pan

Oh pan, oh pan
you fry my food so greasy and fine
your glorious shape is so divine
all black and grey, you make my day
every time I cook you lead my way
put it in the pan, it's nice and quick
that tasty bacon is juicy and thick
wake up in the morning, your pan is there
there's some glorious food for people to share.

Ellin Drewry (11)
Charnock Hall Primary School

SATs

S ilence as the teacher gives our papers,
A nxious looks on pupils' faces,
T ension in my brain like a panic attack,
S ATs have begun; no turning back.

Lydia Fay (11)
Charnock Hall Primary School

Summer

S is for soon we'll be moving up to secondary school.
U is for upset about leaving primary school.
M is for moving on in life.
M is for me, enjoying myself all summer.
E is for ecstatic about the long break.
R is for reading books, revising for my new life.

Ashley Wilson (11)
Charnock Hall Primary School

Bikes

B is for bouncing on the bumps,
I is for indicating left and right,
K is for kicking the pedals round and round,
E is for extreme off-roading, having fun,
S is for safety first - always wear a helmet!

Declan Naylor (11)
Charnock Hall Primary School

Leaving Primary

When we leave primary,
we will always think of you,
we think you're great,
we think you're good,
we don't know why,
but we've got to say bye.

James Moore (10)
Charnock Hall Primary School

Brown Horse

Brown horse standing in the meadow
Head held high
Foal standing by her side
Hiding behind Mum, small and shy
Manes running down their backs
In the distance, a flowing tide
Fisherman waiting for a catch
While the rabbits are playing in the hatch
Grass blowing in the wind
Hay bales rising
While the farmer gathers crops
The faintest mooing of cows can be heard
The food basket is overflowing
The trees are dancing in the breeze
A wagon is rotting in a corner of a field
A ladybird is flying through the air
The horse's swishing tail making flies fly away
The sun is slowly setting over the hill.

Lilly Reynolds (10)
Charnock Hall Primary School

My Best Friend Nicole

Her eyes are green as grass
As helpful as a doctor
Healthy as an apple
She's got red rosy cheeks
Bright as the sun
Clever as a mouse
And always as cheerful as Santa.

Laura Jones (10)
Charnock Hall Primary School

Trains

T rains are wicked to me and some of my mates.
R ailways are my thing whether they are old or new.
A train journey will always make me happy for the day.
I can't resist a train going past me at full pelt.
N ewer models will still fascinate me and so will older ones
with a snorting sound.
S illy boys who don't like them much - but I'm still friends
with them.

Adam Barber (11)
Charnock Hall Primary School

Shopping

Today I'm going shopping,
It's only down the road,
I can't wait to get there,
I'm going to spend a load.

Tell me what to buy,
Jewellery, like a ring,
For tonight I'm going
To a concert to sing.

I'm going to have my dinner,
I don't know what to eat,
In fact, some chicken soup
While I'm sat upon my seat.

I think it's a goodbye,
It's time for me to go,
I've got everything I want
So I don't feel low.

Alex White (10)
Charnock Hall Primary School

My Mate

My best mate's cool
like a cat on hot bricks
loves to get sticky
but mud's so icky
loses everything she gets
she's got two pet cats
likes wearing pet shirts
when silly she's always getting hurt
pink's cool but lilac's cooler
she's a bit of a fooler
she's quite a good dancer
but an excellent pouncer
every day a smile spreads on her face
she is oh so ace
Riding's to the end
she's my best friend
when things get muddled
she sticks at it
funny as a frog
Angel's her dog
creative and drawing lover
mega speedy and cheers you up
I'm sure you can guess
this is my best mate Bekky.

Lydia Watters (10)
Charnock Hall Primary School

22 Facts On Fiona

She's very crazy
She's never lazy
Her hair is brown
She acts like a clown
She always carries chewing gum
She's really, really, really fun
She's 'kid film' mad
She's never sad
We always go to the cinema
My dad always takes us in the car
She never checks her emails
You'll always catch her in the sales
She's always on a footie pitch
She hates my impression from 'Lilo and Stitch'
She loves chips, in special dips
Her American accent is really great
She really makes a perfect mate
Line dancing is her thing
She doesn't really like to sing
We always talk about my school
She'll always be nice to you
Did I mention she's 22.

Holly Ramsay (10)
Charnock Hall Primary School

Deep In Grandad's Cupboard

Deep in Grandad's cupboard
where he keeps his socks and pants.

Deep in Grandad's cupboard
where he keeps his book of chants.

Deep in Grandad's cupboard
where it's as dark as night.

Deep in Grandad's cupboard
you'll get a fright.

Deep in Grandad's cupboard
where there's a golden racket.

Deep in Grandad's cupboard
where there's the code, you must crack it.

Alastair Shephard (10)
Charnock Hall Primary School

School Trip

I can't get to sleep tonight,
Tell me what to do,
I'm worried about my trip
And I really need the loo.
Good morning everyone,
Today is the day,
The bus is going to be rough,
Oh I wish it wasn't the third of May.

Maybe I could miss the bus
And pretend I'm sick at home,
But then again it wouldn't be great,
I'd be sat there all alone,
Maybe I should forget about it
And on the bus take a kip,
In fact I've decided,
I'm going to enjoy my school trip.

Lucy-Mae Bashforth (10)
Charnock Hall Primary School

Why?

Why do we have to get up?
To brush our teeth and hair.
Why do we have to drink out of a cup?
To drink tea and coffee.

Why do we have to go to school?
To learn to read and write.
Why do we have to obey a rule?
To be sensible, to avoid trouble.

Why do we have to go to work?
To make money and friends.
Why is work such a jerk?
To be an idiot, to be a fool.

Why do we have to sleep?
To not to be tired and fall asleep.
Why do we store things in a heap?
To waste space and to not be tidy.

Daniel Parlett (10)
Charnock Hall Primary School

Maxx

Maxx is the motorbike master
He is as funny as a joke book
Slow as a snail
As daft as a headless chicken
But as beastly as a dragon
Hungry like a hippopotamus
As cheerful as a cheetah
Smells like sugar
As strong as Clinton Woods
Can swim as good as a seal.

Harry Lidster (9)
Charnock Hall Primary School

It's All About Friends, It's All About Charlotte!

She's cooler than cool,
She thinks boys drool,
She's fab at cricket,
I can never hit her wicket.

She's got a fab trend
And she's my best friend!

She makes me laugh
And she's as tall as a giraffe!

She's a bed head
And is really quite a chatterbox,
She also has the brain of a very clever fox.

That is my friend and it will stay like this for evermore,
It has been like that since we were four!

Her thing is pink,
Her theme is prawn crackers.

She's be great for playing 'Stan Laurel'
Because she's quackers!

It's all about friends,
It's all about Charlotte!

Lidia Bell (10)
Charnock Hall Primary School

Best Friend

Swims as good as a mermaid,
And as fast as a minnow fish,
A brill friend with her bright gold door always open for me,
She's as ticklish as a puppy,
When she laughs you can't help but laugh too,
She's as smart as a dolphin,
As funny as a clown,
As light as a feather.

Charlotte Arnold (9)
Charnock Hall Primary School

My Best Friend

Normally your best friend is a dog,
But mine is just as bad but needs more training.
He can eat chocolate ice cream for the country
But he'll always save some for me - maybe not!
He acts like a loon,
He always watches SpongeBob cartoons!
That's my best friend.
He doesn't care how he dresses,
Or how much he messes!
He takes us on little trips,
We love to eat fish and chips
And he always has small kips.
His paintings are amazing,
You will often see him lazing.
He knows some really bad jokes,
Knows hundreds of folks . . .
That's my best friend,
Uncle Howard!

Charlotte Turner (10)
Charnock Hall Primary School

Warwick

He's a cat on a hot brick
He's football mad
He's loves riding his bikes
He loves reading books
He likes watching Doctor Who
Obsessed with Pokèmon
Goes hyper
Loves ICT
Likes Star Wars.

Joshua Heap (9)
Charnock Hall Primary School

My Dance Teacher

My dance teacher's called Kirsty,
She is always very thirsty.

After dancing all the time
She sometimes has a little wine.

Always ready to help,
When she does splits she gives a little yelp.

She is active like a puppy,
She helps with the super yuppy.

Never ever down,
As active as a clown.

Always jumpy as a frog
And as mad as a barking dog.

Olivia Ford (9)
Charnock Hall Primary School

Joe

He's as funny as a bunny
Never down, like a clown
A very good friend, there is never a bend
He likes lots of food when he's in the mood
He watches TV with glee
He is sometimes lazy but can be crazy.

Harry Hague (10)
Charnock Hall Primary School

Lydia

Lydia is a jack-in-the-box, a monkey,
even a clown,
she's a joke book and cheers you up
when you're feeling down.

She's a paper chain person
and sticks with her crew,
she's daydreamy, an artist
and tries anything new.

She's a rocket at running
and would win any race,
she is like a queen
because there is always a smile upon her face.

Elyse Bingham (9)
Charnock Hall Primary School

My Baby Brother

He's football mad,
Chocolate and custard creams too,
CBeebies lover,
He's as funny as a clown,
Speedy as a tortoise,
Plus runs in a very funny way,
A sleepy head,
His hair's like a bear,
Cute as a kitten
And always hungry.

Lewis Hobson (10)
Charnock Hall Primary School

My Grandad

He's a good cook
A joke book
He's a clown and golf crazy
And always lazy
His hair is grey and white
He is very, very bright
He's always like fizzy Vimto
Fizzy, fizzy, fizzy
Someone you can trust
You must meet him, you really must
The smell of sweets
But best of all he's my grandad.

Abbie Culf (10)
Charnock Hall Primary School

My Best Friend

She's a glamour puss
A shopaholic
Queen of glitter
She's a pretty girl
Amazing friend
Friendly and fun
A gossip glossy
She's my best friend
With a heart of gold.

Frances Smith (10)
Charnock Hall Primary School

Grandad Paul

He's always there when I need help
He's as chatty as a monkey
He's a really good crabber
Likes having chocolate cake
Rubbish at football compared to me
Likes playing cards with me
Likes playing on PS2 and PSP
But rubbish really
Loves beer and shandy
His flat is nice and tidy
And really good at rounders.

Charlie Caseley (10)
Charnock Hall Primary School

Josh

He's a cat on hot bricks
He's like a chatterbox
He never stops rollerblading
Hair is as bright as gold
Plays Star Wars 24/7
Likes quizzes
Likes playing out on his bike
Likes ICT
Likes comedy programmes
Likes watching Doctor Who.

Warwick Shepherd (10)
Charnock Hall Primary School

My Friend Joseph Laycock

As bright as a cherry,
As light as a feather,
A jumping joey,
A sharp hawk.
As healthy as a tomato,
As fizzy as a can of pop,
As cool as a dude.
Most of all he's my friend.

Harry Dixon (9)
Charnock Hall Primary School

My Friend Dan W

He's as fast as a Ferrari,
As thin as a pin
And his eyes are blue as the sky.
His hair is as brown as mud,
As mad as a monkey,
Also rushes like reeds.

Philip Hustler (10)
Charnock Hall Primary School

My Friend Florence

Her eyes are like sapphire Neptune,
A jumpy dolphin,
A wild elephant.
She's a joyful jolly clown,
Hair as golden as a sunflower,
As nice as a piece of fudge.
Most of all she's my best friend.

Grace Hustler (10)
Charnock Hall Primary School

Tammy And Candy

My little cat is as cute as can be,
leaping the garden, looking for me.
With her enormous emerald eyes and her purring fur,
she still likes to cuddle up on my knee.
My fat cat is as miserable as can be,
she won't come and play or sit on my knee.
She growls at bedtime and hisses at me,
the only time she's happy is when she's having her tea.

Helena Bottomley (11)
Charnock Hall Primary School

Daisy

There once was a girl called Daisy,
She was always very, very lazy.
She loved to eat fruit pastilles,
They made her have lots of funny hassles.
She was as scary as a rabbit,
Eating Dairylea Dunkers was her habbit.
She had brown curly hair,
She loved to stare at my hair.

Olivia Walker (10)
Charnock Hall Primary School

Green Springs

I went to Green Springs
I saw trees
The trees were rattling
Like rusty keys
I also saw some rabbits and geese
I had to phone the animal police.

Lewis Butcher (8)
Doncaster Road Primary School

Listen! What Can You Hear?

Listen! What can you hear?
The small sound of the wind rustling trees.
Listen! What can you hear?
The little bit of sighing in the sea.
Listen! What can you hear?
The autumn leaves falling off trees.
Listen! What can you hear?
The sound of a person coughing.
Listen! What can you hear?
The sound of people humming to the song.
Listen! What can you hear?
The sound of paint on the children's hands
Painting on the paper.

Rhiannon Kitching (6)
Doncaster Road Primary School

Listen!

Listen! What can you hear?
The tip-tap of a keyboard
typing letters to influence you.

Listen! What can you hear?
The creaking of an old spooky house door
being opened by an old lady.

Listen! What can you hear?
The whistling of the wind outside,
it makes you feel cold and shivery.

Eve MacDonald (6)
Doncaster Road Primary School

Listen!

Listen! What can you hear?
The wind rustling through the corn
making the leaves dance.

Listen! What can you hear?
The crackling campfire,
a deer calling.

Listen! What can you hear?
The hoot of an owl
swooping from tree to tree.

Listen! What can you hear?
A flower swaying
in the breeze.

Listen! What can you hear?
The laughter of children screaming and laughing,
cheering with happiness.

Listen! What can you hear?
The sounds of autumn,
incredibly near.

Amelia Gamble (7)
Doncaster Road Primary School

Listen! What Can You Hear?

Listen! What can you hear?
A mouse squeaking in a house.
Listen! What can you hear?
A twinkling star in the open sky.
Listen! What can you hear?
A pencil dropping on the floor.
Listen! What can you hear?
A football bouncing.

Jamie Farnsworth (7)
Doncaster Road Primary School

Happiness

She skipped in the room quickly with her lips a ruby-red,
Her teeth were a gleaming white,
Her eyes were like sapphires, bright blue and sparkly,
Her face was a bright red and was held high to the sky,
Her shoulders held back, her chin was really high,
The sun was shining a bright gold
And you could almost see the biggest smile on its golden face.

Bethany Horbury (8)
Doncaster Road Primary School

Spider

You may think I'm stupid
You may think I'm a fool
But I'm telling the truth
There's a spider on you.

It's on your back
So give it a whack
And now it's flat
And not coming back.

Callum Mellor
Doncaster Road Primary School

Ice Cream

Ice cream, ice cream, all fluffy and white
Ice cream, ice cream, what a delight
Ice cream, ice cream, bits and juice
Ice cream, ice cream, you can choose.

Elliot Foye (8)
Doncaster Road Primary School

Seaside

S eashells by the seashore
E agles flying in the clear blue sky
A dults lifeguard, taking care of children
S apphire blue sea
I ce cream is as cold as can be
D eep blue sea
E verybody enjoys a day at the seaside!

Brooke Fenton (9)
Doncaster Road Primary School

Bedtime

Bedtime is the best,
It's better than the rest,
You close your eyes
And get a big surprise,
Dreams come alive,
You won't believe your eyes,
In the morning you feel good,
Just like you should.

Bradley Lawrence (8)
Doncaster Road Primary School

Chips

Chips, chips go to your hips
Biscuits and buns go straight to your tums.
Sweets and treats can cause decay
So brush your teeth every day.
Running or jogging to keep you fit
To keep your heart healthy do your bit.

Joshua Armstrong (9)
Doncaster Road Primary School

The Ready Rhino Poem

Ready rhinos, ready rhinos are smart and ready
They like to work and play to get through the day
Ready rhinos, ready rhinos, they all think alike
Because Mrs Angel is able to make them work
We like our Fridays
We like our learning
But most of all we like to earn them
Ready rhinos, ready rhinos all like to talk
Before they go for a walk.

Courtney Markham (8)
Doncaster Road Primary School

Happiness All Around

Happiness all around,
people having a great time.

No one pushing, no one shoving,
people having a good time round.

Good and great people having glittery eyes,
no one spoiling the good best times.

Some people having a frown,
no need because I'm coming round.

People having a brilliant time,
children playing all the time.

Happiness, happiness all around,
having a fabulous time.

Santana Sykes-Bailey (9)
Doncaster Road Primary School

Barnsley FC

C ome on you Reds!
O h when the Reds are marching in.
M ichael McIndoe went to Wolves.
E verybody's cheering.

O n the day with Barnsley got in the final
N ardiello scored a fantastic goal!

Y ou are the losers, we are the champions!
O verall the best.
U nder 21s are the best.

R un away from us because we will score some goals.
E verybody ran on the pitch.
D aniel Nardiello, goal kick.
S o come on you Reds!

Dan Scott (9)
Doncaster Road Primary School

A Poem Of Happiness

She quickly walked in the house
with a smile covering her face
as a present quickly came to her joyful face
because it was her birthday today
she was joyful as can be
everybody cheering for a party
yippee, yippee, she was so pleased
the volume was so loud
she was hurting my ears
I think her eyes were sparkling like a cloud.

Abby Grant (9)
Doncaster Road Primary School

Ice Cream

Ice cream is my favourite food
It makes my heart go boom
Ice cream gets me in the mood
To dance around the room.

The reason I like ice cream
Is because it tastes so cold
Mint choc chip flavour is my dream
It's my dad's too, even though he's old!

In the summer when it's hot
The ice cream runs down my hand
Everybody likes it a lot
Especially on the sand.

Georgia Lodge (8)
Doncaster Road Primary School

Vegetables

V egetables are healthy
E at 5 a day
G et all your vitamins
E at the healthy way
T urnips, potatoes, broccoli and peas
A re all very healthy, have them for your tea
B aked potato with cheese, oh yes please
L eeks, sprouts, carrots too
E xciting, delicious, put them in a stew
S o many vegetables I can't choose,
all lovely and delicious, why not try some too.

Charlotte Lindley-Wood (8)
Doncaster Road Primary School

Autumn Song

Autumn come
and autumn go
leaves glow . . . winds blow
winds blow
winds blow
winds blow
winds blow.

Rainbows come
rainbows go
long days slowing . . . raindrops rolling
raindrops rolling
raindrops rolling
raindrops rolling
raindrops rolling.

Storms come
clouds go
leaves flow . . . trees glow
trees glow
trees glow
trees glow
trees glow.

Lauren Fisher (9)
Elsecar Holy Trinity CE Primary School

Winter Song

Winter come
And winter go
Snowflakes blow . . . icy winds
    Icy winds
    Icy winds
    Icy winds
    Icy winds.
Jack Frost comes
And tingling feet go
But still . . .
    Icy winds
    Icy winds
    Icy winds
    Icy winds.
Cold hands come
Slippy roads go
But still . . .
    Icy winds
    Icy winds
    Icy winds
    Icy winds.

Brooke Ireland (8)
Elsecar Holy Trinity CE Primary School

Summer Song

Summer come
And summer go
Summer long . . . summer fun
    Summer fun
    Summer fun
    Summer fun
    Summer fun.
Blue skies come
And wet weather goes
Summer day shines . . . summer glow
    Summer glow
    Summer glow
    Summer glow
    Summer glow.
Seaside delight
And sunburn stings . . . birds sing
    Birds sing
    Birds sing
    Birds sing
    Birds sing.

Harry Gill (9)
Elsecar Holy Trinity CE Primary School

Autumn Song

Autumn come
And autumn go
Leaves blow . . . rainbows show
    Rainbows show
    Rainbows show
    Rainbows show
    Rainbows show.

Sunshine comes
Rain falls go . . .
Rivers flow . . . leaves glow
    Leaves glow
    Leaves glow
    Leaves glow
    Leaves glow.

Winds come
And sunshine go . . .
Flowers grow . . . clouds down low
    Clouds down low
    Clouds down low
    Clouds down low
    Clouds down low.

Tilly Ihnatyszcz (9)
Elsecar Holy Trinity CE Primary School

Summer Song

Summer come
and summer go
roses bloom . . . bumblebees buzz
    bumblebees buzz
    bumblebees buzz
    bumblebees buzz
    bumblebees buzz.

Seaside delight
sunburn stings . . . holiday fun
    holiday fun
    holiday fun
    holiday fun
    holiday fun.

People sing
ice cream melts . . .
people smack the bees away
    people sing
    people sing
    people sing
    people sing.

Jack Guest (8)
Elsecar Holy Trinity CE Primary School

Spring Song

Spring come
And spring go
Rivers flow . . . farmers sow
    Farmers sow
    Farmers sow
    Farmers sow
    Farmers sow.

Flowers come
And seeds go
Soil flat . . . birds chat
    Birds chat
    Birds chat
    Birds chat
    Birds chat.

Tulips come
And squirrels go
Animals awaken . . . lambs appear
    Lambs appear
    Lambs appear
    Lambs appear
    Lambs appear.

Megan Doughty (8)
Elsecar Holy Trinity CE Primary School

Summer Song

Summer come
and summer go
but sunshine glow . . . waters flow
waters flow
waters flow
waters flow
waters flow.

Roses bloom
then bees buzz
but sunburn stings
sunburn stings
sunburn stings
sunburn stings
sunburn stings.

Blue sky come
then boats sail
but everyone's pale
everyone's pale
everyone's pale
everyone's pale
everyone's pale.

Thomas James (8)
Elsecar Holy Trinity CE Primary School

Hunger

It reminds me of an earthquake,
Hunger is white like Heaven,
It sounds like a cat purring,
It feels like maggots wiggling inside you,
It looks like a dog moaning,
It smells like the wind,
It tastes slimy like a worm.

Shauna Pawson (10)
Hollybush Primary School

Happiness

Happiness is green like the leaves,
It reminds me of laughing hyenas,
It feels like butterflies tickling me,
It tastes like bubbling bubblegum,
It looks happy like a floating princess,
It sounds like hearts beating,
It smells beautiful like perfume.

Tia Dhers (10)
Hollybush Primary School

Fear

It reminds me of a raging bull,
Fear is black like a mystical magic,
It tastes like cold shaking in your brain,
It feels like steam running through your back,
It sounds like a rhinoceros leaping through your ears,
It smells like a burning fire.

Jake Flatley (10)
Hollybush Primary School

Fear

Fear is black like a bat,
It smells like petrol,
It tastes like it is in your blood,
It sounds like someone screaming,
It feels like someone biting you,
It reminds me of blazing fire,
It looks like someone crying.

Emma Paley (10)
Hollybush Primary School

Fear

Fear is like a cold spine shivering.
Fear is white like the sun's glow.
Fear reminds me of darkness.
Fear smells like when it has rained.
Fear looks like a rain cloud.
Fear tastes like a rotten strawberry.
Fear sounds like a person screaming.

Daniel Keenan (10)
Hollybush Primary School

Fear

Fear looks like the rage of the bull.
Fear is black like the night sky.
Fear reminds me of red blood.
Fear feels like ice in your brain.
Fear smells like the steam of a train.
Fear looks red like a devil.
Fear tastes like the sourness of lemons.

Christopher Dodd (9)
Hollybush Primary School

Sadness

Sadness is blue like the sea.
It sounds like a kettle pouring.
Sadness reminds me of a funeral.
It tastes like sour milk.
Sadness smells like the salty seawater.
It looks like raindrops running.
Sadness feels like blood splattering down your face.

Erica Wallace (10)
Hollybush Primary School

Darkness

It sounds like a bull raging forward.
It looks black like coal.
It feels like pins and needles.
Darkness is black like a black jumper.
It reminds me of a dark night.
It tastes like sour lemons.
It smells like sadness when you're all alone.

Caitlyn McLean (9)
Hollybush Primary School

Darkness

It feels cold like a ghost hovering over your grave.
It sounds black like a black horse galloping over the hills.
It reminds me of a creature lurking over the hilltops.
It looks gloomy like a pale white face.
It smells like a breeze of fresh air.
Darkness is black like ash.
It tastes like an old burnt field.

Molly Basnett (10)
Hollybush Primary School

Sadness

Sadness is blue like pouring rain,
Sadness sounds like a giant baby crying,
Sadness reminds me of animals fighting,
Sadness tastes sour like lemon,
Sadness smells like horrible frogs,
Sadness looks like an exploding child,
Sadness feels like you want to blow up.

Joshua Johnstone (10)
Hollybush Primary School

School Times

I think schools are boring and dull,
When I'm having my dinner I'm not full.

When it's playtime there's nothing to do,
Sometimes I like to pretend to have the flu.

But PE is good to do,
When I'm bored I pretend to want the loo.

Home time is the best bit ever,
It's best to sit on my sofa that's made of leather.

After the TV I've always been fed,
After that it's time for bed.

Darryl Keir (9)
Hollybush Primary School

Slowly Things Happen

Slowly the snail leaves a trail of slime.
Slowly the sun begins to climb.
Slowly the bird moves its wings.
Slowly the day begins.

Connor Knill (9)
Hollybush Primary School

Wake Up

Slowly the sun rises up in the sky,
Slowly the babies look up, they cry.
Slowly the people start to awaken,
What's for breakfast?
Eggs and bacon!

Chloe Naylor (9)
Hollybush Primary School

Fairies

I heard fairies dance all day
but mostly they dance in May.
They have pink wings
and lots of things,
that's why they're called fairies.

I heard wizards use magic
even though their lives are tragic,
they have a stick
and they're very thick,
that's why they're called wizards.

Claire Richardson (9)
Hollybush Primary School

A Tarantula - Haiku

It might poison you,
It has lots of sticky legs,
They make lots of webs.

Chloe Clayborough (9)
Hollybush Primary School

The Spider - Haiku

Eight long furry legs
Spinning lots of sticky webs
Waiting for his prey.

Ben Taylor & Lewis Johnstone (8)
Hollybush Primary School

Fairies

Fairies are so beautiful,
They sparkle out with glee,
Fairies are so wonderful,
They take my teeth from me.

Fairies are so fantastic,
They are magical to be,
Fairies are so excellent,
They need to be with me.

Hannah Walker (9)
Hollybush Primary School

Sadness

Sadness is blue like the sea.
Cold like snow.
Tastes deadly like ice.
Smells wet like rain.
Like birds dying and suffering.
Revolting like a squashed bird.
It reminds me of a gigantic death.

Jayde Shillito (9)
Hollybush Primary School

Pizza - Haiku

Do you like pizza
Because of the cheese and sauce
Or of the spices?

Hannah Simpson (9)
Hollybush Primary School

Fear

Fear is as black as a spider,
Creeping along, waiting in an abandoned house.
It makes you feel like dying inside.
Smells like rats carrying diseases.
It sounds as quiet as a deserted wood.
Looks like a monster,
Reminding me of a pitch-black hole.

Jessica King (10)
Hollybush Primary School

Happiness

It is as blue as the sky.
Happiness is like air,
It feels like a hint of a touch.
As smelly as a pink flower,
It tastes so fresh.
It sounds like bubbles popping,
Reminding me of a lovely blue sky.

Bethany Wilkinson (10)
Hollybush Primary School

Fear

Fear is bulky like a bull,
Smells like a rotten toad,
No one can change the fear in you,
Now look at yourself,
You think it's not true?

Adam Hedley (10)
Hollybush Primary School

Happiness

Happiness is red like a rose.
Smooth and soft like the clouds.
As smelly as lavender.
As tasty as creamy chocolate.
Sounds like the birds singing in the morning.
As lovely as a feather.
Reminds me of the sun shining upon you.

Abigail Shipp (9)
Hollybush Primary School

Fear

Fear is black like the night sky.
All alone in the dark you can't stop fear.
Then just now you wonder what to do.
Reminding me of a dark hole.

Joshua Catchpole (10)
Hollybush Primary School

Loneliness

Loneliness is as blue as a frozen heart
It feels like a punch in the stomach
Smells like a dreadful rotten apple
And tastes like dreadful salty water
Loneliness sounds like a lost little baby crying and hurt
Reminding me of death.

Hannah Burrow (10)
Hollybush Primary School

Sleeping Cats

(Inspired by 'Cats Sleep Anywhere' by Eleanor Farjeon)

Cats will sleep anywhere
next to a bear
on a chair.
Cats will sleep anywhere
on a bed
on one leg.
Cats will sleep anywhere
in a shoe
or on the loo.
Cats will sleep anywhere
in a car
or on the bar.
Cats will sleep anywhere at all!

Danielle Hope (9)
Hoylandswaine Primary School

Storm

Angry thunder above.
God bashes his drums.
Floods are made
As tears fall from the sky.
As the storm goes on the war goes on.
The crashes are like a bomb.
Will it ever end?

Samuel Mirrlees (9)
Hoylandswaine Primary School

My Magic Box

(Based on 'Magic Box' by Kit Wright)

My magic box will contain . . .
My chocolate coloured cat purring for a cuddle.
A light blue dolphin swimming in the shimmering sea.
The finest dark chocolate melting in the sun.

My magic box will contain . . .
A girl doing gymnastics and a seal bouncing a ball on its nose.
A lady with a shopping trolley and an owl flying in the sky.

My magic box will have . . .
Seven silver shimmering stars on the top.
Bright red roses around the sides
And gold dark glitter decorating the sides.

My magic box will go to . . .
The highest mountains in the world
To see what I can see.

Chloe Humphrey (9)
Hoylandswaine Primary School

Sun

Yellow and bright it shines in the sky.
It gives happiness.
As yellow as a daffodil.
You like to go to the beach
When it is hot and play in the sea
And you do not have to wrap up warm.
You like to play outside.

Rebecca Gibbons (9)
Hoylandswaine Primary School

My Magic Box Will Contain ...

(Inspired by 'Magic Box' by Kit Wright)

My magic box will contain
my brown and white furry hamster's cute red eyes,
my loveable grandma's playful dogs,
a CD of 'O Let Me Be Your Teddy Bear'
by the fabulous Elvis Presley.

My magic box will contain
a sedate old lady dancing in a disco,
a disco dancer in a wheelchair,
a sea without any waves and black snow.

My box is made out of fire, ice and wind for the sides,
earth and water cover the lid.
The clenched teeth of a lion form the lock.

I will go to Sweetie World and I will eat
all the sweets there are.
After that I will go back in time to
when the dinosaurs were born.

Ben Jackson (8)
Hoylandswaine Primary School

Snow - Haiku

Snow is freezing cold
Snowflakes fall from the high sky
Ice is shiny bright.

Tom Humphrey (8)
Hoylandswaine Primary School

My Magic Box

(Based on 'Magic Box' by Kit Wright)

My magic box will contain . . .
My baby cousin's big, bold, brown eyes,
A goldfish's golden skin shimmering in the water,
A horse grazing on the heather covered hills.

My magic box will contain . . .
My silky dog's ears between my fingers,
A pale secretive unicorn's glimmering horn,
A seahorse swimming glamourously in the ocean.

My magic box will contain . . .
A gorilla balancing a ball on its nose,
A seal swinging through the trees,
A boy in a high chair and a baby playing the electric guitar,
An elephant on the computer and a boy at the zoo.

My box is made of my dog's fur,
The sides are rabbits' hair,
The hinges are made of a toe joint from a lion.

I am going to surf on the gentle Caribbean Sea,
I wish to wash up on a beach of golden hot sand.

Georgia Lancaster (8)
Hoylandswaine Primary School

Snow - Haiku

Snow, icy, falling
on my head, on the floor, cold
a blanket of snow.

Sebastian Schmidtke (9)
Hoylandswaine Primary School

Sunset

Red
On the horizon
Bright
In the evening
Orange
Ninety-three million miles away
Hot
Nice to watch
Pinky

Sunset.

Oliver Webb (9)
Hoylandswaine Primary School

Ice - Haiku

As clear as a cloud.
Slipping and sliding on ice.
A crystal clear sheet.

Holly Ward (8)
Hoylandswaine Primary School

Rain

Cold
Clouds
Downpour
Water
Wet
Fast flowing rivers
Flooding drains
Squelchy mud
Damp
Fresh smell.

James Friggens (9)
Hoylandswaine Primary School

What Am I?

Fresh
    crunchy
            pretty
                don't have to wrap up warm
looks like crystals
                pale sun shines
melts easily
            makes the grass look mystic
pale blue skies.

Jasmin Hall (9)
Hoylandswaine Primary School

Snow Kennings

Wet,
Cold,
White.
Fun to play in,
Slippery,
Soft,
Nice,
With a happy feeling.

Thomas Brain (8)
Hoylandswaine Primary School

Snow - Tanka

Icy, wet and cold
Slippy, slidy and slushy
Fluffy, crunchy, white
Falling from the gloomy clouds
Soft, pretty, damp and funny!

Aimee Shiel (9)
Hoylandswaine Primary School

Sun

I like the sun
because it's nice and warm
and you can play outside.
I like having parties in the sun
which is so much fun.
I like walking everywhere
and walking in the beautiful air.
I can see from a distance
and like to see the lovely view.

Joseph Blair (8)
Hoylandswaine Primary School

Sun

I like playing in it
Blue skies
Things grow
Warm
Hot
I like being on the beach in it
Dry
Green grass
I go on holiday in it
Orange
Yellow
Round and golden.

Gaby Mather (8)
Hoylandswaine Primary School

Snow - Haiku

Snow is really cold
It is like a soft feather
It is white and smooth.

James Exley (8)
Hoylandswaine Primary School

Snow - Tanka

Snow is fun and cool
because it's just like crystals
and like a blanket
and it is very slippery
to have some fun in.

Alex Scanlan (8)
Hoylandswaine Primary School

Snow

Snow is very cold
It drops like a blanket, white
It is fun to play in.

Nikita Wragg (8)
Hoylandswaine Primary School

A Teased Girl

I went to school
I looked very cool
I teased a girl
She looked like a pearl.

When I got home
I did homework on my own
Then I felt guilty of what I'd done
I knew I shouldn't of done it.

The next day I went to school
They were teasing another girl
It wasn't very cool
They asked me to join in
And I said, 'I'm not in.'

Melissa Sibanda (10)
Hunslet Moor Primary School

Dreams

I have a dream that one day I will play in the Premiership
and play with my favourite players
like Thierry Henry, Van Persie, Fabregas and lots more.
If I don't get a chance I would like to be a boxer
so I can make history and live my life.

Arbaaz Mahmood (9)
Hunslet Moor Primary School

The Countries I Dream

In my dream I think of Peru
All the mountains side by side
I imagine me sitting on a camel.

In my dream I see Nigeria
I wonder what some bits are like
Some are poor, some are not
Nothing can beat it
It still is a beautiful place.

In my dream I see Australia
I see a kangaroo hopping up and down
I see the sea going in and out
I see a spider, I see a redback one.

In my dream I see Iraq
Bombs crashing down
I see people under rubble, people dying
Kids in the dustbin searching for food
I get so upset.

In my dream I see Brazil
With massive houses
I see footballers like Ronaldinho
I see me going there in July.

Sophia Ifiaz (9)
Hunslet Moor Primary School

I Wonder Why . . .

I wonder why frogs eat flies
I wonder why birds die
I wonder why people are shy
I wonder why cheetahs are fast
I wonder why penguins walk slow
I wonder why cars get you places fast
I wonder why flies can fly.

Luke Gibb (9)
Hunslet Moor Primary School

The Sea

The sea can be angry
The sea can be rough
The sea can be wild
The sea can be tough.

The sea can rip
The sea can tear
The sea can roar
Like a hungry bear.

The sea can be gentle
The sea can be flat
The sea can be calm
As a sleeping cat.

The sea can glide
Over the sand
Stroking the beach
Like a giant hand.

Amy Rhodes (10)
Hunslet Moor Primary School

My Sister Drives Me Crazy!

My sister drives me crazy
She makes me really mad.
My sister drives me crazy
She says you better had.

My sister drives me crazy
She's got a little pet rat.
My sister drives me crazy
She pushed me on the mat.

My sister drives me crazy
She doesn't care a lot.
My sister drives me crazy
Her best friend's name is Dot.

My sister drives me crazy
She's got a boyfriend called Lee.
My sister drives me crazy
She invited him for tea.

My sister drives me crazy
She's got a lovely big house.
My sister drives me crazy
She's replaced the rat for a mouse.

Wendy Milner (10)
Hunslet Moor Primary School

Stay

Please, please stay
I don't have a friend
If you leave I'll cry.

You make me feel so happy and mad.
You make me jump and feel the stars.
Why don't you stay for a little while?

Nicole Sabau (10)
Hunslet Moor Primary School

Who Is It?

Who is it? Who's there?
There's nobody anywhere.
Where are you? You've gone
You have been gone for long.

Help me find you
Or I'll leave you for long.
I want to moan
Are you at home?

Who is it? Who's there?
There's nobody anywhere.
Where are you? You've gone
You have been gone for long.

Are you at home?
I've just found your comb.
Oh tell me where you are!
Did you go to Rome?

Sheri Ibbotson (9)
Hunslet Moor Primary School

Animals

I wonder why cows go moo.
I wonder why ghosts go boo.
I wonder why birds can fly.
I wonder why in rugby they score tries.
I wonder why flies are called flies.
I wonder why bees sting.
I wonder why wasps have wings.
I wonder why I have lots of things.

Arron Applegarth (10)
Hunslet Moor Primary School

Don't Worry, Be Happy

I made you look, I made you see
And now you owe me 50p
So don't worry, be happy.
I will not leave you, no way,
I would like to see you every day,
Yesterday, tomorrow and today,
Don't go away! So stay and play.
You're soft as silk,
White as milk,
Sweet as honey
And full of money.

Mostafa Almousawi (11)
Hunslet Moor Primary School

Friendship

Friends are cool
Friends are nice
Friends are pretty
They don't act like mice.

They can be kind
They can be wonderful
They can be fashionable
They're all careful.

We all can be fashionable
We can all be good friends
We can be polite
We love building dens.

They're so good
They're so funny
They're so posh
Which makes them sweet like honey.

Tashnima Ali (10)
Hunslet Moor Primary School

Dreams

I had a dream, a dream about a dragon.
My dad drives a big, big wagon.

I had a dream about a cat
And it was sat on my nana's mat.

I had a dream about a dog
And it was sat on my playing log.

I had a dream about a frog
And it was hopping on a lilypad.

Tanisha Fagg (10)
Hunslet Moor Primary School

I Wonder . . .

I wonder why we see
Or who we like or hope to be.
I wonder why we love or hate
We can be early, mostly late.
I wonder why grass is green
people have feelings, don't be mean.
I wonder why people are kind
those people are hard to find.
I wonder . . .

Bethany Thompson (9)
Hunslet Moor Primary School

Untitled

I'm all in a cage, no one can see
All in a cage, in misery
The life I want cannot be mine
So I wait and count the time.

Amin Hasnat
Hunslet Moor Primary School

I Have A Dream

I have a dream to play in the Premiership.
Striker, winger or even a defender.
As long as I get to play with my favourite players,
Henry, Van Persie, Fabragas and trust me it goes on and on.
Arsenal are my team
And if they don't win this year
They will the next
And the next
And the next . . .
Well hopefully they will!

Nasim Abdul (10)
Hunslet Moor Primary School

I Wonder Why

I wonder why the sun is hot?
I wonder why it rains a lot?

I wonder why the sky is blue?
I wonder why a cow goes moo?

I wonder why the clouds skip by?
I wonder why a bird can fly?

I wonder, will the lesson end,
Before I'm driven round the bend?

Leana Miah (11)
Hunslet Moor Primary School

Animals

Cheetahs are fast
Penguins are boring
Polar bears are cold
Naked meerkats are bold.

Lions are strong
Giraffes' necks are long
Cats can scratch
Dogs can catch.

Dylan Fletcher
Hunslet Moor Primary School

Homeless Person

Hunger is grey like a poor, ill elephant.
It sounds like a haggard old lady
Screaming in a dark, damp street.
It tastes like a mouldy melon that's been left for years
and years on a dusty old shelf.
It smells plain like the smooth cold air.
It's blank, I can't see anything.
It reminds me of when my mother starved me,
That was when I ran away.

Ben McGettigan (10)
Lady Elizabeth Hastings School

Nature's Knight In Stubbly Armour

Shiny, almost glowing.
The horse chestnut enclosed in its rough stubbly shell,
protecting it from the dangerous depths
of the grinning leaf-covered surface below.

Hanging, unable to drop or climb just able to
sway, to and fro, to and fro.

Conker, peeping through its shield.
The nut is like a magnificent knight in shining armour.
Its beautiful beady eyes lost in the giant tree-huddled forest
of brightly-coloured plants and fascinating creatures.

'I'm lost, I'm falling
my protection destroyed!'

The collection begins.

Maeve Emmott (11)
Mylnhurst Preparatory School & Nursery

Kennings

Silk spinner
Fly dinner
Eight by eight
Insect wait
Furry body
Venom injector
No trespassers
Web liver
Spider.

Jack Parmar (11)
Mylnhurst Preparatory School & Nursery

Teleporting

Teleporting's a sensation,
You transport from nation to nation.
You will reach your destination,
If you follow your location.

Yes, teleporting's really fantastic,
And no, you don't need a tactic
And when you do something really drastic,
You might even make a teleport out of plastic!

So now we know about place drifting
But I'm sorry you're not allowed to take anything,
And yes it is the end of space moving,
So now you need to learn about time shifting.

Sam Green (9)
Mylnhurst Preparatory School & Nursery

An Apology

Sorry Sir, for doing it wrong.
Sorry Sir, for singing the wrong song.
Sorry Sir, for upsetting the class.
Sorry Sir, for smashing the glass.

Please Sir, can you forgive me?
Please Sir, can I go home for tea?
Please Sir, are you sad?
Please Sir, I'm really not bad.

Thank you Sir, for letting me go.
Thank you Sir, for letting me be in the show.
Thank you Sir, for letting me feed the fish.
Thank you Sir, you granted my wish!

Joseph Skull (9)
Mylnhurst Preparatory School & Nursery

Hairs In The Bath

Hairs in the bath are my greatest fear,
I move away when they come near,
They stick to my skin it's hard to get them off
If they go in my mouth I would always cough.

I search the bath for random hair
Then climb in, if I dare,
When I'm in, I search about
Then open my mouth to shout.

Arrgghh!

Daniel Downing (10)
Mylnhurst Preparatory School & Nursery

Flug

Flug is a remarkable pet,
He's even been flying in a jet!
I've never seen anything like him before,
I found him on the beach he was washed up ashore.
He's my new pet called Flug,
But he drinks toxic waste from a mug!
He really is quite smelly,
And he likes to play golf in his wellies.
He has smelly breath,
And a girlfriend called Beth.
Imagine what she looks like.

Rebecca Gill (11)
Mylnhurst Preparatory School & Nursery

Summer

Summer is the year's middle,
The holidays and the rush to the plane.
Hooray! Hooray! No more school for eternity
And the longest days for play.

The days are the coals in the fire,
The evenings the dying sparks,
Midnight, the ashes from the day's burning inferno.

Summer is made for fun,
Though gone like a bullet,
The memories last
From the days of the sun.

Joshua Barr (11)
Mylnhurst Preparatory School & Nursery

My Pets

I have many different kinds of pets,
And they go and see lots of vets.
Dogs, cats, chickens too
But not enough to make a zoo.
Big, average, medium and small,
Whatever size I love them all.
I have a dog that is quite snappy,
But all the rest make me happy.

Edward Harrison (10)
Mylnhurst Preparatory School & Nursery

Cricket

I was dressed in my whites
On a hot summer's day
With a hundred runs in my sight
On the fourth day of May.

My position was *wicky*
Behind those wooden stumps
It can be rather tricky!

We were playing in the ashes
The bowler spins the ball
For a run the batsman dashes
Howzat! Out goes Paul!

What a wonderful catch
I dive on the grass
It's the end of the match

We go off the green
With our heads in the air
Happier than we've ever been
Or dreamed to dare.

Strawberries and cream
And a hot cup of tea
Then I woke up from my dream!

John Forde (10)
Mylnhurst Preparatory School & Nursery

Kennings

Venom spitter
Slithering critter
Vermin killer
Fear filler
Scary creatures
With scaly features.

King cobra!

Connor Williams (11)
Mylnhurst Preparatory School & Nursery

Simpsons

My name is Bart,
I am cool,
But not so clever,
When at school.

My name is Lisa,
I am just smart,
And I am also,
Better than Bart

My name is Homer,
I like to drink,
And five plus five,
Is two I think!

My name is Marge,
I do the cooking,
And Homer thinks,
That I'm good looking.

I'm Abraham,
That's all I know,
So sit back now,
And enjoy the show.

I'm Santa's Little Helper
Ho, ho, ho,
And I just hate,
That barman Moe.

Next it's us snowballs,
Numbers, two and three,
And that the end
Of the Simpson family!

Don't forget me
Little baby, baby,
Baby, baby
Maggie!

Zoe Collins (9)
Mylnhurst Preparatory School & Nursery

Trees

My tree is as old as a granny.
As long as a canal.
As green as grass.
As smooth as brass.
My tree is as thick as a building.
As brown as night.
As stiff as a statue.
As bare as a skeleton.
My tree is as mouldy as fertiliser.

Rehana Abrar (8)
Rawthorpe Junior School

Madness

Madness is pitch-black like a bat.
It tastes like poisonous blood.
It smells like petrol.
It looks like killed people.
It sounds like a gunshot.
It feels like murder.

Kudzai Mubika (10)
Rawthorpe Junior School

Happiness

Happiness is bright green bogies.
It tastes like chocolate cake.
It smells like honey.
It looks like a bright sun.
It sounds like a boy crying.
It feels like wind blowing on me.

Kieron Faulkner (9)
Rawthorpe Junior School

Feelings

Hate is an old star in the dead of night.
Love is a white dove taking flight.
Both can help and both can hurt,
They can also catch you not alert.

It twinkles in your eyes,
It can make you cry and cry.
You cannot predict it,
You cannot shift it.
With it everyone has their time,
Love is blind.

Anger is a spear in the heart,
Happiness is a stallion stuck in a cart.
These feelings can be as bright as the sun
Or as dark as when the day is done.
These feelings may gleam or so it may seem.
The moods creep in, the world is shrouded,
The day has gone, the night is clouded.

Ewan Michael Stephenson (11)
St Dominic's Catholic Primary School, Barnsley

My Guitar

My guitar is magic with its built-in amplifier.
With beautiful coloured designs, it's brilliant to admire.
The six strings sit on saddles like glorious shiny silk.
The white scratch plate on the body is like clear normal milk.
The strings are all in letters from E to E again,
The frets go down in numbers and sometimes go past ten,
It's not a large image but it fits inside my car,
And every day I play it, my glorious black guitar.

Thomas Ford (11)
St Dominic's Catholic Primary School, Barnsley

Greedy Pig Vs Jamie Oliver

Greedy Pig who always ate,
and never thought about his weight.
He went into a restaurant,
and ordered a French Croissant.
He filled it with jam.
and then asked for a ham.
He finished with his dream,
strawberries and cream.
When he got home,
he ate his dad's shaving foam.
He stopped for a drink,
and within time to think.
Jamie Oliver tried to put him on a diet,
and it turned into a great riot.
His flab never goes,
all that exercise never shows.

Darryl Storrie (11)
St Dominic's Catholic Primary School, Barnsley

Christmas Snow

I love the snow,
as you know.

I love to play,
all day.

The misty wind blows,
as it snows.

People play,
all day.

The frost nips your ears,
cold enough to freeze your tears.

Oh, I love the snow,
as you know.

Aimee Brammer (11)
St Dominic's Catholic Primary School, Barnsley

Le Penguino

You're black and white, tall and small
and trapped between four walls.
You slide along ice, but you pay the price
by living in the middle of Spain.
Do not fright, it'll be alright,
we're going to let you free tonight.
So pack your bags and go home
to the ice and frosty weather.

James Green (11)
St Dominic's Catholic Primary School, Barnsley

School

School, school, school!
It's definitely not cool.
In maths, English and science
There has to be compliance.
The teachers here are good, even though . . .
Miss Flood . . . in her chair
She was combing her hair
Whilst she drank her water
And she saw her three daughters.
Year 6 were doing maths,
She came into the class.

Joshua Waterhouse (11)
St Dominic's Catholic Primary School, Barnsley

Inside The Mum

Inside the mum, the love,
Inside the love, the happiness,
Inside the happiness, the softness,
Inside the softness, the anger,
Inside the anger, the care,
Inside the care, the mum.

Daniel Jordan Atkinson (10)
St Dominic's Catholic Primary School, Barnsley

Mystery Mum

She's as much fun as a tiger,
She's as much fun as a bear,
She as much fun as a rabbit,
But she has got fair hair.

Who is this mystery woman?

She can be moody,
She can be a bully,
She can be a bit mad,
But she can be a bit cuddly.

The moody part gives me a clue.

She has got fashion,
She has got passion,
She has got love,
She is like a dove.

I've got it - it's Mystery Mum!

Bethany Corbett (11)
St Dominic's Catholic Primary School, Barnsley

My Dog

My dog is black and white with white toes,
He is a bundle of happiness!
Which is why I love him so.
With long ears and a curly tail,
He's as fluffy and as cute as a dog can be.

Katie Taylor (10)
St Dominic's Catholic Primary School, Barnsley

The Cat

She purred softly as rays of sunlight gleamed on her ginger coat,
Making her as bright as the sun.
She began to groom herself.
She licked her paw and swiped it across her face.
Soon she got bored and leapt onto the garden fence.
Ready and alert.
The bird swooped,
But she was too quick,
Pouncing and biting it in the neck.
She had made her kill.
She took it proudly to her owner.
She sat there looking at her owner
And dropped it on the carpet.
Her owner screamed, 'Oh no!'
No matter how much she thought,
She could not understand the world of humans.

Asheligh Pearce (10)
St Dominic's Catholic Primary School, Barnsley

Frederick Eatalot

'Frederick oh Frederick!' his wife said.
'Carry on like this and you'll be in your deathbed.'
Frederick ignored his wife's pleas
And tucked into strawberries and cream.
'I'm not a fatty,' he replied.
'Oh Fred I'm terrified.'
'Stop this now, or I'll scream,'
Then he ate a chicken supreme.
Just then baby Burt cried out
His eyes terrified at the sight in his eyes,
His dad Fred, he was dead.

Sian Cooper (11)
St Dominic's Catholic Primary School, Barnsley

War

Inside the man is, the life.
Inside the life are, the memories.
Inside the memories is, the war.
Inside the war is, the death.
Inside the death, are the memories of life.
Inside the memories of life is, the life.
Inside the life is, the man.

Ellie Frow (11)
St Dominic's Catholic Primary School, Barnsley

The Horse

The wind was hitting my face,
Mane forced back,
Air gushing past me.
Blinded nearly,
Tail flicking sharp,
Mud flying over my back.
My hooves were thudding on the ground
Like the sound of thunder.
Sweat was dripping off my face.

Megan Wilson (11)
St Dominic's Catholic Primary School, Barnsley

The Shark

Silly little girl swimming in the sea.
Silly little girl didn't see me.
I, the shark, had her for tea.
Silly little girl couldn't see me!

Joseph Sennitt (11)
St Dominic's Catholic Primary School, Barnsley

The Great Old Tree

The tree looked like an old man sitting in a chair,
The leaves were like a wild man's hair.
The leaves of the tree were like a bee flying by,
Through the sapphire, clear blue sky.
The tree was bathed in silver light,
Sometimes it caught the flying kite.
The wind in the tree that was flowing around,
The wind was blowing the leaves to the ground.
The old tree's roots were like the old man's boots,
Sitting in the soil.

Harry Black (9)
St Martin's Ampleforth School, Gilling East

Trees

The trees smell sweet like fresh dew,
They smell like herbs and smoke,
Like wild garlic in springtime.

The trees can hear you snapping twigs,
They hear you rustling below in the leaves,
Like toddlers flying shopping bags.

The trees feel like sharp stones,
They are crispy and rough,
Bumpy as baked beans in a pan.

The trees look like flowing water,
They are like tall skyscrapers,
High as the clouds drifting by.

The trees are wonderful things,
Like Grandpa on a happy day.

Georgina Eglinton
St Martin's Ampleforth School, Gilling East

The Tree

The tree is like a giant matchstick which has just been lit
With a fluttering flame on top.

The tree is like a huge skyscraper
With millions of floors and workers.

The roots are like laces that go for miles
Getting thinner as they go lower.

The bark feels like sharp knives
And razorblades.

The surrounding has a strange smell of wild garlic
And smoke rushing through the air.

Alex Pearce (9)
St Martin's Ampleforth School, Gilling East

The Tree

The tree was tall,
It went right up to the sky.
Its arms were as strong as my dad's.
The green leaves covered it
Like a woolly jumper.
The bark was like flowing water
Bumping, waving down the hill.

The trunk was shaped like a catapult
Ready to take its aim.
You could hear the birds in the background
Singing their songs.
The tree has been here for hundreds of years
And will be here for hundreds more.

Henry Laird (9)
St Martin's Ampleforth School, Gilling East

The Old Tree

A chocolate brown tree
As straight as a matchstick.
The golden knot, the eye of the tree.
The wrinkly smoky old bark.
The tree cries tears of sap.
The leaves are like a canopy covering you from the rain.
The roots are like shoelaces tying the tree to the ground.

Harry Everett (9)
St Martin's Ampleforth School, Gilling East

Spring

Spring is a lovely time of year,
Birds chirping, tweeting, you can hear.
The trees waving to you and me,
The leaves are twirling in the air so free.
Fresh dew lies upon the grass,
The patterns on the tree are like a river going past.

Daisy Pern (8)
St Martin's Ampleforth School, Gilling East

Fun

Fun feels like the softest cushion in the world,
Fun looks like 1,000 people having fun.

Fun sounds like the laughter of children,
Fun reminds me of the beautiful Earth,
Fun is the colour of every colour in the rainbow,
Fun smells like 10,000 spearmint sweets.
Fun tastes like a hot McDonald's.

Matthew Turner (8)
St Mary's CE(A) Primary School, Barnsley

Anger

Anger is the colour of red for doom!
Anger reminds me of a volcano erupting.
Anger smells like smoke from a house chimney.
Anger tastes like a red hot chilli pepper from a pizza shop.
Anger looks like a tornado on a windy day.
Anger feels like rage and fury clashing together.
Anger sounds like rock music from darkness!

Harrison Brook (9)
St Mary's CE(A) Primary School, Barnsley

About My Dog

Scooby is funny, he can run very fast.
He is very cool and he rules,
And he runs faster than a horse
And he hates running on a course.
He is good once or twice
But his best course is to catch fish alive.
He is so nosy, you would hug him once or twice.

Ben Hunter (9)
St Mary's CE(A) Primary School, Barnsley

Anger Poem

Anger is red like a burning fire,
Sounds like a scream, wretched.
It tastes like burnt toast,
Smells like a devil's hotpot.

It looks like the monster of all eternity,
Feels like you're going to die,
Reminds me of the terrible times
Of the monster creeping up from my bed.

Caroline Todd (9)
St Mary's CE(A) Primary School, Barnsley

Darkness

Darkness sounds like children screaming in their nightmares,
Darkness is the colour of 100 devils,
Darkness reminds me of my terrible dreams,
Darkness smells like rotten milk,
Darkness feels hard and bumpy,
Darkness tastes like four-year-old rotting tomatoes.

Robert Mitchell (9)
St Mary's CE(A) Primary School, Barnsley

Gazelle

The gazelle racing through the savannah,
Being chased by a cheetah, will it escape?
It bounces over the crisp grass,
Will it escape? We don't know.
The cheetah on its tail, running as fast as 60mph,
The gazelle's horns slowing it down.
The cheetah slowing down, getting tired,
The cheetah will have to go hungry,
The gazelle got away.
Will he get caught next time? Nobody knows!

Niall Thomas Egan (9)
St Mary's CE(A) Primary School, Barnsley

Darkness

Darkness tastes like burnt toast,
It sounds like a devil's screech,
It reminds me of when I was beaten up.
Darkness feels like I am all on my own,
It is the colour of blood,
It smells of a devil's hotpot.
Darkness is like a terrifying spider.

Jonathan Harry Bennett (8)
St Mary's CE(A) Primary School, Barnsley

Rabbit

As the rabbit runs frantically through the field,
The wind flies quickly behind,
Children watch as the rabbit hops up and down.

The rabbit has extremely brown soft fur
That sticks up in the wind.
Its big brown eyes bulge out at you
When you see its face.

Rabbit is faster than the wind!
As the wind tries hard to keep up,
However, it just can't.

Jodie Higgins (9)
St Mary's CE(A) Primary School, Barnsley

Humpty Dumpty Clock

My Humpty Dumpty clock,
Goes *tick-tock, tick-tock!*

Round the clock goes,
Where it ends who knows.

It's now the end of the day,
Still ticking away!

It still ticks at night,
What a lovely sight!

My little clock, what a lovely fit,
What would I do without it?

If it was to break,
It would be a big mistake!

Olivia Barker (9)
St Mary's CE(A) Primary School, Barnsley

The Shark

The shark likes to lurk under the wet sewers,
Getting from A-B as quick as a flash,
When any living things come near him,
He leaps, then catches them with excellence.
The shark loves to show off,
Jumping through hoops with excellence,
But when you meet him he's not that valiant,
Scared in the sewers.

Callum Michael Gillott (9)
St Mary's CE(A) Primary School, Barnsley

My Teddy Called Flower

My teddy, my teddy,
She's always sweet,
And she is there for me to meet!

My teddy, my teddy,
She eats fish,
I don't
Then she gets selfish!

My teddy, my teddy,
She's called Flower,
While I am saying Flower,
I always eat something sour!

My teddy, my teddy,
I love you teddy,
Even though you are dirty,
You are cuddly as well.

Jessica Rose Nixon (9)
St Mary's CE(A) Primary School, Barnsley

Darkness

Darkness feels like a fear coming true,
Darkness smells like your worst food.
Darkness sounds like ghouls in the air!
Darkness reminds me of a monster eating people,
Darkness looks like a headless ghost,
Darkness is black like a grave,
Darkness tastes like a rotten carrot.

Daniel Jubb (9)
St Mary's CE(A) Primary School, Barnsley

My Darkness Poem

Darkness looks like the Devil,
Darkness feels like a knife stabbing you,
Darkness tastes like mud from a field,
Darkness reminds me of losing my teddy,
Darkness smells like rotten banana,
Darkness is the colour of pitch-black,
Darkness sounds like a thunderstorm.

Rhys Barker (8)
St Mary's CE(A) Primary School, Barnsley

Kitten

Round, misty-blue eyes.
So small, so cute.
Small nose and ears.
Small butting paw.
Intelligent swish of tail.
Perfect.

Ellie Bamforth (9)
St Mary's CE(A) Primary School, Barnsley

The Squirrel

I looked out of the disgraceful window,
Guess what I saw,
A red squirrel it was,
I started jumping on the floor.

Collecting yummy nuts,
For the squirrel's family,
I shot up in the air,
I think they're so wonderful.

Some people don't like squirrels,
I don't know why,
I looked through the window the next day,
It made me cry till my eyes went red.

The squirrel wasn't there,
It doesn't like me,
I wish it was there,
But it doesn't matter to me.

Hope Ashley Musgrave (9)
St Mary's CE(A) Primary School, Barnsley

Happiness

Happiness sounds like a boy yelling for joy.
Happiness feels like skipping through a meadow.
Happiness looks like a newborn baby puppy.
Happiness reminds me of eating candy.
Happiness is a pink flower growing.
Happiness smells like melted chocolate.

Isobel Oliver-Haste (9)
St Mary's CE(A) Primary School, Barnsley

My Teddy Called Dotty!

My teddy,
Cuddly and sweet
Always the one I want to meet.

Very special,
Sits alone,
Waiting for me to come home.

Having tea parties,
So much fun,
We always share the last bun.

In the evening,
Time to go,
Snuggle up in bed,
The morning is due to come,
Rest your sleepy head!

Bethany Jane Green (9)
St Mary's CE(A) Primary School, Barnsley

Summer

The colourful gleaming sun,
All the kids having fun,
All eating a hamburger bun.
Green as green grass,
The sun is yellow as cheese,
The sky as blue as a sapphire,
Strawberries as red as rubies,
As purple as bluebells.
The little birds in the sky,
It makes me think of pie.
You can go to Cyprus or Spain
And you can take an aeroplane.

Jake Thompson (9)
Wavell Junior School

Autumn

When the trees begin to die,
Crunchy leaves fill the sky.
Leaves are . . .
Orange, brown and even red,
Those are the colours above my head.

When the conkers fall to the ground,
There seems a chilly wind around.
Fireworks banging late at night,
Some of them are really bright.
In the oven there's berry pie,
And there's a little hedgehog sweet and shy.

When the snow begins to fall,
I make a giant igloo wall.
I have a snowball fight with my friends,
I wish this time would never end!

Molly Grace Bullock (10)
Wavell Junior School

Sunny Days

The sun was shining,
The seagulls were whistling,
Barbecues were burning,
The ocean was waving,
Making castles in the soft sand.

The children were playing,
The neighbours were sleeping in,
The boys were swimming,
Dolphins were squeaking.

Tom Mark Cousin (10)
Wavell Junior School

Summer!

Summer is great when it comes
Because you can smell barbecues in every garden
And you can hear people having fun
And you can see the beautiful summer sun
And I wish summer was never over.

Arron Simpson (10)
Wavell Junior School

Summer Days

Its colours are yellow as golden sand
And a red rose shining in the sun.

It smells like ice cream
Cold, white and delicious to eat!

It sounds like the sea
Rushing up on the sand.

It tastes like strawberries,
Sweet, soft and juicy.

It reminds me of my birthday
All the time.

Sophie Pattison (10)
Wavell Junior School

Spring

It has all the snow melting,
More birds singing all day long,
More sun than rain,
Eggs from the Easter rabbit
Birthday . . .
Beautiful leaves.
The cold has gone -
See you next year!

Callum Johnson (10)
Wavell Junior School

Summer Poem

Summer reminds me of staying up late,
Mine and Jake's birthdays.

Summer tastes like melted chocolate,
Fudge, toffee, caramel, pizza and ice cream.

It sounds like the world is going
When the summer storms begin.

It smells like you are surrounded by fire
And like a fresh barbecue.

Stewart McDermot Alexander (9)
Wavell Junior School

Winter White

Winter white is as snow,
Snow that has a sparkling glow.
Cold as a big pile of snow,
I wonder when it might go.
Christmas comes then it goes,
Present wrapping all over your toes.
Christmas trees all colourful,
Winter is the best season ever.

Nishu Chhantyal (10)
Wavell Junior School

Summer

Summer is the smell of freshly cut grass,
The taste of ice cream,
The sea glistening in the sunlight,
The barbecue smells are delicious,
A breeze cools you down.

Chloe Ann Wild (9)
Wavell Junior School

Winter Poem

Winter, it makes me feel as if I'm in Heaven,
It tastes like an ice cube in your mouth melting,
It smells like roast chicken and hot chocolate,
Its colour is white, it reminds me of my soft warm bed,
It sounds like little animals sleeping and keeping warm,
White as Santa's beard, giving lots of presents,
Snow, snow-white and glows, see it sparkle and then glow,
Animals sleeping through the winter snow, purring, howling
and miaowing,
It feels like an angel's cloud coming down from Heaven to
a snowy town,
People singing and digging in the snow,
Winter is fun, it will never be gone,
Winter I love, winter you can play with snow and make snowmen.
Winter, winter what a day,
It's going to start another day.

Bishnumaya Dura (10)
Wavell Junior School

The Sounds In The Kitchen

The bacon sizzles in the pan,
The pop goes *fizz* and *bang,*
The tea is steaming hot,
The pots and pans go *clang!*

Aaron Calis-Dale (8)
Wavell Junior School

My Seasons

The sun shines bright in the sky,
Above your heads the birds fly.
Little lambs run around,
On the green grass daisies are found.

A time of year when it is too hot,
Out in pools quite a lot.
The lovely lick of ice cream,
And the nice smell of sun cream.

Fireworks making pictures in the sky,
Berry picking and making pies.
Crunching leaves under our feet,
Hallowe'en, trick or treat!

Snowflakes gently fall to the floor,
Carol-singers at my door.
Snowmen stand tall and proud,
Father Christmas comes without a sound.

Mollie Boynton (10)
Wavell Junior School

Summer

I taste the tangy lollipops inside my mouth.
The flowers are as sweet as kittens.
Suddenly when summer comes
The sky turns a bright blue!
It smells smoky with a barbecue smell.

Kayleigh Melissa Kneen (10)
Wavell Junior School

Summer

Summer reminds me of ice cream,
It reminds me of the taste as it shivers in your mouth.

Summer reminds me of the sweet smelling grass.

Holidays are the best because you get to sunbathe
on the beach.

The barbecue always smells good,
The burning sun, you sweat with the heat.

The water is always cool,
Bright colours like yellow, glow in the sun.

The red sun burns on the beach,
The sand tingles your feet.
Summer is the best time of year.

Rebekah Hewitt (10)
Wavell Junior School

Spring

I like it because it is my birthday.
It is not too cold or hot
And it does not snow.
It is a time when things grow back.
There is fresh grass and leaves.
It tastes like chocolate.
A new beginning.

Kurt Metcalfe (10)
Wavell Junior School

Summertime

Summertime, summertime,
Tastes tangy like a lolly.
Summertime, summertime,
Tastes delicious like a barbecue.
Summertime, summertime,
Tastes sweet like orange juice.
Summertime, summertime,
Sounds fun like laughter.
Summertime, summertime,
Smells like chlorine in a pool.
Summertime, summertime,
Feels full of joy.
Summertime, summertime,
The colours - yellow, green and blue.
These are the signs of summer times.

Tamsin Edge (10)
Wavell Junior School

Winter

Turkey roasting in the oven,
Fires blaring orange, yellow, red,
Christmas trees green with tinsel,
Baubles hanging shiny gold.

Angel hanging on the tree,
Snow, crunchy, white and cold.

Winter is a time of happy thoughts,
Like Christmas, birthdays, Christmas Eve.
Winter is the best season ever.

Freya Williams (10)
Wavell Junior School

Three Episodes Of Star Wars

Two Jedi walk from a ship
And the battle droids take a slip.
Along came Darth Maul who flattened Qui Gon-Jinn,
The hole Darth Maul fell in.

Jango Fett comes and goes
Quite suddenly
There was Jedi battle
With Kit Fisto and Shaak Ti.

General Grevas gets shot in the heart
By Obi Wan
Anakin turned into Darth Vader
Young Skywalker's life is done.

Thomas Griffiths (8)
Wavell Junior School

Night-Time Sounds

Tick-tock goes the clock,
As the children snore.
The dog barks really loud,
Then someone will knock on the door.

Mum and Dad went back to sleep
And the knocking stopped.
The children still slept soundly,
So their ears were blocked.

Emily Wright (8)
Wavell Junior School

Under The Sea

Sea, sea, lovely sea,
Fish play all day.
Mermaids find gold and treasure,
Dolphins are wonderful and clever.

Linnea Southam (8)
Wavell Junior School

Dreaming

Every time you sleep in your bed,
You go on an adventure in your sleepy head.
The adventure you go on is full of fun,
And you will get a lot, lot done.

One night when a little girl was dreaming,
She dreamed that she was singing.
She had a magic locket that was shaped as a heart,
Then her singing fell apart.

She pressed the locket in the centre,
Her singing was much, much better.
When she came home her popularity went really high,
Now she is no longer shy.

Beth Roberts (8)
Wavell Junior School

The Autumn Fox

Hair red like a tiny autumn leaf,
Eyes like the smallest raindrops,
Runs like the trees waving in the wind,
Legs like the branches, holding white
    and all sorts of other coloured leaves,
Body gold, as it shines in the fresh autumn morning.
Ears listening as if autumn is speaking.
Autumn is here, 'Hooray!'

Jade Costello (11)
Wavell Junior School

Magic Box

Open the lid of a magic box
And see what's inside.
Rainbows above the clouds with fairies dancing,
Ponies waiting for you to ride.

Georgia Nicole Lougher (8)
Wavell Junior School

Autumn

Autumn, a treasure of beauty,
That you create everywhere you walk.
Your hair a-billowing, burning crimson
Of the bonfire flame.

Your dress, a golden glimpse of glory,
Eyes a shower of amethyst,
A cloak like a stained-glass window of
Glittering golds, shimmering oranges,
Scarlet rubies and glowing auburns.

The mist left behind is like a creeping linger
Of ghosts gliding through the trees.

You leave us when
You are finished being
With your last creation
In its dying moments
Yet you are ready for
The next vibrant creations.

Mindy Reid (11)
Wavell Junior School

Autumn Creature

Nearly ruby-red fiery feet.
The style of robins' feet.
A golden pointed beak.
Your body can camouflage with crystal clear water.
Your eyes are like an emerald reflection.
You make a misty trail as you move.
You make a cloudy breath as you breathe out.
A sparkling frill above your head.
Leafy green wings
And a nettle tail.

Cal White (11)
Wavell Junior School

Autumn

Autumn is when the children have Hallowe'en,
Where the kids have sweets and treats all around,
When leaves, seed and tree fruits fall from the sky,
Big fruits start to fall from the trees to the ground
Ready to eat.

You go on holiday and go around the world,
It gets darker at night,
It starts to rain more,
School starts again,
We have more parties.

Josh Baker (9)
Wavell Junior School

Winter Fun

W inter is a cold season mostly in December.
I ce-cold winter everyone likes.
N ice warm fire like a bonfire.
T he snow, icy cold.
E veryone likes their new presents.
R ide a horse through the snow like a slide.

Louis Glistrup (10)
Wavell Junior School

Winter Fun

W inter feels like a clown,
I n December snow comes down,
N o Christmas is ever old,
T he snow is very cold,
E veryone likes a Christmas dinner,
R oast dinners don't make you thinner.

Liam Cook (9)
Wavell Junior School

Summer

S unny as the hot boiling sun,
U nder the parasol, bathing on a deckchair,
M um is sweating like mad,
M elting chocolate is so luxurious,
E njoying the hot sun beaming on my body,
R eally, really tired. I've had a very long day at the beach.

Christie Hodgkins (10)
Wavell Junior School

Summer

S ummer, as colourful as a rainbow.
U nder a parasol, hiding from people screaming for joy.
M outh full of salty seawater.
M ountains of ice cream on top of your cone.
E xploring the creatures in the baby-blue sea.
R eturning back from a long sunny summer day.

Shannel Milne (10)
Wavell Junior School

Winter Fun

W inter is such fun,
I like to eat a chocolate bun,
N early everywhere it snows,
T hen the wind blows,
E at a chunk of turkey,
R eady for Santa to have some jerky.

Jacob Alexander Dennison (10)
Wavell Junior School

Summer

S ummer, everyone's favourite time, with colours like a rainbow
in the sky.
U nlike winter, people are screaming with joy.
M ums are angry at children's red faces.
M ost places look like a pot of colourful flowers.
E veryone wants ice cream as cold as the North Pole.
R emember going on holiday with all your family.

Charnelle Smith (10)
Wavell Junior School

Springtime

Springtime is coming hip hip hooray,
Daffodils growing in the sun, shining in my happy eyes,
Trying to escape from the sky.
Easter's coming, jump and scream,
Playing basketball with my team,
Flowers are growing from the ground,
Sticking out like a crown.

Chelsea Payne (9)
Wavell Junior School

Winter

W here does snow come from?
I n ice-cold winter, snowflakes fall,
N aughty people will never get toys,
T urkey is in all Christmas dinners,
E xtravagant is all parents do,
R osy cheeks everyone gets.

Calum Brown (9)
Wavell Junior School

Spring

S pringtime is coming, the birds start to sing.
P oppies are popping out of the soil.
R abbits poke their heads out of their burrows.
I t is very sunny and hot.
N owhere is a sad place in springtime.
G oats are giving birth to baby kids.

Janet Greene (9)
Wavell Junior School

Spring

Spring is warm and the sun begins to shine.
My ewe is having cute baby lambs.
She gives birth to nine.
Spring comes before it is summertime.
Bees are buzzing around the trees.

Shannon Crockett (10)
Wavell Junior School

Sounds

The crisps go *rustle*,
The pan goes *sizzle*,
The biscuit goes *crunch*,
The pop goes *fizzle*.

A snake goes *hiss*,
A cow goes *moo*,
A mouse goes *squeak*,
An owl goes *tu-whit tu-whoo*.

Brittany Dennison (8)
Wavell Junior School

The Stables

The horses rip the hay,
Their shoes go clip-clop,
The horses say *neigh,*
The water goes drip-drop.

The saddle goes flop,
The bit jangles,
The door goes *boom,*
The horse goes chomp.

Laura McDermott (8)
Wavell Junior School

Playground Games

My friends and I were having fun,
Playing on the playground,
Having a game of polo
With an enormous bound.

My friends and I were having fun
Playing on the playground,
Having a game of Doctor Who
With some Dalek sounds.

Charlie Skelton (8)
Wavell Junior School

Food And Drink

The bacon sizzles,
The carrots crunch,
The Coke fizzes,
The children munch.

The children slurp,
The biscuit crumbles,
The cornflakes crunch,
The children's tummies rumble.

Amy Caris (7)
Wavell Junior School

Angry Words

Angry words are like being poked in the eye
with a sharp stick.
Like hitting your head on a radiator.
Angry words are like running into a
tall tree.
Like trapping your fingers in a car door.
Angry words are like falling down the stairs.
Like having bones pulled out of your body.
Angry words are like bricks being
catapulted at you.
Like having a red-hot poker on your forehead
Straight from the fire.
Angry words are like being thrown
into a fiery furnace.

Owen Prescott (9)
Wavell Junior School

Football On The Playground

On the playground
A game of football
Running around
Lots of sound.

I was in goal
Someone shot
I saved it
Everyone was happy
But the sad thing was
I never got to shoot.

Connor Haley (8)
Wavell Junior School

Angry Words

Angry words are like sharp
Shark teeth stuck in your flesh.

Angry words are like a furious bull
Hitting and stomping on your face.

Like hard hailstones falling on your face.

Angry words are like going mad
And committing suicide.

Like being bitten by a snapping
Turtle, hard on the nose.

Angry words are like your
Heart being cut by a Samurai sabre.

Like being poisoned by the toxic fumes
Of a fungus.

Angry words are like being slashed
By a fierce tiger.

Conor Porritt (9)
Wavell Junior School

Angry Words

Angry words are like hot, big stones,
Like icy wind and lightning storms,
Angry words are like sharp teeth,
Tearing your skin with flesh,
Like cold freezing winds with snowstorms,
Angry words are like burning glass.

Nathan Gammie (9)
Wavell Junior School

Angry Words

Angry words are like falling from the tallest tree in the world.
Like falling from the clouds.
Angry words are like getting cut by a dinosaur's tooth.
Like getting struck by lightning.
Angry words are like getting hit in the face by hailstones.
Like getting hit with a sledgehammer.

Joel Vout (8)
Wavell Junior School

Angry Words

Angry words are like being chucked
on spiky-topped icicles.
Like breaking your back.
Angry words are like being pushed
onto a really hard brick wall.
Like smashing your head on a metal bar.

Chloe Bradbury (8)
Wavell Junior School

Winter

I like having snow fights as well as turkey.
Sun has gone and snow has come.
So has Santa with lots of toys.
Time to wear trousers and jumpers.
When you look out your window
Jack Frost paints a white coat of snow.

Daniel Theyers (10)
Wavell Junior School

Having Fun On The Playground

My friends and I were having fun,
Playing crazy football.
Scoring goals all day long,
Having loads of fun.

When I was playing rounders,
Batting the ball so far.
Catching the ball in the air,
Having tons of fun.

Curtis Wyeth (8)
Wavell Junior School

Summer

Its colours are as bright as the sun
And all the kids have lots of fun.
You can feel the chocolate melting in your hand,
The smell of flowers and feel of sand.

The taste of ice cream swirls around my mouth.
I shiver when I step into the pool
And then I say, 'Summer rules!'

Chloe Simpson (9)
Wavell Junior School

Autumn

Autumn is Hallowe'en.
It feels like you are in the clouds.
Its colour is orange.
Leaves falling from the sky
And green apples falling from the trees.
It tastes like sour fruits from the trees.

Alex Savage (10)
Wavell Junior School

The Breakfast Poem

The cereal *crunches*
The cereal goes *pop*
The cereal goes *snap*
The cereal goes *chomp*.

The milk *splashes*
The bowl *dings*
The milk *dribbles*
The kettle *sings*.

Callum Fraser (8)
Wavell Junior School

Blank Mind

I can't think what to write,
My mind is feeling blank.
I feel like my brain
Is playing an annoying prank
On me!

What type of poem?
Haikus, acrostics and rhyme.
Too many different types -
Please, one at a time!
Not three!

My entry will be late
For the competition for poems.
No, wait a minute
Here's one I can throw in!
Yippee!

Eleanor Hill (10)
Westways Primary School

Holidays

H appy memories
O f a happy time
L icking a soft, creamy ice cream
I n the peaceful charm of the sea
D olphins curve in perfect arches
A s the setting sun gives off a million different colours
Y achts zoom on the glittering water
S ailing home after a day at the seaside.

Joanna Lee (11)
Westways Primary School

My Garden

My favourite place I like to be
is in my garden by the tree.
I love my pond with fish and frogs
I have a cat that can't stand dogs.
I like to bounce on my trampoline
then fall exhausted in the grass so green.
Picnics are a special treat
with buns and cakes and lots to eat.
Washing hanging on the line
while I play and have a good time.
Grandpa sitting in his chair,
Oh my goodness - he has no hair!
I like to laugh and have a giggle
while the blackbirds tweet and the
earthworms wiggle.
The moon appears in the sky
The sun goes to bed and so do I.

Ruth Whitehead (10)
Westways Primary School

Dogs Don't Dance!

Dogs play fetch,
Dogs jump high,
Dogs run a long way,
But dogs don't dance!

Chow-chows are nice,
Terriers are cute,
Labradors are active
But dogs don't dance!

Pretty poodles look funny,
Dalmatians are very spotty,
Dogs meet every year at Crufts
But dogs don't dance!

Jacob Pountney (10)
Westways Primary School

Spring

The smell of tree sap
Hanging in the air
From newly opened tree buds
Turning into flowers.

The sound of birds
Chirruping at dawn
As the days get longer
And warmer.

A sense
Of freshness
And new growth
Strong in the air.

Tanya Sciamanna (10)
Westways Primary School

Friends

Friends can be kind,
Friends can be mad,
Friends can be on my mind,
Friends can be bad.

Friends like to run,
Friends like to be fun,
Friends like food,
Friends get in a mood.

Friends hate boys,
Friends love to dance,
Friends make some noise,
Friends never prance.

But the best thing about friends
Is they're *caring!*

Eleanor Woffindin (9)
Westways Primary School

Holidays

H aving fun in the sauna,
O h! My gosh it's getting warmer,
L icking lollies by the sea,
I wonder what else could possibly be.
D ays like these are such fun,
A lso because we're in the sun
Y ippee! The beach stalls,
S trange but wonderful beach balls.

Megan Powell (10)
Westways Primary School

Caroline Dude

I'm Caroline Dude,
People call me Caroline Rude.
I always have to lie,
My best one is pigs can fly.

I'm Caroline's friend,
She drives me round the bend.
She always walks around nude,
She is very rude.

I'm Caroline's mother,
She always fights with her brother,
Never tidies her room,
She hits me with her broom.

I'm Caroline's father,
Caroline wants to be called Martha.
She has a boyfriend,
She says her love will never end.

I'm Caroline's brother,
People say I look like my mother,
But Caroline never will,
She never pays her telephone bill.

I'm Caroline Dude,
People call me Caroline Rude.

Phoebe Parsons (9), Katie Hart & Suhayla Hizam (10)
Westways Primary School

All Cats Like . . .

All cats like,
To claw the furniture,
Eat lots of food,
And to fall asleep.

All cats like,
To be stroked,
Lie on the sofa,
And to fall asleep.

All cats like,
To kill birds,
Eat live mice,
And fall asleep.

All cats like,
To explore the garden,
Chase butterflies,
And fall asleep.

All cats like,
To lie in the sun,
Eat meat,
And fall asleep.

All cats like.

Nuala Leake (9) & Frances Catherine Coombe (10)
Westways Primary School

The Ocean

As I walk down to the glistening ocean,
Dolphins greet me with their song,
The sun shines down on my smiling face,
My shadow before me dark and long.

When I gaze up at the bright blue sky,
Away from pollution, smoke and devastation,
This world suddenly seems a perfect place,
The most peaceful and beautiful scene in the nation.

I must bid farewell to the dazzling ocean,
And leave the scene just as it was,
Only take with me the memories,
And leave behind only footsteps because . . .

I would not destroy this serene world,
And spoil another's view,
Litter and pollution are things of the past,
A future especially for you.

Meg Plowright (11)
Westways Primary School

My Lovely Clock

Ting! The clock shows the time
Ting! The clock is mine
Ting! The clock goes round and round
Ting! The clock it makes a little sound
Ting! The clock is not working any more
Ting! The other clock is on number six
Ting! I think I need a fix
Ting! The clock is now working
Ting! It needs to wake me up next morning
Ting! The clock is on number two
Ting! Oops . . . I like my watch and I like you too
Ting! No thing, no ting, no sound
Ting! My clock is lost and never found.

Ghadeer Alqattan (10)
Westways Primary School

I Feel Like I'm Invisible

I can steal all the sweets or at least most,
I can scare my friends by being a ghost.

I feel like I'm invisible!

I don't have to tidy my room,
I feel like I can jump over the moon.

I feel like I'm invisible!

I can pull a prank and not be caught,
I can take things that I have not bought.

I feel like I'm invisible!

I won't have to eat that horrible fruit,
And yeh! I don't have to try on that itchy suit.

I feel like I'm invisible!

Although it sounds the brilliant way,
There is one thing I would like to say,
And that is that not being seen
Makes you feel lonely.

Amy Walkley (9)
Westways Primary School

A Visit To Egypt

A visit to Egypt
Is a visit to the sun.
Look for the magnificent sphinxes
With glowing amber eyes.
The glistening sand
Shining between my feet.
Though it may sound like the desert
It's the best place for me.
Oh listen to all the sounds
Vibrating in my ears
Ever heard such brilliant music?
Egypt, where the sun never goes down . . .

So-Jeong Yoon (10)
Westways Primary School

Dreams

Dreams are happy
Dreams are sad
Dreams tell the future
Dreams can be bad
Dreams are dark
Dreams are light
And the darkest dream
Is mysteriously bright.

The light that shines
When entering the dream world
Makes eerie shimmers
Upon your face
The trees in the dream world
Are twisted and gnarled
And the ocean is wide and deep.

Misty dreams are reality.

Rowan Drury (11)
Westways Primary School

Seaside

I saw glittering water for miles and miles,
And people surfing the waves,
Children everywhere were wearing smiles
As they searched mysterious caves.

I heard the whizzing of a Frisbee,
And all the people talk,
Oh, phew the ball just missed me,
As I heard a seagull squawk.

I could taste melting ice cream,
And sea salt on the end of my lips.
As I sat in a sunbeam,
I looked out to see a magnificent ship!

Kitty McCarthy (10)
Westways Primary School

True Love

Love is like a violet
And you are the seed.
You are the only thing in life that I need.

You are my starlight that shines from above.
I know in my heart it must be true love.

I see it and feel it in your tender kiss,
Loving you is truly true bliss.

Silky blue dresses
And pink fluffy bunnies.
Twinkling stardust
And warm milk and honey.

My dear
You are all of these things,
Sparkling diamonds
And shimmering rings.

True love is something
I feel from within,
I feel it from my feet to my chin.

Your beauty is radiant,
Your perfume is sweet,
When I see you my heart skips a beat.

You make me happy when I am blue,
When I'm in trouble you help me through.

You make my heart go all of a flutter,
When I see you my heart turns to butter.

You make me feel like I can fly,
Love has no reason, so don't ask me why.

Oh chocolate bar . . .

Rowan Sumption (11), Amy Bond,
Ruby Marshall & Issy Petersen-Adams (10)
Westways Primary School

Young Writers Information

We hope you have enjoyed reading this book - and that you will continue to enjoy it in the coming years.

If you like reading and writing poetry drop us a line, or give us a call, and we'll send you a free information pack.

Alternatively if you would like to order further copies of this book or any of our other titles, then please give us a call or log onto our website at www.youngwriters.co.uk

Young Writers Information
Remus House
Coltsfoot Drive
Peterborough
PE2 9JX

(01733) 890066

DAN JENKINS

A BIOGRAPHY

Dan Jenkins

A Biography

His Life and Times in Cardiganshire and Carmarthenshire

ALAN LEECH

y Lolfa

Dedicated to Rod Davies of Croesmaen, Llanfihangel-ar-arth, for his encouragement and invaluable help in making family contacts with Dan Jenkins' grandchildren.

First impression: 2011

Cover design: Y Lolfa
Cover photograph: Dan Jenkins' scrapbooks

ISBN: 978 184771 316 2

FSC

Published and printed in Wales
on paper from well maintained forests
by Y Lolfa Cyf., Talybont, Ceredigion SY24 5HE
website www.ylolfa.com
e-mail ylolfa@ylolfa.com
tel 01970 832 304
fax 832 782

Acknowledgements

I am very grateful to a large number of people who have shared with me their photographs and documents relating to Dan Jenkins. I especially thank members of his family: grandchildren Aeron Jenkins (Pentrefelin, Talsarn); Ifor Lloyd (Derwen, Pennant); Evan Lloyd (Aberaeron) and Mary Davies (Nantwich, Cheshire); great-granddaughter Eleri Davies (Aberystwyth); great great-granddaughter Gwyneth Jones (Blaen-waun-ganol); great-granddaughter of Dan's sister Eleanor, Myfanwy Gate (Ffos-y-ffin) and Jackie Armitage (Llanrhystud) who married granddaughter Myfanwy. All were very supportive and cooperative. Without their support and preparedness to talk to me, along with their sharing of papers and Dan Jenkins' scrapbooks which they had acquired from their parents or other family members, this book would not have been possible.

I have also been helped considerably by various people in both Ceredigion and Carmarthenshire, who have assisted me with interpretations, and more especially translations, from Welsh to English. They are: Islwyn Walters of Maes-y-deri, Ffaldybrenin; Eleri Davies of Pentre, Llanfair Clydogau; Deborah Jones of Llanfair Fach, Llanfair Clydogau; Dan and Aerwen Griffiths of Pengarn, Llanfair Clydogau; Gwyneth Jones of Noyadd, Llanfair Clydogau; Myfanwy Lloyd of Derwen, Pennant; Eleri Davies of Aberyswyth; Gwyneth Jones of Blaen-waun-ganol; Glenys Jenkins of Pentrefelin, Talsarn and the Rev. Aled Williams of Lampeter. I am pleased too about access and support with regard to my research from the National Library of Wales, Ceredigion Archives, Lampeter University Library, Bangor University Archives, Aberystwyth University Archives, Warwick University Library, National Newspaper Library at Colindale, Carmarthenshire County Archives, the Rev. Goronwy Evans of Lampeter, the Rev. Stephen Morgan of Trefilan, Joan Jones of Buarth-yr-oen, Ffarmers; Jen Cairns of Parcau, Cilcennin and Andrew

Jones of Cwmgwyn, Pentrebach. I thank, too, my editor at Y Lolfa, Eirian Jones. I apologise in advance if I have forgotten anybody.

I made a decision to try to produce this biography when I first came across the name Dan Jenkins whilst undertaking research with regard to the history of Llanfair Clydogau parish in Ceredigion. Upon further scrutiny, I became impressed with the way in which he had lived his life, the extent to which he had been involved in important initiatives, actions he had taken and his engagement in campaigns, which were designed to make a difference to the life of ordinary people and the country in general. His record can be seen in the articles and books which he produced: his fight for tenants' and teachers' rights; the organisations which grew and thrived through his participation; the elevated status of the Welsh language and the evolution of the National Eisteddfod.

Researching the life of a 90-year-old man and providing detail of his wider family background has been challenging, fascinating and enjoyable. I have done my best to check dates, names and relationships. There may well be errors of fact. I apologise in advance for any failures, the responsibility is mine. I thank also, my wife Sally, for her hard work, support and encouragement, and also her skill in working on the layout of the book prior to submission to the publishers.

Alan Leech
April 2011

Introduction

Most people are lucky if they receive one mention in a newspaper during the whole of their lives. Daniel (or Dan) Jenkins was different: there were dozens and dozens of reports featuring or mentioning some aspect of his busy, unusual and spectacularly successful life. He was a man of action, a campaigner, a creator and an originator, whose ideas helped to contribute to the shaping of the cultural and countryside landscape of Wales. He retained much of the detail of a lot of the things he did and those things which happened to him, in a range of large books in which he stuck documents. These have become known as his scrapbooks.

It was a life which spanned 44 years of the 19th century and 46 years of the 20th century. By choice, it was a life spent in rural mid and west Wales, in what today's political commentators are fond of describing as the Welsh heartlands. Born of a literary farming family in the Aeron valley of Cardiganshire, in what is now known as Ceredigion, he inherited and acquired an interest and curiosity in history, family, folklore, folk songs and poetry, as well as customs of both the past and the fast disappearing present. He saw a great many of the traditions and practices, including the Welsh language, under siege from rapid change, poverty, rural depopulation, and the overriding importance and status given to the English language in schools, government institutions, communication and the law. Yet, he also saw the opportunities associated with the changes: education for all, the possibility of the ending of illiteracy, more printed newspapers, a widening of the electoral franchise, better transport links and improvements in farming.

He grasped these opportunities to show that Welsh could, and should be taught in schools alongside English, and that the Welsh nation had much to celebrate and record of its people, distinctive culture, spoken and written word, singing, poetry and public speaking. As a farmer and headteacher of three schools located in Cardiganshire and Carmarthenshire, he used these institutions to demonstrate and display what could be done to further his ideas. He did much to develop the curriculum of what the modern Welsh school of the early 20th century might look like, through his activities at Llanycrwys School. He was one of the leading figures in the move towards recognising and celebrating St David's Day each year. He was also an important man of ideas, a communicator through his extensive correspondence with many literary and political personalities across the country.

His entry in the National Library of Wales's Welsh Biography Online, refers to him as a devotee of Welsh literature and music. Yes, he was. Yet, he was much more than that. He was a farmer, singer, organiser of concerts and eisteddfodau, recorder of poetry and folk songs, as well as the publisher of *Cerddi Cerngoch* and *Cerddi Ysgol Llanycrwys*. He was a Liberal politician, a campaigner for farm tenants' rights and the employment rights of school teachers, the latter through his active involvement in the National Union of Teachers (NUT).

A quiet, little known, but supplementary activity, was his collecting of small pieces of local news from the region, or Welsh gossip, as his liaison journalists called it, on behalf of both the NUT's weekly newspaper, *The Schoolmaster* and various local newspapers of mid and south Wales – in both English and Welsh. His pieces appeared in the *Cambrian News*, the *Welshman*, the *South Wales Daily News*, the *Carmarthen Journal*, the *Welsh Gazette* and others.

Summarising the achievements and character of Dan Jenkins in a few words is not easy. The *Cambrian News* described him in 1897 as "a Radical". The *Western Mail* in 1914 said: "he was one of the best-known educationalists in Cardiganshire". The *Daily Mail* in 1936 referred to him as the "Archdderwydd y Maes" or archdruid of the field in respect to his National Eisteddfod activities. In 1946, the *Welsh Gazette* commented that he was "King of the Beekeepers" in view of his long and distinguished period as a beekeeper. In the 1930s Sarnicol (T J Thomas) wrote:

> Daniel Jenkins is a tall gentleman, strong proportionate, beard turning grey, wide forehead with cheeks like August apples, two blue eyes, country bashfulness in his eyelid. He is a mixture of aspect of a teacher, preacher and farmer. That is Dan Jenkins, Cardi at his best. He is not a bard or literary man, but something rarer – a collector and appreciator of great literature. He is a great respecter. It is worth travelling far to meet a respecter.

Chapter One

Dan Jenkins – family background

An examination of the Jenkins family background shows it centred in and around the vale of Aeron in the central part of what is now Ceredigion, but was formerly known as Cardiganshire. The river Aeron rises in the hills around Blaenpennal and flows south/southwest, passing Llangeitho, Abermeurig and Tal-sarn, before swinging north-west and then west to the sea at Aberaeron, passing Felinfach and Ciliau Aeron along the way. Our focus is the valley in the area east of Tal-sarn, which is surrounded by relatively steeply sloping hills, which rise to about 850 feet in places. These valley sides are often covered with broadleaved trees, whilst the land around the river is largely very fertile pasture and is the home today of dairy farming. It is a beautifully green and pleasant land. The terrain some way from the river is also attractive and is important farming country. It is this general area of the Aeron valley which is the heart of where the wider Jenkins family grew, developed and thrived from the late 1700s onwards.

In the 18th and 19th centuries this was a remote and economically poor area. The predominant employment was farming, with the population either making a living in a farmhouse with land, or working as a farm labourer or farm servant. Those who, because of some combination of family circumstance, luck, or enterprise and hard work, happened to have possession of a farm were usually tenant farmers. They held the tenancy, normally on an annual rental basis, through an agreement with the local landowner who was often rich, and sometimes a member of the gentry. Quite a large part of the central valley of the Aeron was owned by several wealthy individuals, one of whom was the Earl of Lisburne.

To understand the life of Dan Jenkins it is necessary to have, not only some comprehension of his background, but also knowledge of the various generations of the Jenkins family which preceded him, and who surrounded and nurtured him with their ideas and way of life. This is to enable an identification of, not only the influences, values and ideas which affected him, but also the character and lifestyle of family members. Dan had such a proud regard for both his background and wider family that he went to great lengths to keep in touch with his relatives.

Dan Jenkins' grandparents

Dan Jenkins' grandparents were Jenkin Jenkins and his wife Eleanor. They lived at the important farm of Blaenplwyf, near to Tal-sarn, in the early years of the 19th century. According to the tithe agreement of 1839, the farm had 185 acres of land (rented from Theophilus Jones), plus a further and separate 221 acres (rented from the Earl of Lisburne). They employed a number of farm servants. Blaenplwyf was located about a mile south of the river Aeron on the slightly raised lands, away from the valley bottom, but between the two smaller streams of the

Denis and Dyfel. As a farm it produced butter, eggs, chickens and meat from cows and sheep, either for sale in the local markets, or often for eventual transport (on foot) to England. Jenkin and Eleanor Jenkins had 13 children and a relatively affluent lifestyle in comparison with many of their neighbours, who lived in much poorer accommodation, which was often tied to their employment on a local farm. There was a family background of interest in literary matters. Eleanor's uncle was David Davies of Castell Hywel who undertook a translation of Gray's 'Elegy' into Welsh, and was a very well-known bard, responsible for a number of pieces of good quality poetry. He was a schoolmaster at Castell Hywel Preparatory School, as well as being a Unitarian minister. Two of her brothers, Rees and Joseph, became Baptist ministers at Whitestone Baptist Church near Hereford. Jenkin Jenkins was well known in the area, being "a member of the Board of Guardians" for the administration of the Poor Law, "serving as a juror at the Assize Courts and being an agent to Lord Lisburne of Trawsgoed, one of the local gentry."[1] As parents, both Jenkin and Eleanor had an appreciation of the importance of education for their children and took steps to see that they were able to read and write.

In her book *Pity the Swagman,* which is the story of Joseph Jenkins, a son of Jenkin and Eleanor, Bethan Phillips has written that a private tutor was hired to work with the children on the rudiments of reading, writing and arithmetic. This man, Jac Llwyd, was local, a strict disciplinarian and was 67 years old when he taught some of the children. We also know that sons Joseph and John both experienced additional schooling from the Unitarian minister, the Rev. Rees Davies, in the little village of Cribyn, some five miles away.[2] Another son, Jenkin had a term's education at a school in Herefordshire "where he gained the prize for penmanship".[3]

Dan Jenkins' own scrapbooks provide evidence, by way of a receipt for payment of a school invoice, in relation to another brother, Timothy. This shows that Timothy, in 1855,

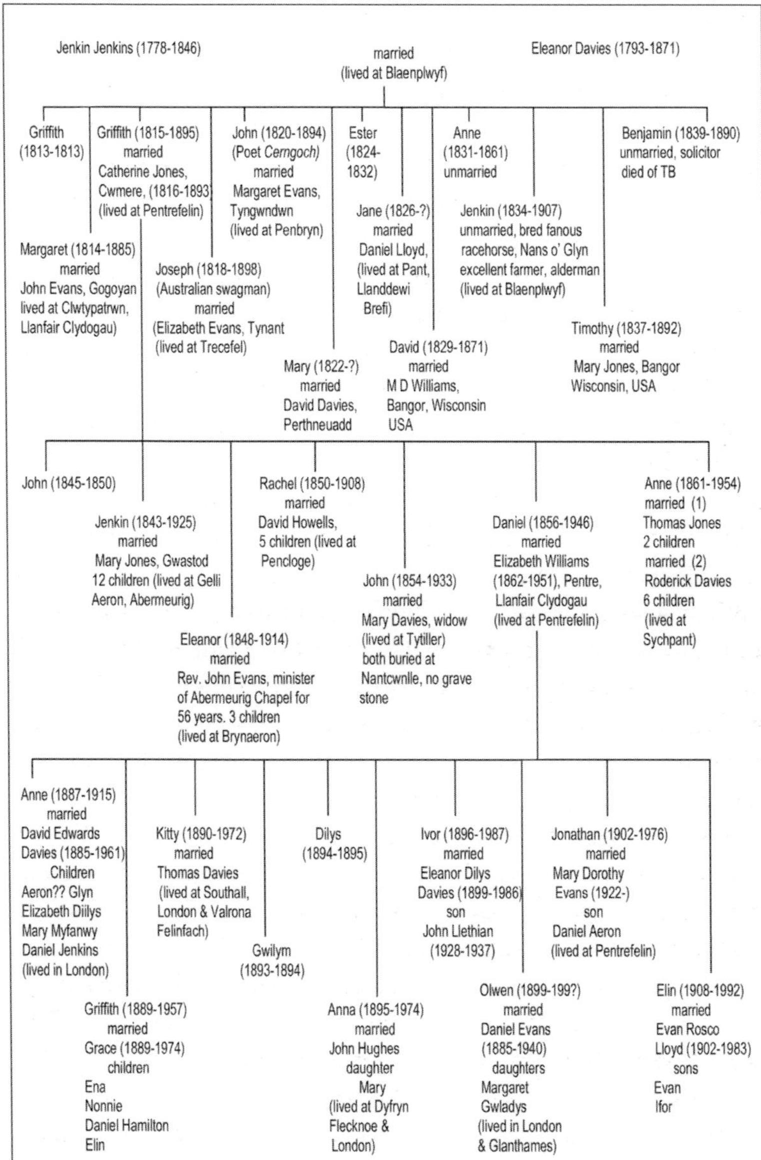

The Jenkins family tree (compiled by Myfanwy Armitage)

attended and boarded at Park Velvet Preparatory School, Carmarthen. His fees for a quarter, including board, were £6 10s. The proprietor was Titus Evans. Further information, again provided by Dan's records, details the education of one other brother, Benjamin. His documents show an undated newspaper cutting of the 1850s which refers to the eighth annual examination at the Park Velvet Preparatory School, by external examiners who then awarded prizes. These prizes went: "to the most deserving: First to Benjamin Jenkins and William Jones, who were equal..." The account went on: "This examination afforded the most satisfactory evidence of the care, assiduity and general abilities of the master, the Rev. Titus Evans, and also on the part of his pupils, twelve whereof are preparing for the Christian ministry, especially those who read Xenophon, Livy and Medea. It evinced a clear proof of the intense application of the mind before they could have acquired such knowledge of the synthetised structure of the writings of the authors as they did." Benjamin Jenkins was the youngest son of the Blaenplwyf household of Jenkin and Eleanor Jenkins.

The 13 children of Dan Jenkins' grandparents

The following family detail has been compiled, drawing upon initial research undertaken by Dan's granddaughter Myfanwy Armitage. The children, who were born over a 26-year period from 1813 to 1839, were as follows:

- Griffith, born in 1813 and who died after nine days.
- Margaret, 1814–85; married John Evans of Gogoyan in Llanddewibrefi, lived at Clwtypatrwn, Llanfair Clydogau; undertook farming.
- Griffith, 1815–95; married Catherine Jones of Cwmere, lived at Pentrefelin in Nantcwnlle; undertook farming; was the father of Dan Jenkins; Dan described his father as a bard in a piece of poetry he wrote in 1904, although we have no examples of his work.

- Joseph, 1818–98; married Elizabeth Evans of Tynant, lived at Trecefel in Tregaron; farmed; was a major force in the community for the development of schools; wrote poetry under the bardic name of Amnon II; kept a diary for 58 years; left his family and emigrated at the age of 51 to Victoria, Australia before returning 25 years later; his diaries have been published as *Diary of a Welsh Swagman* by William Evans and *Pity the Swagman by* Bethan Phillips.
- John, 1820–94; married Margaret Evans of Tynygwndwn, lived at Penbryn; farmed; wrote a large amount of poetry; his bardic name was Cerngoch; his writing was extremely well known in Welsh language circles across the country and he had a strong and appreciative following in Cardiganshire and the surrounding counties.
- Mary, 1822–unknown; married David Davies of Perthneuadd.
- Esther, 1824–32; died of tuberculosis at the age of eight.
- Jane, 1826–unknown; married Daniel Lloyd; lived at Pant in Llanddewibrefi; farmed, with her husband, a large 200-acre farm which in 1881 employed seven servants.
- David, 1829–71; married M D Williams, emigrated and lived in Bangor, Wisconsin, USA; Dan Jenkins obtained and placed in his correspondence a copy of David's 1871 obituary in a Bangor newspaper, which shows an early death at the age of 42, soon after returning from a visit to Wales. The obituary stated: "his heart and purse have always responded to the wants of the needy, to the cause of humanity, Christianity, and benevolence; a man of firm convictions, a true friend and valuable citizen."
- Anne, 1831–61; unmarried; lived at Blaenplwyf; died at the age of 30 from tuberculosis.
- Jenkin, 1834–1907, unmarried, lived at Blaenplwyf in the parish of Llanfihangel Ystrad, Cardiganshire; introduced many new and improved farming techniques to the farm – practices including the breeding of Welsh cobs, Welsh Black cattle and Welsh mountain sheep; was a county councillor

and later, county alderman for Cardiganshire; bred famous racehorses, including Nans o'r Glyn (Nance of the Vale); was a member of the Board of Guardians in Aberaeron for his home parish of Llanfihangel Ystrad; a member of Llanfihangel Ystrad School Board for 20 years. "He was one of the most popular people in the neighbourhood. Apart from the service he gave to the various public posts he held, he was always ready to help others. He was an energetic and thorough Liberal. On account of his service to the Liberal cause, he was made member of the county's Liberal Society." (*Yr Ymofynnydd*, February 1907)
- Timothy, 1837–92; married Mary Jones; emigrated and lived in Bangor, Wisconsin, USA.
- Benjamin, 1839–90; unmarried; was a solicitor.

Of the 13 children, 11 survived into adulthood and largely remained in the general area of mid Cardiganshire, including the vale of Aeron, often renting and operating farms. Jenkin Jenkins, the father, appears to have been able to assist several of his offspring financially in getting them started on the road to independence. For instance, he obtained the tenancy of Penbryn farm for his son John, and upon the marriage of his son Joseph, gave him £200. Three of his daughters married farmers, some of whom ran large farms. For instance Margaret and her husband were, in 1871, farming the 60-acre farm of Clwtypatrwn, in Llanfair Clydogau, whilst Jane and her husband were farming a large lowland area on the outskirts of Llanddewibrefi in 1881.

The Jenkins family appeared proud, not only of its roots in the area and its position within local society, but also of its literary, especially poetic background. With a family connection to Castell Hywel, and two of the eldest brothers, Joseph and John, recognised as beirdd gwlad or country poets, there was a heightened awareness that the family were different from the norm. They also had an interest and commitment to enterprise, education, hard work and literature, along with the celebration of their Welsh culture and its traditions. These important characteristics went on to extend to the next generation of the Jenkins family.

Dan Jenkins' parents at Pentrefelin

As indicated, Dan's father Griffith Jenkins was the eldest son of Jenkin and Eleanor, named after the death in 1813, of his older namesake Griffith. He managed, probably with assistance from his father, to become a tenant farmer in his early 20s, at nearby Pentrefelin farm near Tal-sarn, leaving his siblings at home in Blaenplwyf. This valley bottom farm was in the centre of the Aeron valley. The 1841 census shows him living there at the age of 25, described as a farmer and accompanied by three live-in farm servants. The farm and its lands of 80 acres are shown in the 1843 tithe agreement as owned by Theophilus Jones, who also owned Blaenplwyf. Following Griffith's marriage to Catherine Jones, they had seven children between 1845 and 1861: three girls and four boys. Following the death of the firstborn, John, at the age of five, the other children all survived into adulthood. We know that Griffith sought to provide an education for his

Pentrefelin (largest farm second from the left)
(source: Eleri Davies)

children. Jenkin, the eldest son was sent to local schools at Bwch-llan, then Pontsian, followed by Whitestone School in Herefordshire to learn English.

The *Welsh Gazette* reported that he was an avid reader who "could hold an argument on any subject". As if to emphasise his important ancestry, he was also described upon his death, as "a brother of the literary man Dan Jenkins of Pentrefelin".[4] It seems very likely that the other children of Griffith and Catherine also received a similar type of education, well before it was publicly provided and available in this area of the upper Aeron valley.

The children were as follows:

- John, 1845–50; died at the age of five.
- Jenkin, 1843–1925; married Mary Jones of Gwastod; had 12 children; lived at Gelli Aeron.
- Eleanor, 1848–1914; married Rev. John Evans, minister at Abermeurig Chapel for 56 years; had three children; lived at Brynaeron.
- Rachel, 1850–1908; married David Howells; had five children; lived at Penglogau.
- John, 1854–1933; married a widow, Mary Davies and lived at the nearby three-acre farm, Ffynnon Forgan.
- Daniel, 1856–1946; married Elizabeth Williams and lived at Pentrefelin plus boarding residences as a headteacher at Llanfair Clydogau and Llanycrwys.
- Anne, 1861–unknown; married (1) Thomas Jones, (2) Roderick Davies; lived at the nearby Sychpant farm.

The kind of personal attitudes and values which would have characterised life at Pentrefelin farm throughout the growing-up period of the children can best be summarised by an extract from the newspaper obituary to their mother Catherine, who died in 1893, at the age of 77:

> Mrs Jenkins was well known throughout a considerable district, and to know her was to respect and love her. There were several

> traits in her character commanding the respect and admiration of everybody: orthodox and tolerant, meek and firm, devotional and cheerful.

Five ministers of religion officiated at the funeral. These embraced church as well as chapel.

Dan Jenkins taking over at Pentrefelin

Griffith and Catherine Jenkins had three surviving sons as they moved into middle, and then older age. It was the norm of the time that the eldest son of a family would succeed to the family farm, in the case of a tenant farm, with the approval of the landowner. Yet, this did not happen, as the farm tenancy ended up being held by the youngest son Dan. Compiler of the family tree, Myfanwy Armitage, has offered an explanation of the succession route. She pointed out the eldest son, Jenkin, married Mary Jones of Gwastod in 1865. She wrote:

> He lived at Gilfachyfan for a time and later farmed at Tyncoed. Both farms were on fairly high ground and were not very productive, so he supplemented his income by working on other farms and also worked on the roads, cutting hedges and repairing the highway. And thus, he was constantly employed and had a steady income. Pentrefelin farm was the largest and best farm of those owned by the Blaenplwyf estate, and the rent, tithes etc. that were to be paid were no doubt high and more than Jenkin could afford.[5]

Hence, it seems likely that at the time of a succession of Pentrefelin being sought, that Jenkin was strongly engaged in his other farming and working arrangements.

The second Pentefrelin son was John. The 1881 census shows him living at Pentrefelin when he was 27 years old, with his parents also in residence. It must have been assumed that he would take over the farm upon their retirement. Myfanwy Armitage states:

> This however, did not happen. John had fallen in love with a girl who lived at Bwlchddwyallt, near Llangeitho and he hoped to marry her. Her name was Mary Jones. Mary, however, decided to marry John's second cousin, David Jones of Perthneuadd, near Tal-sarn. This was a heart breaking blow for John and he decided to leave both his home, and Wales, in order to start a new life in America. He sailed shortly afterwards and found work in Colorado as a lumberjack. After being in America for 12 years, John received news that David Jones, Perthneuadd, had died and Mary was left with five young children to rear on her own. He returned as soon as possible.

Sadly, by the time he arrived back, his mother had died. This loss is all the more significant when one reads the poem (below), which he had written and sent from Colorado some years before.

Once back home, John Jenkins married Mary Jones. They then farmed at Gorswen, Pennant and later Ffynnon Forgan,

Griffith and Catherine Jenkins with Dan's daughter, Ann.

Dan Jenkins' scrapbooks

John Jenkins (Ffynnon Forgan)

Dan Jenkins' scrapbooks

near to Pentrefelin. The written account from Myfanwy Armitage went on:

> John was a very popular character and he had the same gift of writing instant poetry as his uncle John Jenkins [Cerngoch]. His rhymes were very humorous, but often rather lewd.

He adopted the bardic name of Ffynnon Forgan.

The third Pentrefelin son was Dan Jenkins. He was always interested in farming and although he had become the headteacher at Llanfair Clydogau Board School at the time his brother John left for the USA, he took over the farm tenancy in 1882. His parents retired in due course and moved to a nearby cottage at Glanthames, not far from Pentrefelin.

This is the poem that John Jenkins sent to his brother Dan, with a note asking that he sings it to his mother. It was later translated into Welsh by his cousin Aeronian.

Take this letter to my mother

Take this letter to my mother,
Far across the deep blue sea,
It will fill her heart with pleasure,
She'll be glad to hear from me;
How she wept when last we parted;
How her heart was filled with pain
When she said 'Goodbye, God bless you,
We may never meet again.'

Take this letter to my mother,
It will fill her heart with joy,
Tell her that her prayers are answered, –
God protects her darling boy,
Tell her to be glad and cheerful,
Pray for me where're I roam,
And ere long I'll turn my footsteps
Back towards my dear old home.

Take this message to my mother,
It is filled with words of love,
If on earth I'll never meet her,
Tell her that we'll meet above,
Where there is no hour of parting,
All is peace, and love and joy,
God will bless my darling mother,
And protect her darling boy.

John Jenkins

CHAPTER TWO

Dan Jenkins – early years (1856–78)

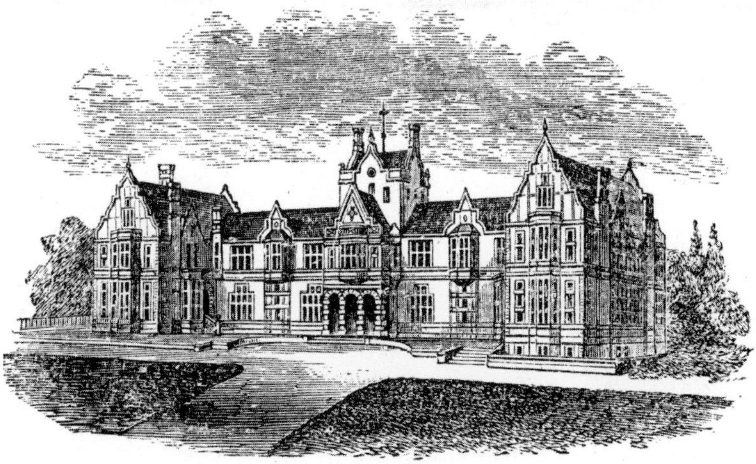

The Normal College, Bangor.

DAN JENKINS WAS the fifth child of the family at Pentrefelin and his early life suggests that he must have been well regarded by his parents in terms of his personal inquisitiveness and interest in learning. He was born on 7th November 1856, on the night of the day when the local Tal-sarn fair was annually held. He received many more educational opportunities than his brothers and sisters. His parents spent a great deal of money sending him to different schools, at some of which he had to board and be transported long distances, at a time when transport links were difficult. He was sent to receive his earliest education at Bwlch-llan School (a forerunner of the later board school), in the parish of Nantcwnlle, north-east of Tal-sarn, a short distance from his home. From there he was sent to Whitestone School, Herefordshire. Dan wrote an article in the *Welshman* about his time there. He outlined the tradition which had been established (until the arrival of the board schools under the requirements of the 1870 Education Act), whereby "a custom developed among farmers in mid Cardiganshire, of sending some of their younger boys and girls to Herefordshire to learn English. Boys went to Whitestone, Kington or Hereford. The girls went to Kington, as it was a mixed school." Whitestone was established in 1827 by the Rev. Joseph Davies, brother to Dan's grandmother Eleanor. It was attached to the Baptist chapel there. Dan wrote: "I was at Whitestone from September 1870 to June 1871. The Rev. Murrels Plaice was pastor and schoolmaster. He was one of nature's gentlemen. I boarded in." He wrote how he would sing the song 'Shall we gather at the river?' in Welsh to the people. In his article he referred to another important link between the two counties, with a custom of 9, 12 or 15 men going to Herefordshire with "sickles of special make, to cut the wheat, which ripened weeks earlier than on our uplands. One 'binder' to two cutters. One who could speak a little English was chosen as foreman."[1] Dan started at Whitestone when he was 13 years old. The census of 1871 shows him living at Whitestone Chapel with the Rev. Murrels Plaice and wife and 17-year-old daughter Julie, who is described as "teacher". Dan is referred to as a "boarder and scholar". He left Whitestone at the age of 14.

He subsequently went on to The Academy, Holt, near Wrexham in north Wales. This institution was generally known as Holt Academy. Records do not exist to show us how long he was there. The school was founded by Ebenezer Powell in 1865 and a later proprietor was Mr J Oliver Jones. Dan's scrapbook notes show that he was there in 1875 and that also in attendance at that time were John Lloyd, Rhydygroes; Richard Jones, Edward Davies and J J Jones of Temple Bar.

As a building it was not very large, with a schoolroom measuring 37 feet by 21 feet and an accompanying house, containing nine bedrooms, where the owner and boys who were boarding, stayed. Its title of The Academy perhaps suggests something grander, larger and more impressive than the reality. The school ceased to operate in the 1920s and was put up for auction in 1925. A prospectus dating from the 1890s (at least 15 years after Dan had left) stated:

> Young gentlemen are carefully prepared for middle-class examinations. The advantages of Holt Academy as an educational institution are various and important. Holt is proverbially healthy and being five miles from any market town, the pupils are not exposed to the annoyances and temptations incident to more populous localities.

The prospectus emphasised "a sound English education, together with Greek and Latin, or Grammar and French". For young men preparing for college the charges were £7 10s. per quarter.[2]

He must have agreed with his parents that it would be beneficial for him to attend Holt Academy, since the education on offer suggested it would help him in later life; especially with the emphasis on "a sound English education". The world of the professions: law, government, commerce and industry were all heavily dependent on a high degree of competence in the English language. It was the main language of official communications across Wales. Attendance at Holt, with its leaning towards college preparation, would also help him obtain a higher education place in a college. He was being educated in the manner of a rich, middle-class young man.

So, we know that as Dan approached his late teenage years, he was a man of success who had received an exceptional education for a person of his country background in the 1860s and 1870s; an education which was very far removed from that normally afforded a son of a farmer from the fairly isolated and rural mid Cardiganshire area. He could speak and write well, in both Welsh and English; he could mix easily and confidently socially, and had a self-sufficiency which enabled him to live away from his home. However, although the emphasis at Holt was on the education of 'gentlemen' in a forum which was very English-centred, it is clear that Dan never emotionally or spiritually travelled far away from the Wales he remembered as a child, with its own language, large attendances at church and chapel, plus its own character and customs in farming, singing, entertainment and public performing.

There was an inherent curiosity and excitement within him about his Welshness and his family background and roots in the Aeron valley, combined with an interest in political and social developments. We can see and sense his curiosity, interest in history and literature and naturally quizzical nature, from the documents and mementos of his life which he sought to obtain and subsequently retained, in his extensive scrapbooks. Similar personal characteristics have subsequently travelled well to his children, grandchildren, and amazingly to his great- and great great-grandchildren, who express enormous interest and commitment to celebrating their background and family history.

Prior to starting his higher education at Bangor Normal College, Dan spent three months in 1875, working as a student teacher at Llanddewibrefi School, Cardiganshire, when the schoolmaster Rhystud Davies was ill. He wrote:

> Llanddewi had been very close to my heart for many years. I used to spend part of the holidays from school and college, staying with my uncle and aunt at Pant, which was three fields away from the village.[3]

Dan also collected items which illustrated the society and times of which he was a part. For instance, he obtained and retained the original tickets for a concert at the British School, Llancrwys in May 1873, along with an invoice issued in the 1820s by a local medical practioner, John Harries (shown right). This invoice reminds the recipient that if the aforementioned amount for treatment is not paid "adverse means will be resorted to for the recovery".

Another historic document which he collected was an I.O.U.

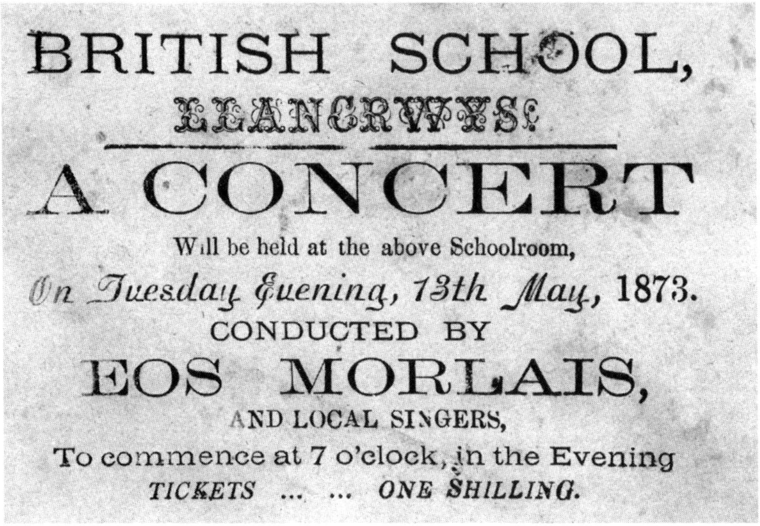

BRITISH SCHOOL,
LLANCRWYS.

A CONCERT

Will be held at the above Schoolroom,
On Tuesday Evening, 13th May, 1873.
CONDUCTED BY
EOS MORLAIS,
AND LOCAL SINGERS,
To commence at 7 o'clock, in the Evening
TICKETS ... ... ONE SHILLING.

Dan Jenkins' scrapbooks

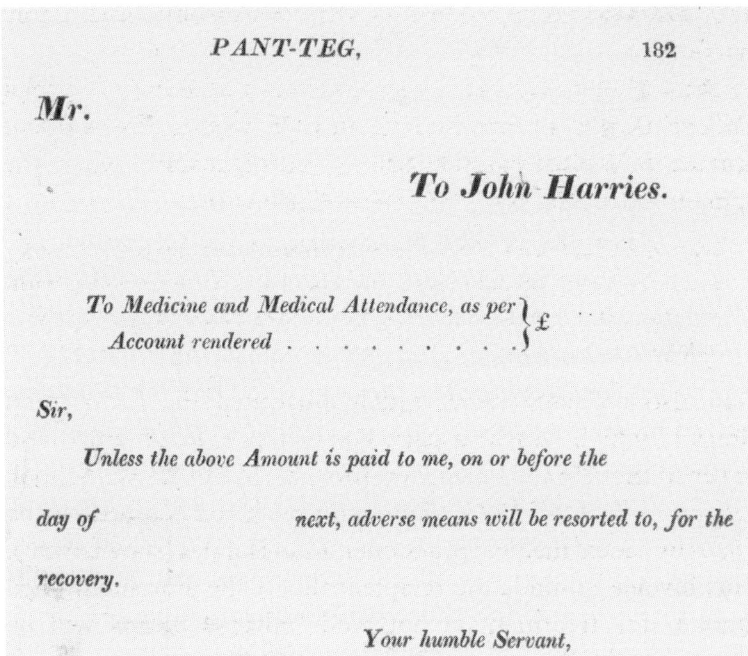

PANT-TEG, 182

Mr.

To John Harries.

To Medicine and Medical Attendance, as per Account rendered . . . . } £

Sir,

Unless the above Amount is paid to me, on or before the day of next, adverse means will be resorted to, for the recovery.

Your humble Servant,

Medical invoice

Dan Jenkins' scrapbooks

(I owe you), of April 1845, from the Rev. Morgan Williams, the minister of St Mary's Church, Llanfair Clydogau, for 5s. which he had borrowed from local farmer, Thomas Richards of Pentrelan. Morgan Williams eventually borrowed more money to engage in lead and silver mine speculation and was imprisoned for debt in Cardigan jail, where he died in 1859.[4]

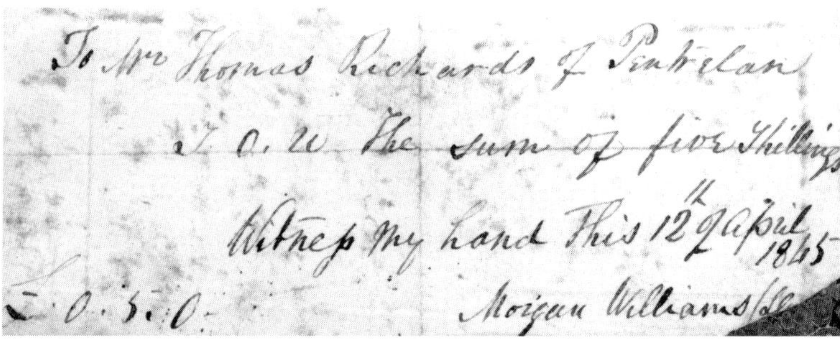
To Mr Thomas Richards of Pentrelan
I O U the sum of five Shillings
Witness my hand This 12th of April 1845
£ 0. 5. 0. Morgan Williams

Morgan Williams I.O.U.
Dan Jenkins' scrapbooks

Bangor Normal College

Bangor Normal College was an independent teacher training college, dating from 1861. It was founded by the British and Foreign Schools Society with the aim of training teachers for non-denominational primary schools (that is, not affiliated to any church). Dan Jenkins attended the college in 1876 and 1877. The college archivist writes: "he completed his course, having passed in the second division."[5] (This is regarded today as a second class degree.) The archives do not contain any further information about his studies. However, Dan was enthusiastic about his time there and, in line with his keenness to record history and events, he collected comments and autographs from his lecturers and those who had worked with him on his teaching practice placements, and pasted them in his scrapbooks. The principal, Daniel Rowlands, wrote about him: "sings well and altogether we can recommend him as

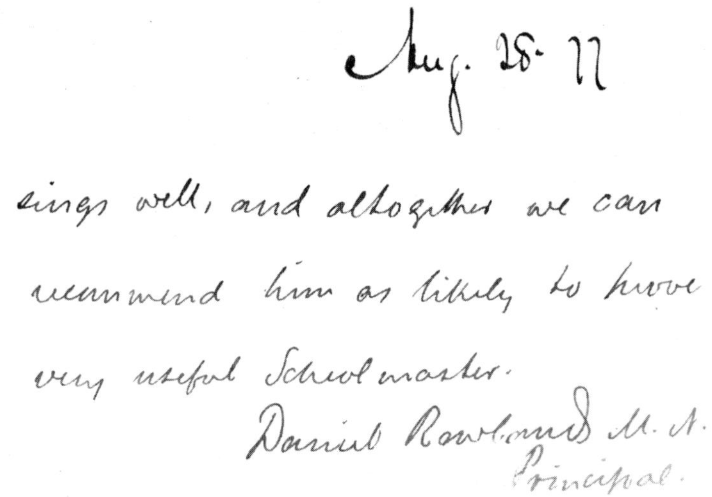

Aug. 28. 77

sings well, and altogether we can recommend him as likely to prove a very useful Schoolmaster.

Daniel Rowlands M.A.
Principal.

Bangor College comments

Dan Jenkins' scrapbooks

likely to prove a very useful school master." His scrapbooks also contain the autographs of various staff members such as John Price, vice principal, R N Phillips, art tutor; his maths tutor and staff at his practice schools of St Paul's and Garth. Note the emphasis in the principal's comment on Dan's singing. This aspect of his ability was enormously important to all parts of his later personal and professional life.

Myfanwy Armitage has written: "a black and white photograph taken of him whilst at Bangor showed him to be a slim, tall young man and very good looking. He was clean-shaven with fair hair parted on the right hand side and combed back from his forehead, with the back and sides cut short." She added that: "the photograph showed him dressed in a light grey, well tailored waistcoat suit, and his whole appearance was of gentry class. Unfortunately, no trace of this photograph or the album in which it was contained can now be found. In the same album there were photographs of some very elegantly dressed young ladies whom he said were

Family recollections suggest that Dan is on the back row, fifth from the left on this Bangor College photograph of 1875–7

Dan Jenkins' scrapbooks

students at the college while he was there."[6] However, the photographs to which she refers may well be the ones shown here, which I have taken from Dan's scrapbooks.

As he came towards the end of his two year course, Dan looked for a teaching job in the burgeoning elementary school sector (catering for all ages of children). All across England and Wales new schools were being built as a result of the recent legal requirement for children to attend school and for communities to provide the facilities. There was a surge in the demand for teachers. He was appointed to his first permanent job at Cilcennin, Cardiganshire.

Essay competition

Sometime in the middle years of the 1870s, Dan entered a Cardiganshire-based essay writing competition. Entrants were required to produce an essay in Welsh entitled: 'Cynnydd Llanbedr Pont Steffan', an essay on 'The development and improvement of Lampeter, 1863–78'. The 24-page long handwritten tract which he produced was awarded first prize in the unspecified competition. It appears under the signature of ap Tulas, a bardic name used by Dan at this time.[7] The neat handwriting of the essay is clearly his.

Cilcennin School

Cilcennin is a small village to the west of Tal-sarn and about four miles from Dan's family home at Pentrefelin. The board school was erected in 1876 under the impetus of the 1870 Education Act, with accommodation for 96 pupils. A note from his daughter Elin Lloyd, refers to Dan being paid £60 per year for his work as the master of the newly established school. It was to be a short stay, as he commenced work on

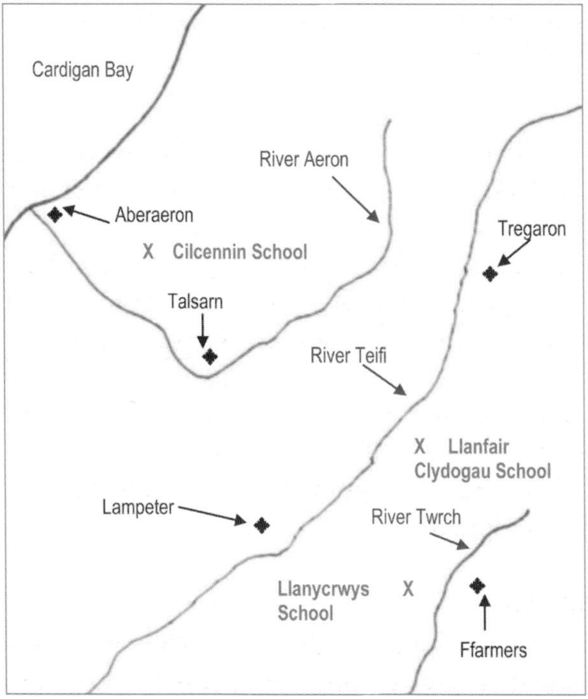

Schools at which Dan Jenkins was headteacher

Dan Jenkins is shown on the back row, far right (1875–7)
Dan Jenkins' scrapbooks

24th December 1877 and left on 9th October 1878. The reason seems to be a clash about policy between Dan and the school board. Like all schools at this time, the Welsh language was not to be used with the almost exclusively Welsh-speaking children. Officialdom in the form of the government had decreed this for all schools in Wales. The task for the teacher in charge, or headteacher as he would have been called, was to change the children from speaking Welsh, their language of the home, into a new language, English, which policy stated would be the language of schools.

Unfortunately, neither the school logbook nor the minutes of the school board covering this early period have survived. Later years are covered by documents held by Ceredigion Archives office. Hence, sadly we have no information about the issues and challenges which this 21-year-old man faced, or officially why he left after such a relatively short space of time. One account in *Y Byd o Ben Trichrug* (The world from the top of Trichrug) describes Dan and the opening of Cilcennin

School. The author refers to the children waiting for their new teacher to arrive and states:

> All of a sudden this well-dressed young man came in. He looked with a schoolmasterly eye at us. He was Dan Jenkins of Pentrefelin. He came straight from college to teach us as someone with authority. He soon won the respect and admiration of the children and the community. He was a good singer and worked hard in the chapel especially with the singing. People would remember for a long time the religious fervour of the two anthems sung under his instruction, namely 'Datod mae rhwymau caethiwed ein teyrnas' [Untying are the bonds of our nation] and 'Wylwyn' [Weeping/wailing]. I understand he was about nine months there.[8]

Several sources shed some light on the severe problems which he encountered at Cilcennin. These were rooted in two key issues: the Welsh language and the extent of religious instruction within this state school. The issue of Welsh related to his approach and attitude towards its use and position in school. A note by one of his daughters, written many years later, describes her recollection of what he had told her, of one of the children going home after school and telling her parents that the 'Lord's Prayer' had been recited in Welsh, rather than the expected English. This use of Welsh enraged members of the school board who were keen to see English, the language of trade and commerce, promoted, developed and embedded within the school. The issue of the Christian religion's overall place within this new, untried and undeveloped school was also significant. Dr T I Davies, a pupil at the school from 1918–26 (40 years after Dan left), presumably recalling the folklore of the village over the years after his departure, wrote in the centenary publication of the school:

> The new school was bedevilled for a while by sectarian religion. The first headmaster, Dan Jenkins, Pentrefelin, came straight out of the nonconformist Normal College in Bangor, indoctrinated with the idea that religion should be left to the Sunday schools. He'd have none of it [religion] in the day school. This got to the

> ears of the school board, whose red-haired chairman was not unlike Dan Jenkins to look at, except that he had lost one blue eye in the Crimea. At a celebrated meeting of the board, the chairman let rip and said: 'Go fetch the headmaster. I will make the devil pay.'[9]

Granddaughter Myfanwy Armitage gave a different slant on the dispute. She wrote:

> Welsh reading and writing was taught on Sunday in chapels and churches and in the Sunday schools associated with them. This was to enable people to read the Bible. But it seems that Daniel Jenkins considered that enough scripture was learnt on Sundays and it was necessary for children to be able to read and write fluently in Welsh, their native language, and he started to teach Welsh reading and writing instead of the morning scripture lesson in English at the school.[10]

The Cilcennin centenary publication summarised the situation as follows:

> At the end of nine months Dan Jenkins was gone. His subsequent record at Llanycrwys proves that Cilcennin had lost a man who, as a teacher, was all of 100 years ahead of his time. He was replaced here by a monoglot English-speaker by the name of Savage.[11]

This comment is correct; Dan Jenkins was way ahead of his time in considering what should be taught, the position of the Welsh language and also the central position of the school within the life of the village and indeed, the parish. After he had left, a school inspector said publicly that it was a great tragedy that Cilcennin had lost such a good headmaster. It was also a sad loss for the cultural activities in Cilcennin, as a newspaper article, written years later in 1936 states:

> Dan Jenkins came direct from college and soon won the respect of the children of the neighbourhood. He was a fine musician, and hard working in the chapel, especially with the singing. Cilcennin was first in the school gymanfa at Tynygwndwn that year and the young school master conducted the singing.[12]

Life in Cardiganshire in the late 19th century

In the early years of the century, the population of the county had grown steadily as its main area of employment, agriculture, was augmented by an expansion in lead mining. Transport links were improved, with greater care being given to the roads, and the arrival of railways. Welsh was overwhelmingly the spoken language of the people. Yet, a great wave of change began to occur at about the time when Dan Jenkins, as an adult, began to make his way in the world. For instance, as already recounted, English became the required language of the new school system; major change to the electoral system occurred and, in addition, the basic economy of the county underwent a profound alteration. These changes affected every facet of society: social, financial, political and religious. One writer has commented:

> In the early 1880s, Cardiganshire, like every other county in rural Wales, was in the grip of a prolonged recession. This was intensified by the collapse in the price of foodstuffs that afflicted the farming community from 1879 onwards, as the effects of American and Russian competition came to be felt.[13.]

Rural depopulation began to take place on a large scale, especially in the eastern lead mining districts of the county. Overall, the population of Cardiganshire declined dramatically, falling from 71,000 in 1871, to 59,000 in 1911. The reduction was almost 10 per cent in the years between 1881 and 1891. The birth rate was high, with many large families, but the rate of emigration was spectacular, especially of young men. The arrival of the railway had helped many more to secure an easy transport route to the coalfields of Glamorganshire and Carmarthenshire where they could gain work in the mines. So great was the flood of population towards the south, that the 1891 census showed that in the Rhondda valleys, there were almost 6,000 men who had been born in Cardiganshire.[14] Others left to develop the milk trade in London, including members of the wider Jenkins family.

The county at this time had one of the highest proportions of its working population engaged in agriculture, as farmers or labourers. Most of these were tenant farmers or smallholders on newly enclosed lands in the eastern, more marginal upland areas. A lot of this land was of poor quality and it was difficult to sustain the livelihood of a family. Some got round the problem by the male member moving away to work for most of the year in the coal mines, leaving behind women and children. This characteristic was very prevalent on Llanfair mountain in the eastern part of the parish of Llanfair Clydogau. Dan Jenkins became very aware of this during his long period of work at the board school there. As one historical account of the county states:

> On all sides therefore, Cardiganshire manifested the grim symbols of a depressed area. The loss of young males, the high prevalence of idiocy and deaf mutes in the county, the preponderance in its age structure of the 45–65 and over-65 groups, and a truly staggering surplus of unmarried females. The proportion of females to males was the highest for England and Wales recorded in six successive censuses: in 1891, there were 1,274 females for every 1,000 males. The census commissioners quaintly attributed this phenomenon to the difficulty that monoglot Welshwomen from Cardiganshire found in gaining employment in domestic service outside the county.[15]

Balancing the problems of decline was the growth in the population of the developing urban settlements such as Aberystwyth, and the efforts being made to improve the agriculture within the county. In this respect no area was more important than the vale of Aeron, with its fertile soils and the production of butter and cheese. The Lampeter Agricultural Society helped to play a part in this and was encouraged by the very active local landowner, Mr J C Harford of Falcondale near Lampeter, who was not only a leading participant in farming, but also a county councillor.

This was the background to the life of Dan Jenkins. He saw at close hand the impact of mass emigration on the farming communities, the people who lived there and the social consequences for education, church and chapel and a general way of life that had been in place for a long time. He saw the impact on the Welsh language, the economic hardship of people and the loss of family and social structures which helped to maintain the traditions of the past such as folk singing, public performing, the writing and reciting of poetry and local eisteddfodau. He saw two of his uncles emigrate to the USA and a third, leave for Australia.

Yet, he chose to stay in Cardiganshire, and not join the exodus to south Wales, England or the new world. Instead, with his high level of ability, inquisitiveness, interest in history and the collection of local literature, combined with commitment and energy, he set about making a contribution to society and the economy, plus the retention and celebration of old and ancient traditions and practices. He helped to participate in the development and revival of farming. He was at the vanguard of the arrival and expansion of the elementary school in rural communities and helped to shape both the education process and society, so that within them, an important place was found and occupied by the Welsh language and culture.

Chapter Three

The Llanfair Clydogau years (1878–97)

Capel Mair, Llanfair where Dan Jenkins was married in 1886
Cyfrol y Jiwbili

After leaving Cilcennin in October 1878, Dan Jenkins joined Llanfair Clydogau Board School, located in Cardiganshire, north of Lampeter in the river Teifi valley, on 28th October 1878. He was described as 'master', or what today would be called headteacher. There were 65 children on roll. The school was newly built following the implementation of the 1870 Education Act. Under this act, a school board had been set up for Llanfair Clydogau parish and a decision taken to build a school on land bought from the Lord of the Manor, William Jones, a bank proprietor and major landowner, who lived at Glandenys mansion, in the nearby village of Betws Bledrws.

Prior to this, educational provision was largely unavailable for the vast majority, with a few children attending small fee paying 'schools' in the homes of industrious local residents. The first headteacher of the school had been Mr Pritchard of Machynlleth, who worked from the autumn of 1877 until September of 1878. One of Dan's scrapbooks shows a small newspaper advertisement for the job he got, as follows:

> Llanfair Clydogau; wanted by 1st October, a trained certified Master, single, for a new mixed school under the above board; accommodation for 110 children; salary in first year £80; apply to Mr D Jones, Old Bank, Lampeter.

The man to whom applications had to be made, David Jones, was manager of the Lord of the Manor's bank. He was also responsible for providing secretaryship to the Llanfair Clydogau School Board and, in addition, acted as agent for William Jones in the administering of his estate with its many tenant farms in the area of Llanfair and Cellan. This close linkage of roles, and the connection with the affairs of the major landowner was significant. It added to the existing pivotal position occupied by William Jones. He had influence, a degree of control and, as the major wealthy establishment figure of the locality, aura and image. He had links with 30 to 40 tenant farms which he owned, the agricultural economy, banking, finance, the church and, in many ways, topped the social class hierarchy in the area.

The school logbook indicates that on the 4th October 1878, as an emergency measure, the school was in the charge of temporary master, John Jones of Lampeter Board School, who had been "preparing for his scholarship". He was there following the departure of Mr Pritchard and "until Mr Jenkins comes to take charge". Dan's first day was 28th October, following his departure from Cilcennin School.

Living in Llanfair

Once appointed, Dan Jenkins had to live away from his home at Pentrefelin, since the journey of approximately seven miles by road made it impossible to travel on a daily basis. Journeying home would have entailed walking. The evidence shows that during his stay in Llanfair from 1878–97, he lived in several locations, but, because of his love of farming, he travelled back home from the outset to the family farm very regularly. He wrote:

> I spent six very happy years lodging with John and Anne Davies at Ty Canol – the middle of the three single floor houses known as Silver Mine and no tall person dared go to bed in the gromlwyd [crog loft].[1]

However, the 1881 census shows him lodging at the house called Office Fawr (large office) in Llanfair; a building constructed to serve the once thriving Llanfair lead and silver mines nearby (the mines had closed in about 1862). Also, in 1895, after the building of a schoolhouse close to the school, he moved to this new more independent and autonomous location.

Establishing the school

His immediate task upon arrival in Llanfair was to continue with the establishment and development of the new institution in this very rural area. Up until this time there had been no tradition of attending school, except the Sunday schools belonging to both St Mary's Church and the non-denominational Capel Mair, or the small unregulated private 'schools'. He later wrote that hitherto: "not a great effort was placed by parishioners to educate their children."[2] The task was how to get all the parents to send their children to school, especially when (though attendance was compulsory), there was a requirement to make a payment towards their child's education. Equally necessary, was to put into place a teaching curriculum, obtain enough books and teaching equipment and set about the work of introducing the entirely Welsh-speaking youngsters to English, the required medium of instruction. As stated, Welsh was not a recognised school subject, nor acceptable as a medium of conversation or instruction in

Llanfair Clydogau former school building (2010)

schools. It was a task of some magnitude, especially with a pupil age range of five to thirteen years, divided into several teaching groups, with little space and equipment. Heating during winter was inadequate; water was taken manually from the well and toilets were primitive. Children often had to walk three miles to reach the school, which was located on the steep hill on the eastern side of the Teifi valley, above both the site of St Mary's Church and the former manor house of Plas Llanfair. The building was converted into a family home after its closure in 1976.

By today's standards, conditions were grim, with often tired, wet and puzzled children. During his first week Dan noted that:

> … the children behave badly. They do not even wish either 'good morning' or 'good evening' to a person passing on the road. In addition, there are no pens and folders for writing and writing in the upper standards is but fair.[3]

It seems likely that he knew the Llanfair area before he applied to work here. After all, one of his father's sisters, Margaret Evans, lived with her family at Clwtypatrwn farm in the parish. Myfanwy Armitage wrote in the 1990s:

> At first it seems the residents of Llanfair were not too pleased with him, as they thought he should spend more time in the village, attend the local chapel and be a help and adviser to the community. But it was soon realised that he was an excellent master and he became fully appreciated.[4]

After a short time at Llanfair he received his certificate as a qualified teacher (right), following an assessment by a school inspector, and by May of 1879, a further inspection of the school gave rise to a log entry as follows: "The new master seems to have done his best to improve the school during the few months he has been here." Both sewing and singing were praised. The school logbook shows Dan Jenkins, over the years, working with an assistant teacher, usually a woman, and pupil teachers, who were learning their trade. In 1885, the annual inspection concluded: "the school appears to be well conducted, and is on the whole, well instructed. The scholars passed, on the whole, a good examination in English and in elementary subjects." Specially praised was the practical work undertaken in singing where "the scholars sang with much taste and they did fairly in singing from notes." This shows Dan achieving a lot through his high-quality singing skills.

Llanfair, like all board schools, received its funding from three sources: the parental fees, the school board for the parish and the annual grant from the Department of Education in London. The latter was based upon firstly, the number of children on roll and secondly, the quality of work undertaken within the school in the opinion of the inspector carrying out the annual visit. This 'payment by results' saw Llanfair receive the highest grants possible during the five years 1892–97 under Dan Jenkins' leadership, along with the 'excellent' award in drawing in 1896 and 1897. Saturday morning classes also occurred at various times in the 1880s. In the 1890s, he started an evening continuation school in order to provide extra opportunities for the older children, the majority of whom did not go to secondary school, but remained in Llanfair. These Saturday classes would have made it even more difficult to get over to Pentrefelin during a crowded weekend.

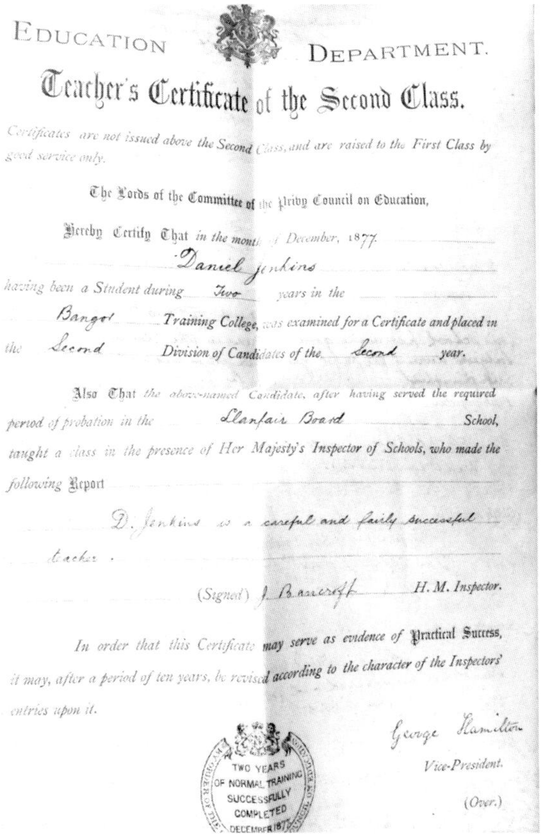
EDUCATION DEPARTMENT.

Teacher's Certificate of the Second Class.

Certificates are not issued above the Second Class, and are raised to the First Class by good service only.

The Lords of the Committee of the Privy Council on Education,

Hereby Certify That in the month of December, 1877.

Daniel Jenkins

having been a Student during Two years in the Bangor Training College, was examined for a Certificate and placed in the Second Division of Candidates of the Second year.

Also That the above-named Candidate, after having served the required period of probation in the Llanfair Board School, taught a class in the presence of Her Majesty's Inspector of Schools, who made the following Report

D. Jenkins is a careful and fairly successful teacher.

(Signed) J. Bancroft H. M. Inspector.

In order that this Certificate may serve as evidence of Practical Success, it may, after a period of ten years, be revised according to the character of the Inspectors' entries upon it.

TWO YEARS OF NORMAL TRAINING SUCCESSFULLY COMPLETED DECEMBER 1877

George Hamilton
Vice-President.

(Over.)

Teacher's Certificate

Dan Jenkins' scrapbooks

Personal life

Dan's life at Llanfair was, from the beginning, very busy. He was a single man, living in lodgings, and by the standards of today, he was very young, at the age of almost 22, to be the headteacher of a school. A great deal was asked of him and, according to the inspection reports, he responded well and with considerable success. Whilst at Llanfair, he first met the young woman who would some seven years later become his wife. Elizabeth Williams was born in Llanfair in 1862, the third of the seven children born to William Williams and his wife Anne. Prior to 1871 the family was living at Pentrelan, a farm on the edge of Llanfair mountain, close to the Roman road of Sarn Helen. By 1871, they had moved to the much larger and more prosperous valley farm of Pentre and Elizabeth's mother had died. She (at 18 years of age), was the eldest daughter still at home and was running the domestic side of a household which included her father, two older brothers, two younger brothers and two farm servants. They were a very well-known family because of their size and the length of time they had been within the parish, with the two younger boys attending Llanfair Board School. They were amongst the first to enrol at the new school in October 1877. Elizabeth's sister Margaret had married David Richards, who farmed the nearby large and desirable farm of Penlan. Myfanwy Armitage has written of

Dan Jenkins in his early years at the school
Dan Jenkins' scrapbooks

her conversation with Elizabeth, who was then aged 79, as she recalled how she first met Dan Jenkins:

> She was 17 years old when a tall, well-dressed young man called at the farm to introduce himself to her father. Two of her brothers were attending the school where he was the headmaster, he told her. She was washing the family clothes in a tub of hot water in the front yard of the farmhouse and she was embarrassed as she had to lift her apron to wipe her hands before she could shake his. She didn't say it was love at first sight, but said he continued to call at her home as he got on well with her father. They also met at concerts and fairs and it was seven years later when he asked her to marry him. By then she was 24 and he was 29 years old.[5]

Dan and Elizabeth married on 29th October 1886 at Capel Mair, Llanfair Clydogau. This is located close to Llanfair bridge shop and the river Teifi. Officiating at the wedding were the Reverends Thomas Thomas (pastor) and John Evans of Abermeurig; the latter being a brother-in-law of the groom. The *Cambrian News*[6] reported the wedding as follows:

> The bride and groom were cheered lustily, greeted with flags, arches, rice, mottoes and other means of congratulations, and also the firing of guns. The bride's father provided an excellent dinner for scores of relatives and friends and the evening was spent speech making, poetry reciting, and toasts were made, drinking in honour of the happy couple, who were deservedly popular in the vales of Aeron and Teifi.

The well-known bard Carolan (Benjamin Carolan Davies) wrote the happy couple a special poem which wished them a happy and long life. Probably because the two families were well known and important in the region, a newspaper published the poem:

> **Verses written for the wedding of Mr Dan Jenkins, Llanfair Board School and Miss Elizabeth Williams, Pentre, Llanfair Clydogau.**
>
> What is this special skill
> That ties two people together,
> Before many people
> On bended knee,

The passion in the eyes,
Sad faces become happy,
It plays around the gentle lips,
It weaves around the heart.

Who will trace its origin?
It is like an electric current.
Dan and Lizzie will reply
That it is love.
Who can give a better explanation?
For a word so full of fire,
They specialise in the topic,
They deserve a song.

Within the wedding ring of love
I see a boy and girl,
Their hearts tied together
With the silver threads of love.
Dan can sing a solo
A time full of happiness,
He conquered a beautiful girl
He won her total love.

He won her heart
and she won his,
Their union will be blessed
by smiles from heaven.
Blessed be your journey
And may it be long and happy,
And heaven – the home of true love
May it bless their journey to the end.

May your future world be full of happiness
May the sun shine upon you,
Dear Dan and Lizzie
Until the end of time.

Carolan (translated by Aerwen Griffiths) [ref 1]

Commenting upon the wedding day many years later in 1946, Dan told the *Cambrian News*: "There was no fuss in those days. We walked to the chapel and went in a horse and trap to Llanybydder fair for our honeymoon."

The tenancy of Pentrefelin and married life

Precisely where the newly married couple lived in 1886 is unclear. A letter to Dan Jenkins in Llanfair, from Jenkins and Evans, solicitors of Cardigan in February 1883, refers to his taking over the tenancy of Pentrefelin, retrospectively from Michaelmas 1882. It looks like he took this over from his brother, since the 1881 census shows the 'head' of the house as being brother John, who was described as a farmer with 70 acres. Also living in the house in 1881 were his father and mother, Griffith and Catherine, then aged 65 and 68. There is an inscribed stone in the wall at Pentrefelin which states 'D Jenkins 1886'. It is presumed this signifies in some way, the beginning of his possession of the farm as a married man. What we can deduce is that upon their marriage, the newly wedded couple moved either to Pentrefelin, though Dan of course would have had to be back in Llanfair to run the school during the week; or they moved to Dan's lodgings at Office Fawr; or alternatively they stayed at Elizabeth's father's home of Pentre. It seems likely that during the first few years from 1886, they adopted some form of complex living arrangement. Elizabeth's first child Anne was born in Llanfair Clydogau in 1887. Census information tells us that all her other nine children were born in the parish of Nantcwnlle, presumably at Pentrefelin. As recorded on the family tree compiled by granddaughter Myfanwy Armitage, the children were: Anne (1887–1915); Griffith (1889–1957); Kitty (1890–1972); Gwilym (1893–94); Dilys (1894–95); Anna (1895–1974); Ivor (1896–1987); Olwen (1899–199?); Jonathan (Jack, 1902–76) and Elin (1908–92).

To add to our understanding of the complexity of the family's living arrangements, the school records of Llanfair

Dan Jenkins and family *c.* 1902–03 after he had left Llanfair Clydogau.
Dan Jenkins' scrapbooks

show Anne being admitted to the school as a pupil, just before her fifth birthday in 1891 and six-year-old Kitty Jenkins joining in July 1896. Yet, their brother Griffith, born between Anne and Kitty did not attend Llanfair. So perhaps the family was geographically split at this time, with some in Llanfair and some in Pentrefelin with a gathering together at weekends.

The above photograph, which has been labelled by one of Dan's daughters, shows the growing Jenkins family a few years after he had left Llanfair. Whilst still employed at the school, census night in 1891 shows Dan and Elizabeth, along with

Inscription at Pentrefelin dated 1886 (2010)

three children and two farm employees, recorded as resident at Pentrefelin with Dan shown as farmer and schoolmaster. So we know he was not away from home on that night. Yet, what is clear is that Elizabeth had a major job to do in overseeing and running the farm during the weekdays when Dan was away in Llanfair. She would have had many of the skills needed to undertake this work in view of her major role, both as a farmer's daughter, and as the senior woman in her father's household from a relatively early age.

If we summarise the time up to 1894. Dan was a busy man running an all-age school, where there were pupils in excess of a 100 some years. He was living at first in temporary accommodation, commuting at weekends between Llanfair and Pentrefelin. He was working with his wife to successfully farm and pay the annual rent on the tenancy. He became a father to five children. He was contributing much to Llanfair parish through his work at the school and his many contacts both with parents of schoolchildren, and his own relatives by marriage, the Williams and Richards families.

Wider community involvement

Not content with running the school and teaching full-time, Dan involved himself in a number of the major social and political matters of the day. The many changes in UK society which characterised the second half of the century gathered momentum at this time. For instance, following on from the development of elementary schools for all, a further initiative was the arrival of intermediate education after 1889, which saw the building of new schools for older children in Lampeter, Tregaron, Aberaeron and Cardigan. This development witnessed a further demand for teachers and hence more had to be trained. Accompanying this educational development was the creation and then rapid growth of the National Union of Teachers (NUT): a body which aimed to campaign for educational opportunities for all, along with improved working conditions for teachers. There was no laid down salary scale for teachers; it was entirely a matter for the local school board to determine the wages of staff. Nor was there any pension scheme for employees. Dan was in the forefront of some of the campaigns on these developments in that he was an active member of the NUT, and experienced at first hand the power of the parish's school board in terms of it arbitrarily determining his salary and contract of employment.

The publicity for Trefnlen Cyfarfod Llanfair (agenda for a meeting in Llanfair) of 1886, shows Dan as the secretary of the organising group. The 29 items of entertainment and competition which were to take place from 4.30 p.m., included singing, wood crafts and poetry. The compère was the bard Aeronian (Dan's cousin, and the son of the famous bard Cerngoch). This event was an evening of celebration of the local culture – in many ways a mini eisteddfod.

The English and Welsh languages within Llanfair School

From its founding, everything officially recorded about the school was required to be in English. That was the language of teaching, writing, music, correspondence with the government, inspection and with the five-man Llanfair Board of Education. The inherent Welshness of the children was overwhelmed by a remorseless flood of the English language and of English accoutrements such as in the few books they had, and also through the songs they were required to learn and sing.

The then current attitude towards the Welsh language was conditioned by the kind of comment in the *Report of the Committee of Council on Education* of 1868, which reported that, although the Welsh language in Wales "was very prevalent and may be said to be the language of the people, the inspectorate (HMI) were opposed to its use in the classroom."[7] As an indication of the position of the Welsh language, below is an extract from the school logbook, written by Dan, which lists the songs prepared for the annual school examination in 1888. All are in English.

Evidence of a gradual increasing acceptability of the Welsh language is provided by the school logbook. In 1890, upon a visit to the school, board member Walter Griffiths of Blaen-cwm boldly wrote several sentences in Welsh recording his presence. Thereafter, each time he called to check the number of children present against the official attendance list, he wrote in Welsh. This checking mechanism, but not the use of Welsh, was a requirement of the board system. The only other board member to write in the logbook in Welsh was Evan Abel of the Factory. Others who recorded their call at the school did so in English.

Dan Jenkins and the Welsh language

Dan was highly competent in both English and Welsh. From this strong personal position, he wanted to slow the decline

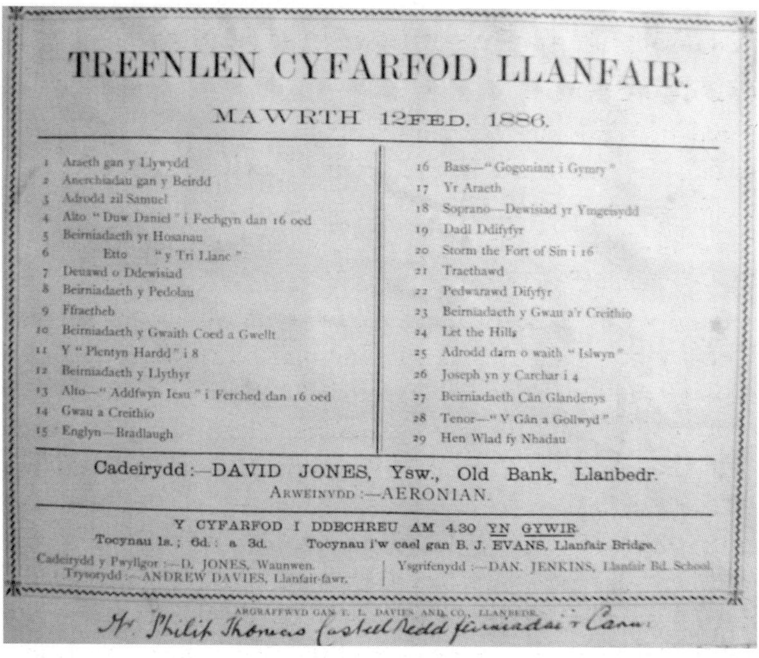

TREFNLEN CYFARFOD LLANFAIR.

MAWRTH 12FED. 1886.

1 Araeth gan y Llywydd
2 Anerchiadau gan y Beirdd
3 Adrodd zil Samuel
4 Alto "Duw Daniel" i Fechgyn dan 16 oed
5 Beirniadaeth yr Hosanau
6 Etto "y Tri Llanc"
7 Deuawd o Ddewisiad
8 Beirniadaeth y Pedolau
9 Ffraetheb
10 Beirniadaeth y Gwaith Coed a Gwellt
11 Y "Plentyn Hardd" i 8
12 Beirniadaeth y Llythyr
13 Alto—"Addfwyn Iesu" i Ferched dan 16 oed
14 Gwau a Creithio
15 Englyn—Bradlaugh
16 Bass—"Gogoniant i Gymry"
17 Yr Araeth
18 Soprano—Dewisiad yr Ymgeisydd
19 Dadl Ddifyfyr
20 Storm the Fort of Sin i 16
21 Traethawd
22 Pedwarawd Difyfyr
23 Beirniadaeth y Gwau a'r Creithio
24 Let the Hills
25 Adrodd darn o waith "Islwyn"
26 Joseph yn y Carchar i 4
27 Beirniadaeth Cân Glandenys
28 Tenor—"Y Gân a Gollwyd"
29 Hen Wlad fy Nhadau

Cadeirydd:—DAVID JONES, Ysw., Old Bank, Llanbedr.
ARWEINYDD:—AERONIAN.

Y CYFARFOD I DDECHREU AM 4.30 YN GYWIR.
Tocynau 1s.; 6d.; a 3d. Tocynau i'w cael gan B. J. EVANS, Llanfair Bridge.

Cadeirydd y Pwyllgor:—D. JONES, Waunwen.
Trysorydd:—ANDREW DAVIES, Llanfair-fawr.
Ysgrifenydd:—DAN. JENKINS, Llanfair Bd. School

ARGRAFFWYD GAN T. L. DAVIES AND CO., LLANBEDR.

Llanfair event

Dan Jenkins' scrapbooks

in the use of the Welsh language and raise its official status, especially in schools. His recorded comments, personal notes and lifestyle show his enthusiasm for this. He can be said to have been a campaigner, a motivator, an inspirer and a conduit for change. When he attended the National Eisteddfod in Aberdare in 1885, he attended a meeting of the Union of Welsh Societies. At the meeting decisions were taken to campaign to change the regulations for schools and so permit and encourage the use and teaching of Welsh. The same meeting also asked four headteachers to write a series of four textbooks to assist the teaching of the language in elementary schools. The evidence suggests Dan was one of these.[8]

It became legally possible to teach Welsh as a part of the school curriculum in 1891. Not all schools responded. Many were extremely reluctant to embrace this new freedom. Yet this opportunity was taken up enthusiastically by Dan at Llanfair. An indication of this is the school logbook which records a major shift in the songs the children had learnt during the year, with many more Welsh ballads used in 1894–5 (shown below).

The formal teaching of Welsh as a classroom subject also began and was a success. On an unannounced visit to the school in June 1894, one of Her Majesty's Inspectors of Schools (HMI) commented: "The first class did creditably in Welsh as a specific subject."[9]

Religion

Dan has written that in Llanfair many familes had an allegiance to either Capel Mair or St Mary's Church, with some families "sharing their allegiance, with one member attending chapel and another, church". It was a very chapel and church centred community, with a large percentage of the population attending one or the other. The parish's population peaked at 614 persons in 1861 and thereafter began a steady decline which was paralleled throughout many rural areas of the county. Dan became a member of the chapel and he says "was happy there, while I lived in Llanfair, close on 20 years. Their religion, like themselves, was simple, plain and good and all homespun. All services were natural." He added: "some tree trunks kept the fire alight, but it's the kindling that keeps the water boiling." He recalled that:

> ... for church and chapel the most important service of the year was the Thanksgiving service (Harvest), with a sermon in church and a prayer meeting in the chapel. It was in fact an overall parish service and always well attended when a number of churchgoers took part in the chapel service.[10]

Music and singing

We know that Dan Jenkins was a good, enthusiastic and avid singer. He had a rich bass voice. He was confident, self-assured and keen to entertain, encourage and train others in the art. As a teenager, he was frequently entertaining an English audience during his short period of schooling in Herefordshire, when he performed without accompaniment, singing in Welsh. He sang in school in Llanfair and encouraged children to do the same. He was very committed to the enjoyment of singing and led by personal example.

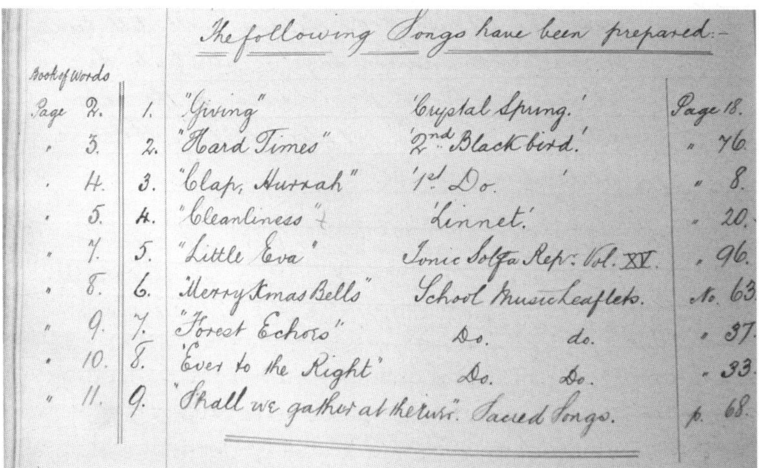

The following Songs have been prepared:-

Book of Words				
Page 2.	1.	"Giving"	'Crystal Spring.'	Page 18.
" 3.	2.	"Hard Times"	'2nd Blackbird.'	" 76.
" 4.	3.	"Clap, Hurrah"	'1st Do.'	" 8.
" 5.	4.	"Cleanliness"	'Linnet.'	" 20.
" 7.	5.	"Little Eva"	Tonic Solfa Rep: Vol. XV.	" 96.
" 8.	6.	"Merry Xmas Bells"	School Music Leaflets.	No. 63.
" 9.	7.	"Forest Echoes"	Do. do.	" 37.
" 10.	8.	"Ever to the Right"	Do. Do.	" 33.
" 11.	9.	"Shall we gather at the river."	Sacred Songs.	p. 68.

Llanfair Clydogau school logbook, songs all in English

Ceredigion Archives

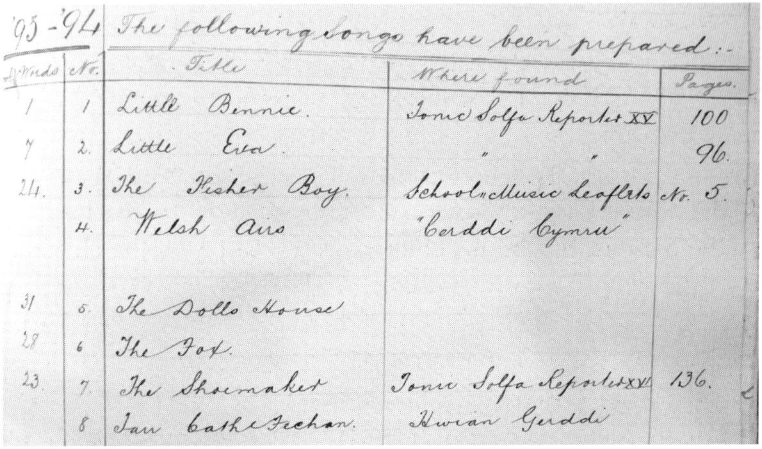
'93–'94 The following songs have been prepared:–

Words	No.	Title	Where found	Pages.
1	1	Little Bennie.	Tonic Solfa Reporter XV	100
7	2.	Little Eva.	" "	96.
24.	3.	The Fisher Boy.	School Music Leaflets	No. 5.
	4.	Welsh Airs	"Cerddi Cymru"	
31	5.	The Dolls House		
28	6	The Fox.		
23.	7.	The Shoemaker	Tonic Solfa Reporter XVI	136.
	8	Iau bach Fechan.	Hwian Gerddi	

Llanfair Clydogau school logbook, 1893–4, Welsh songs now included
Ceredigion Archives

Whilst at Llanfair he was sometimes asked to visit neighbouring parishes to sing, or to lead singing involving others. Islwyn Walters of Ffaldybrenin (Llanycrwys parish) in Carmarthenshire, recounted to me an occasion experienced by his grandfather, Thomas Walters. One evening, Dan Jenkins walked the four to five miles over the mountain from Llanfair to Ffaldybrenin to sing for an audience. Upon being accompanied part way on his journey home to his lodgings, he discussed the superiority of the paraffin lamps in Llanfair by comparison with the candle power in Ffaldybrenin. His part way walking companion joked: "we asked you to come to sing, not advise on lighting!"[11]

About Capel Mair, Dan has written:

> I never forgot that I was a newcomer and refused to do any job that another could do, but at their request I became leader of the ysgol gân [singing school], a task I really enjoyed. I have very happy memories of singing from Lloft Fach. The old lead singer was Walter Griffiths of Blaen-cwm. He had a strong clear voice and I never recall him singing out of tune.[12]

St David's Day

The changing times of the 1890s in terms of the legal position of Welsh within schools provided an opportunity for Dan to do something fairly unusual, if not unique at the time. He decided to allocate school time in order to celebrate St David's Day on 1st March 1894 by holding a concert. In the lead up to the big day, he and his colleagues worked with the children on preparing recitations, songs and Welsh airs. Because of his musical abilities and skill as a singer, Dan was well able to pull together all the parts of his personal vision for the event. He also invited the headteachers of the schools in the nearby parishes of Cellan, Llangybi and Llanddewibrefi to be a part of this inaugural event. His father-in-law chaired the performance.

The *Cambrian News* reported the event as follows:

> On St David's Day the children of the Llanfair Board School held their first Welsh concert in commemoration of the festival of the patron saint. In the absence of Mr B J Evans, Chairman of the Board, Mr Walter Williams, Pentre, presided, and Mr Dan Jenkins conducted. The young performers were adorned with the leek, as were a few of the audience. The programme was a lengthy one consisting of recitations, puzzles, action songs and Welsh airs. The following are a few of the items: 'Dydd Gwyl Dewi' children's choir; 'Llwyn Onn', 'Toriad y Dydd', 'Rhyfelgyrch Cabden Morgan', 'Codiad yr Hedydd', 'Nos Galan' (which was sung by the scholars after the manner of penillion singing) from *Cerddi Cymru*. The recitations were creditably rendered and taken mostly from *Hwian Gerddi* as were also the two tunes 'Robin Goch' and 'Tair Cath Fechan', which with 'The Shoemaker', 'The Dolls House' and 'The Fox' were amusingly given by the infants, conducted by Miss Benbow, the assistant mistress. Miss Hughes sang 'Y Deryn Pur'; Miss Hettie Jones 'Yr Eneth Ddall'; Miss S Richards 'Codiad yr Hedydd'; Mr D Lloyd and Mr Davies also gave solos. There were three items for competition: impromptu speech on 'Y Geninen', best was D Lloyd of Frondale; largest number of words beginning with the letter D, best was A Pugh of Pentre; best wit was J Williams of Llanfair-fach. Mr John Williams, merchant of

> Penygraig addressed the meeting. The finale was 'Hen Wlad fy Nhadau' with the audience standing and singing the chorus.[13]

This was a large and complex event, involving many children and adults. It went down well with the audience. A marker had been put down by Dan of what he thought was important and could be achieved. Good publicity was also forthcoming across Cardiganshire, Carmarthenshire and elsewhere through the newspaper coverage and, equally important, headteacher colleagues had attended and could see the approach adopted. In this respect, Dan Jenkins was seeking to lead public opinion in the direction that celebrating the country's patron saint was important. But, in addition, such a celebration allowed the use of the language, public performances, singing, poetry and the wearing of the leek.

National Union of Teachers

The NUT was founded in 1870 and its membership grew rapidly as the number of schools increased. Dan Jenkins was an early member, active in both the Lampeter and South Wales branches. He attended the NUT's annual conference also on a number of occasions; that was usually held at Easter at various well-known seaside towns. His scrapbooks indicate that he participated in delegations of rural school teachers who journeyed to union headquarters in central London. Their purpose was to lobby and discuss some of the issues of the moment which were of concern to country school teachers, such as wages and working conditions.

Dan's harsh treatment by the Llanfair School Board from 1894 and beyond proved to be one of the major cases used by the NUT in their campaign to firstly, improve the pay of rural teachers and secondly, bring about a greater security of tenure so that staff could not be callously dismissed for any discernible reason. His case assumed, along with a handful of others, a national significance in the struggle for workers' rights.

Before his major battle of 1894, as part of his commitment towards trying to improve the conditions and salaries of headteachers, Dan conducted surveys of local schools in both 1879 and 1886. This detailed comparative data on school wages and staff accommodation and can be seen in one of his scrapbooks. Once gathered, this information was conveyed to NUT headquarters in London, in order to help the statistical case being compiled by the union.

Welsh Land Commission of 1894

In Wales there had, for some time, been concern amongst farmers, especially tenant farmers, about the conditions under which they lived and farmed. Their issues included the lack of security of tenure, size of annual rent due to the landowner, low revenues for farm produce, repair and maintenance of farm buildings and how to secure payment for any self-funded improvements they had made, at the time they were choosing to leave the tenanted farm unit. There was also a strongly held view, supported by specific cases and a lively folk law, about people who had been evicted by Conservative supporting landlords for voting for the Liberal party in the election of 1868. Dan Jenkins would have been well aware of this background history.

Some of these matters came to a head in the 1890s when the government decided to set up a Welsh Land Commission to investigate the many issues surrounding the use, availability and ownership of land. As a result, farmers gathered together in many places in Cardiganshire during late 1893 and early 1894, to discuss how best to present evidence during the forthcoming visits of the commission to the county. At a meeting in Lampeter in 1893, Dan Jenkins, knowledgeable about farming because of his life at Pentrefelin, and also confident and articulate, agreed to be a spokesman and present information on behalf of the central committee when the commissioners took evidence in public in Lampeter. He was aware that his testimony would be aimed at the power and control of elements of the local gentry and the rich land-owning social class. It would focus on what he saw was an abuse of the rights of their tenants; their low level security of tenure and the subjugation and sometimes censure of their voting and religious expression. This was to be a most significant, defining and far-reaching moment in his life.

Dan Jenkins: a "radical"

The actions which he took saw others proudly describe him as a radical. Those who came to oppose him for his testimony and detailed statement before the Land Commission probably saw his actions as a breaking of a taboo and a disregard of an unstated agreement that you don't criticise the local establishment or disturb the balance between the haves and have-nots.

He appeared in public before the commission in Lampeter on the 25th and 28th of April and later in Aberystwyth, on the 31st of October, 1894. His evidence largely consisted of statements which were critical of the conduct of William Jones, the Lord of the Manor of both Cellan and Llanfair Clydogau. As stated, he was an important local man who had sold the land upon which the school was built and whose employee David Jones, was the very man to whom Dan Jenkins had applied, when seeking the headship of the school in 1878 (also whose member of staff was clerk to the Llanfair School Board and whose company acted as treasurer to the board). At the April hearings Dan cited evidence of specific people who had previously received a notice to quit their tenancies, and detailed tenants' agreements which contained restrictive covenants which they were required to sign, in order to waive their rights of protection offered by the Agricultural Holdings Act of 1883. He also referred to what he believed to be preferential treatment given towards church rather than chapel tenants and discrimination towards those who voted Liberal rather than Conservative. He said:

> ... where farms have been vacant, instances could be given of churchmen and Conservatives being preferred for the tenancy when some of the best old tenants were desirous to secure the same... There is a splendid set of tenants on the estate and they are very industrious. The children in most cases work hard without pay, but they (the tenants) are in a state of servility; they do not feel sufficiently free to act independently in any public capacity – school boards, for instance.[14]

After his evidence, which was widely discussed and reported across Cardiganshire, several quite draconian and unfortunate things happened to him, seemingly in an effort to quieten and punish him. However, not being cowed, he decided to recount what had happened to him after giving his initial evidence, once more in public. At the October meeting of the commission in Aberystwyth, his stated purpose in attending was to recount openly and in public, before this officially sanctioned body, detail of the quite severe actions taken in the Llanfair and Lampeter area by members of the Lord of the Manor's staff and others to seek to reject his allegations and, at the same time, censure him for his comments. He was very bold. The Witness Protection Act was designed to protect witnesses, but it did not stop these actions being taken by the agent of William Jones, or some members of the Llanfair School Board which, if successfully implemented, would have caused financial ruin to Dan.

The main actions taken included cutting his salary – probably knowing he would not accept this. For instance, on 9th May 1894 at a meeting of the school board, a motion was carried that the school master's salary be fixed at £70 a year – a reduction on the present amount. The *Cambrian News* reported:

> ... the master was called in and asked if he was prepared to accept this sum, but declined. It was afterwards resolved to call a special meeting of the board to pass a resolution that three months notice from that date be given to Mr Jenkins to terminate his engagement.[15]

In addition, a bank loan he had with the Lord of the Manor's bank for the purchase of Pentrefelin was called in and immediate repayment demanded. Dan had to mobilise himself to fight this threat. In respect to his employment he used the NUT, public opinion and letters which he sent out, asking for support. He dealt with the loss of the bank loan by securing another from a friendlier bank in Lampeter.

After giving evidence, Dan Jenkins was so concerned about what he saw was a personal threat to himself that he, along with two other witnesses from Wales, applied to parliament for enforcement of the Witness Protection Act.

Help for the old tenant of Felin, Llanfair (the mill)

Another aspect of property tenancy problems and Dan's preparedness to stand up for the rights of the oppressed and dispossessed, relates to the former tenant of the Felin, Llanfair. Located on the Llanfair road, this important mill was owned by the Lord of the Manor. A former tenant, who, by the 1890s was an old and poor man, was trying to secure recompence for his investment in new grinding stones at the mill some years earlier. According to one of Dan's daughters, her father "advised him about the law and consulted a solicitor on his behalf". As a result, the case was recounted before the land commissioners in 1894. This caused those who thought he was overstepping his responsibilities to say "he had been hired as a headteacher, not a solicitor".[16]

Freedom of expression

Following Dan Jenkins' appeareance before the Land Commission in April, his comments were widely reported in the *Cambrian News* and other Welsh newspapers. In the Teifi valley area where he was very well known, there was much discussion about his actions. Firstly, his being prepared to speak out on behalf of the tenant farmers; secondly, being confident enough to speak whilst being employed as a public servant in a school, where the staff of the Lord of the Manor acted as both the treasurer and secretary to the board; and thirdly, being prepared to challenge the Establishment in this way. The summer of 1894 must have been a very unsettling time for Dan. He knew the people who were trying to punish him for his statements very well. His lodgings were only a few hundred yards from the school, hence there would have been no easy opportunity for distant mature reflection; instead there was an intensity of action and reaction. Here was the leader (for the past 16 years) of the only school, a person who was probably the best educated person in the parish and pillar of Capel Mair Christian community, being rebuked and treated in this way. The humiliation of deciding to cut his salary and then dismiss him when he refused to accept the decision was further compounded in that the detail of the school board meeting of May was reported in the *Cambrian News* of 18th May.

The Lampeter branch of the NUT discussed the decision to dismiss Dan and this too was reported in the *Cambrian News* of 8th June. The following resolution was agreed at a Saturday meeting of members:

> We heartily sympathise with Mr Daniel Jenkins of Llanfair Board School, under the circumstances in which he is placed by the harsh and high-handed proceedings of the Llanfair School Board, and we pledge ourselves to do all in our power to secure for him justice and fair treatment.[17]

In the event, as a result of the twin efforts to ask for assistance under the Witness Protection Act, and the actions of the solicitor acting for the NUT, in what the union described as a "capricious dismissal", the case was eventually not proceeded with. Nevertheless, an attempt was made to appoint a new headteacher in that the position was advertised across the United Kingdom. However, following an active campaign by the NUT nationally to boycott the post, most candidates withdrew their applications, leaving only one. As he was deemed unsuitable, the dismissal did not proceed.

Public support for Dan Jenkins

The possibility of dismissal, however ridiculous the NUT might have regarded it, and the attack on Dan Jenkins were still very much on the minds of Llanfair residents when on 22nd August 1894, the annual treat of a tea and concert for children at the school took place. An unusually well-attended tea and concert saw 30 former pupils of the school (many visiting their family homes from London and elsewhere), attending to express support and encouragement for the beleaguered headteacher. These old students had received a good quality education at the school and had a fondness and high regard for Dan. This was an impressive show of affection for him. A *Cambrian News* report stated the following:

> As the weather was everything which could be desired, the tea was laid out in a field adjoining the schoolroom, kindly lent by the genial tenant of Llanfair-fawr. Mrs Evans, Llanfair-fach; Mrs Williams, Penygraig; Mrs Jenkins, Pentrefelin; Mrs Abel, Factory; Miss Benbow, teacher; Miss Annie Richards, Penlan presided at the tables... After tea was over, the children and elders held sports. Several races, jumping and tug-of-war competitions were indulged in. There was singing and a bardic address from the chairman, the Rev. J Davies, Independent minister... followed by an address by John Hughes on behalf of the former students residing in London and Bath, who then presented Mr Dan Jenkins with a beautiful and costly album inscribed in Welsh, as follows: 'Knowledge is strength. Presented to Mr Daniel Jenkins, the Board School, Llanfair Clydogau, from many of his old pupils resident in London, as a small sign of their gratitude for the education he gave them, and their admiration of the success of his labour as the school master during the 15 years of his stay in Llanfair, in the hope this secures his services for many years to come and that he has a long life in order to instruct the young of the community, so that their parents would be proud of them, and for the lifelong benefit of the pupils in his care.'[18]

The *Cambian News* commented: "the presentation showed the kindly feelings and pleasant reminiscences of days gone by." Dan Jenkins "returned thanks in very appropriate words and

Former pupils' presentation to Dan Jenkins

Dan Jenkins' scrapbooks

gave 'Hen wlad fy nhadau' with all joining in the chorus." The show of strength from former pupils was an indication of the kind of esteem these young men had for Dan Jenkins. Their comments to him within the inscribed album are an enormous testimony to his position within Llanfair society. They were a major show of solidarity. The fact that the inscription was in Welsh and that the tea and concert also included a bardic address and other aspects of a Welsh culture the headteacher was so proud of and was determined to demonstrate and display, was also highly important. The whole thing showed not only the extremely high regard with which he was held in Llanfair, but also the support which existed for his radical stance in speaking on behalf of local farmers.

Parish Council membership

Even though Dan Jenkins had gone before the Land Commission in October 1894 to recount what had happened to him, and hence publicised the difficult events of the summer, matters did surprisingly calm down in Llanfair as the end of the year approached. By December 1894, work was underway to elect and set up the inaugural parish council. Sixteen men were nominated for the nine-seat Llanfair Clydogau Parish Council, including Dan Jenkins. In the election which followed, he came seventh with 54 votes and was elected. No-one campaigned with a party label, but in the small Llanfair community judgements about a person's views would have been well known from their church or chapel attendance. In Dan's case they were extremely well known because of his regional and national prominence as a spokesman before the Land Commission.

Allotment conflict

At the April 1895 council meeting there was an acrimonious debate about allotments in which Dan was involved. He and another member proposed that the clerk should write to William Jones (Lord of the Manor) to ask if land could be made available and used as allotments within the parish. This was strongly opposed by a majority of members, a number of them tenants of William Jones. They did not wish to be associated with such a request. Dan Jenkins was trying once more, to do something on behalf of others who were less well endowed than himself. Trying to get land for landless farm servants to use, shows an interest in the wellbeing of the people. The fact that it did not proceed is perhaps indicative of the perceived influence of the major landowner, whom tenants, with occupancy based upon annual agreements, did not wish to offend. Or maybe a majority of parish councillors thought the levels of inequality within the parish were an acceptable price to pay for not disturbing the status quo.

1896–97 campaign to oust Dan Jenkins

By 1896, the parish council was very much an established part of village life in Llanfair. At a meeting held in March, the chairman of the council, David Lloyd of Frondale, launched a highly critical verbal attack on the Llanfair School Board of which he was not a member, referring to the "extravagence of the school board". An aspect of this claimed extravagence could well have been their decision taken in 1895, to build a schoolhouse for the headteacher. Forty-six people attended a council meeting to discuss and argue about the board's decision. The bulk of the cost of the construction would be covered by a loan of £250 from the Public Works Loan Board.

By November 1896, such was the interest in the work of the board, that thirteen people were nominated for the five places on the soon to be reconsitituted body. Rather than hold an election, a meeting was held to try to agree by consensus on who the five members should be. Those agreed were: David Jones, farmer from the large Waun-wen farm; David Lloyd (above), Frondale, sheep dealer; Evan Morgan, farmer of the large Nant-y-medd farm; Thomas Davies, shoemaker of Pentre and Evan Abel, spinner of the Factory, Llanfair. Of this group the first four were new members. David Lloyd was the public face of the board as it began to initiate actions throughout most of 1896 and 1897, causing a degree of notoriety to surround Llanfair for a number of years. From the outset amongst the new board, he was keen to curb the waste of money associated with the school. Hence, at a series of some five meetings in January and February 1897, he led on actions which firstly voted to cut the salary of Dan Jenkins and Miss Martha Benbow, assistant mistress; and then, when they refused to accept the reductions, resolved to dismiss them, giving three months notice. The detail of these meetings and letters surrounding them is contained in Dan's correspondence files and his scrapbooks, or was reported in the newspapers.

The reasons for the action of the board in seeking to curb expenditure are scarely credible, as Llanfair was already choosing to pay staff salaries below that of neighbouring schools. Once more, attempts to cause discomfort, humiliation and anxiety to Dan Jenkins were played out in the full glare of the press, with the *Cambrian News* reporting the discussions of the board. Dan's files show that a London official from the NUT, Mr T H Jones, came to Lampeter to meet him in mid-March, travelling on the mail train due at 7.35 a.m., to consider what actions could be taken and speculating that there might well be a link to the events of 1894. A letter to Dan of 18th March 1897 from the NUT's South Wales District branch, referred to a "printed sheet" which had been prepared and circulated by him explaining the actions being taken against him by the school board. The writer referred to the Llanfair School salaries as already "shamefully low" and that "the reduction is a means to an end" (that is, to get rid of him).

The NUT campaigned vigorously nationally once more, in order to try to save Dan Jenkins from dismissal. Challenges were mounted about the legal correctness of the calling of board meetings, the wording of letters and other technical matters. Dan received confidential and kindly help from one of the board members, probably Evan Abel, since copies of correspondence containing his name are found within Dan's notes of the time. These legal and technical arguments were helpful in slowing down the process. As a result, Dan and Martha Benbow were difficult to shift from their posts, much to the frustration of a majority of the board (the voting was 3 members to 2). The *Cambrian News* reported that on the 5th of March, the Lampeter NUT branch debated the situation and resolved:

> Members of this association strongly condemn the action of the Llanfair Clydogau School Board in giving notice of dismissal to their teachers for refusing to accept a reduction in salaries which are already small, and they pledge themselves to do their utmost to secure them fair treatment. They also strongly advise intending applicants for the vacancies to communicate with the secretary of this association before sending in their applications. Mr Jenkins' present salary is £69 with house and coal and Miss Benbow's £40. These salaries the Board have determined to reduce by about £8 each. It should be added that the school is now, and for many years has been, in a highly efficient state, the highest grants being earned as well as the excellent award for drawing.[19]

In May 1897, the South Wales District of the NUT debated the Llanfair situation and passed a motion of "deep sympathy with the teachers serving under the Llanfair Clydogau School Board who have received notice". The district secretary, Mr Willmott, in writing to Dan, hoped he would be able to "show them the error of their ways" and that "the NUT will be able soon to find you more congenial work" in another school.

Protest by school pupils

The pupils who attended the Llanfair night school (an evening continuation activity) and were taught by Dan, also strongly protested against his treatment. Twenty of them signed a petition which stated: "We unanimously beg to protest against the Llanfair School, for their unjust and unmanly action in giving our worthy schoolmaster Mr Daniel Jenkins, notice to quit." (22/3/1897) It was signed by the following: Anne Jones (Pandy), Anne Davies (Silver Mine), Anne Rees (Cefnfoelallt),

Anne Pugh (Pentre), Jane George (Cerrigdrudion), Elizabeth Timothy (Tynlon), John Jones (Pandy), Thomas Pugh (Pencilboa), Solomon Davies (Officefach), David Jones (Silvermine), David Lloyd (Troedrhiwgoch), Daniel Timothy (Tynlon), Thomas George (Pantyffynon), Thomas Davies (Fachddu), Joseph Rees (Cefnfoelallt), Jonathan William (Pentre), David Jones (Tancoed), John Jones (Tycoch), Daniel Evans (Ynysmoch) and John George (Pentre).[20]

Community life

In the midst of the turmoil to force Dan out of Llanfair, normal activities in which he believed, continued. The poster below shows him in March 1897, conducting at a concert to raise money for a Sunday school, believed to be that run by Capel Mair.

Assault on Dan Jenkins

Also in the middle of the tussle with the school board, Llanfair resident Thomas Evans appears to have assaulted Dan. A letter of 23rd June 1897, written to Dan on behalf of Mr Evans, by the Rev. Davies, Congregational minister, states: "Thomas Evans, Troed-y-bryn, Llanfair, begs to apologise for any assault he is said to have committed upon Mr D Jenkins, the Master of the Llanfair Board School. And hereby, he undertakes not to repeat the offence, nor in any way molest your client." (Sent to solicitors Arthur Hughes of Aberystwyth with a copy in Dan Jenkins' scrapbooks.)

Attempt to eject Dan Jenkins from the schoolhouse

By August 1897, the school board had decided to go ahead and appoint a new headteacher and needed to get Dan Jenkins to accept that he had been dismissed and leave the schoolhouse. A problem for the board was that, following the publicity from the NUT, eight of the nine applicants withdrew and they wondered if enough choice was available to them. Dan had also taken a very energetic stance in getting his friends within the NUT to write to the applicants. That would suggest he had inside knowledge on who the candidates were. Dan's files show a letter from a teacher at New Quay Board School on 9th April 1897 which states: "Dear Sir, Note memo by first post. Had a reply this morning. He will forthwith withdraw." At the same time Dan was still arguing that the eviction notice was illegal due to the technical manner of its issuing.

Taking a firm decision, the board decided to bring matters to a conclusion, and in early August applied for a warrant of ejectment against him at a special Petty Sessions held at Lampeter. The magistrates were John Fowden Esq., J C Harford, Esq. and the Rev. T C Edmunds. Dan Jenkins was represented by a local solicitor engaged by the NUT, and the Llanfair School Board had Frank Lloyd of Lampeter acting for them. The hearing was well reported by the *Cambrian News* which stated that: "there were a large number of the friends of both parties present, and the proceedings were watched with much interest."[21]

The County Court bailiff told the court how he had served the ejection notice on the defendant at Llanddewibrefi on 29th July. In reply to questioning from the NUT solicitor, he admitted that he had not read over the notice with the defendant, as was required by the law. This technical and procedural failure caused the board to withdraw its application before the court and decide to issue a fresh notice, the outcome of which was that Dan could effectively remain in the school for another three months. However, it was only a matter of time before he lost the legal argument. The facts were that the law allowed the employer to arbitrarily reduce his wages and to evict him from its property. Confident of an eventual victory, the school board went ahead and appointed the only remaining candidate for the post of headteacher. As a result, they had to pay two people's salaries for the same job for several months, as the new 'master' arrived in the village, took lodgings and waited for his predecessor to leave.

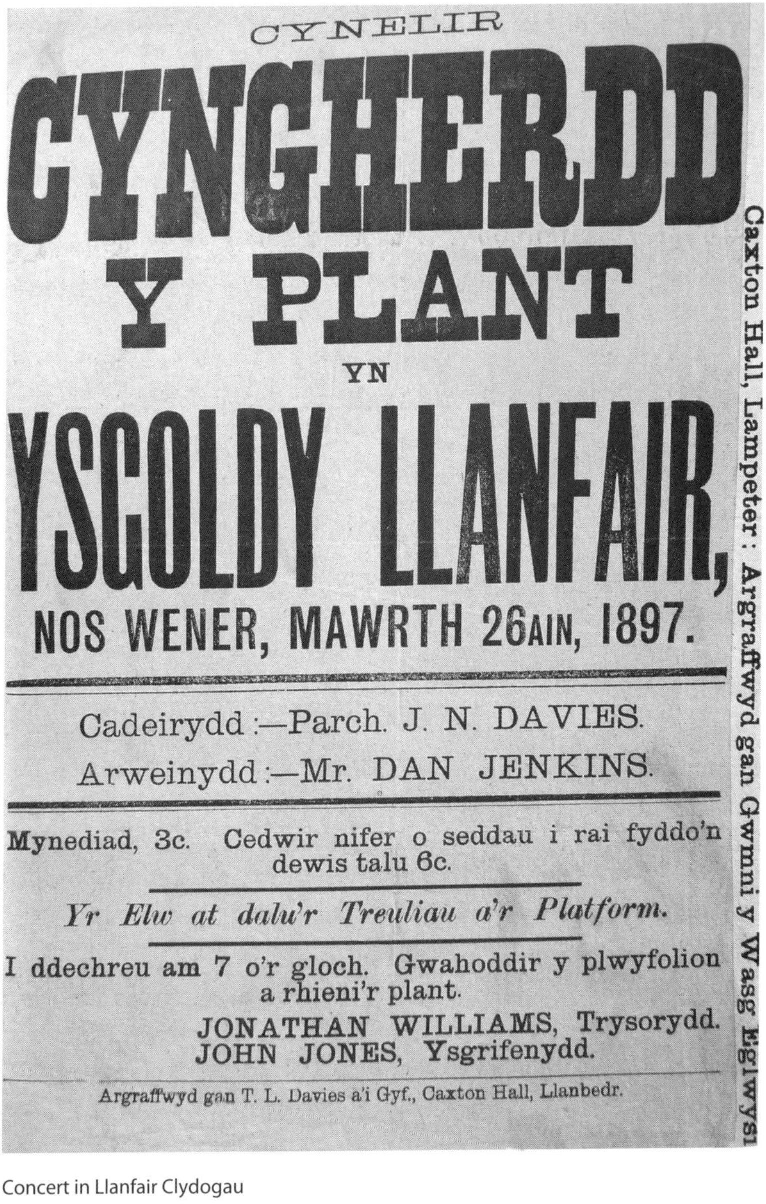

CYNELIR

CYNGHERDD

Y PLANT

YN

YSCOLDY LLANFAIR,

NOS WENER, MAWRTH 26AIN, 1897.

Cadeirydd :—Parch. J. N. DAVIES.

Arweinydd :—Mr. DAN JENKINS.

Mynediad, 3c. Cedwir nifer o seddau i rai fyddo'n dewis talu 6c.

Yr Elw at dalu'r Treuliau a'r Platform.

I ddechreu am 7 o'r gloch. Gwahoddir y plwyfolion a rhieni'r plant.

JONATHAN WILLIAMS, Trysorydd.
JOHN JONES, Ysgrifenydd.

Argraffwyd gan T. L. Davies a'i Gyf., Caxton Hall, Llanbedr.

Caxton Hall, Lampeter : Argraffwyd gan Gwmni y Wasg Eglwysi

Concert in Llanfair Clydogau

Dan Jenkins' scrapbooks

Dan Jenkins' supporters at Capel Mair meeting

On 23rd August 1897, the *Cambrian News* reported that friends and supporters of Dan Jenkins held "a large and enthusiastic meeting" at Capel Mair in Llanfair for the purpose of presenting testimonials and other gifts to the soon-to-be-leaving headteacher and teacher Martha Benbow. These were to be given to the headteacher "as evidence of the respect with which he is held in the district, but also as a protest against his dismissal by the school board". The chapel was crowded with people. The newspaper reported that: "public feeling in the neighbourhood has run very high. Mr Jenkins is very popular with the inhabitants, especially the nonconformist section. Long before the meeting started the seats in the chapel were occupied by an enthusiastic gathering." As supporters got up to speak there was "much cheering".

The importance of the meeting was considerable. It was chaired by the MP for Cardiganshire, Vaughan Davies. David Lloyd-George, MP had promised to attend but was unable to reach Llanfair since the afternoon train did not go beyond Pencader. Mr T J Evans, MP, the chief Liberal Whip in the Commons sent a letter referring to the "odious persecution he had suffered". Other important people present were Morgan Evans JP; J H Davies JP of Cwrtmawr; Tom John of Llwynpia and the Reverends E Evans of Lampeter, J Davies of Alltyblaca, B Carolan Davies of Tynygwndwn and J J Jones BA of Rhydybont. Several old students of Dan Jenkins were there, including W Evans and E Richards of London. The *Cambrian News* commented that every religious denomination was present in the audience, not just non-denominational people. In addition there were a large number of school masters present.

Vaughan Davies referred to a dark cloud hanging over Llanfair. He said: "it was a shame, because they lived in a time when every man ought to be free to think and act as he thought right." He went on to assert: "they were not merely fighting for their locality, but were fighting for the people of Wales." He linked the dismissal of Dan Jenkins to his actions in speaking up before the Land Commission about abuses of tenant farmers and said that it was against the act of parliament designed to protect witnesses. He added:

> They would not have a law for the rich and a law for the poor and expected the law to be enforced... there was sufficient evidence from the records in the school district that Mr Jenkins had done his duty – (applause) – then they had the right to ask why that persecution was taking place. Was it because their children had not been well taught? (Loud cries of 'No'.) Was it because he had neglected his duty in connection with the school? ('No.')

Several presents were given to Dan Jenkins and Martha Davies (formerly Benbow). Mr D Morgan, Pentrelan presented an illuminated address; Mr Evans of Llanfair shop presented a purse of money on behalf of Capel Mair and Walter Griffiths

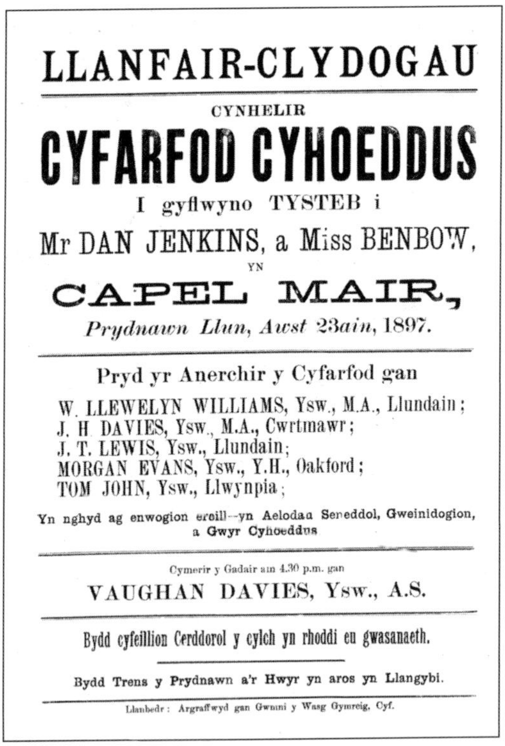

Publicity poster for 1897 Capel Mair meeting

Dan Jenkins' scrapbooks

made a presentation of a gold watch and chain on behalf of the singing class. Mr T J Evans gave a welcome address, and a writing desk was given on behalf of the Llanfair boys in London by Mr E Richards.

Vaughan Williams MP compared the treatment of the two teachers to events he had seen in Russia and was beginning to think that perhaps Russia was not such a bad place after all in contrast to Cardiganshire. The Rev. J Davies of Alltyblaca Church spoke of the "unwarrantable persecution" to which Dan Jenkins had been subject. A telegram from the Llanfair boys in London hoped the meeting would be a means of establishing peace and unity once more within the parish. Evan Richards referred to the unjust conduct and personal animosity shown by a few in forcing him out.

In reply to the audience at Capel Mair, the *Cambrian News* reported on Dan Jenkins rising to his feet: "he was received with long and prolonged cheering" and "said he felt like the man who had blackened his face at night and having for some reason to get up rather early next morning, looked into the mirror and went back to bed, observing he was not the man who was to have got up. (Laughter.) If he had been of any service to them in that place he was very glad. No doubt however, he ought to have done more. But he had done his best, and whatever he had done was meant for the best, and was done with pure motive. (Cheers) The present of a portmanteau to him seemed to indicate that he was to be henceforth ever on the move. In that case it would prove very useful. (Laughter and applause.)"[22]

The *Welsh Gazette* of 25th August 1897 headed its report about the same Llanfair meeting as 'School Board in Pickle'. It was complimentary about Dan Jenkins, describing him "as a gentleman who has made himself so prominent in Cardiganshire ever since his appointment."[23]

The sacking of Dan Jenkins

We will never be able to say exactly why the school board of Llanfair Clydogau decided to proceed to dismiss him. The evidence suggests the following:

1 His decision to appear before the Land Commission in April 1894 and criticise alleged unfair and unjust landlords and tenancy practices, naming the Lord of the Manor, was key. Especially so, in a parish in which such a large amount of land and its allocation and use was controlled by one landowner who had considerable direct and indirect influence on people within the parish.

2 He was known to be a Liberal and in the words of Vaughan Williams MP, a radical and some people did not like his preparedness to speak on matters of freedom of voting and the secret ballot.

3 He was an attendee at Capel Mair and ran the chapel's choir. He was not involved with St Mary's Church in a parish in which there was, in the minds of some, a clear demarcation line between the church and chapel. Yet, he was not known to be antagonistic towards the church.

4 He was a strong proponent of the Welsh language, Welsh culture and customs relating to poetry, the bardic tradition, singing and story telling. In this respect he was in advance of his time, as not all Welsh people attached the same importance to the language and its heritage.

5 The law made it easy to dismiss him. Reasons did not have to be given. The NUT was involved in a number of disputes in the 1890s with school boards which had dismissed their headteachers, sometimes over a refusal to attend church. Dan Jenkins' case was one of a number which helped the NUT campaign for improvements in employment law.

6 The composition of the membership of the school board after the election in 1896 was a significant factor. The *Cambrian News,* in a leader article, classified the board as consisting

of three church members and two nonconformist members, and felt that the church members were heavily influenced by others who wanted to take action against Dan Jenkins for his prominent part in the political and social life of the district. The newspaper referred to the church members as "pliant tools" and wrote: "The treatment meted out to Mr Daniel Jenkins shows that it is still possible for a man to suffer for his principles and for holding views which are distasteful to some of those persons who think it is their special province to rule the earth... our advice to the church party in the parish is to take warning by the signs already made clear and save themselves the humiliation and defeat which will surely follow their present action if it is persisted upon."

The cost of the sacking

There was damage to the image of Llanfair Clydogau and the school board as well as monetary damage to the local population. Dan Jenkins had a number of powerful supporters: the Liberal party nationally, the NUT, a large number of Cardiganshire clergymen and very many people in Llanfair. Almost 70 ratepayers within the parish signed and presented a petition demanding his reinstatement. The NUT almost managed to "save him" as they had in 1894 by taking out advertisements to dissuade applicants for the headship of the school. However, they could not persuade all candidates to withdraw and Mr Cleaton Davies of London was appointed – he being the only candidate who would accept the job. The post, when advertised had requested applicants to not only send details of their qualifications, but also the salary they required. In a leader article in the NUT weekly paper the *Schoolmaster* of 4th September 1897, it was pointed out:

> ... the blundering majority of the Llanfair Board now find themselves in a serious position. Their attempts to oust a good and tried public servant, or lower his already inadequate salary have resulted in a serious loss to the ratepayers, for they have

> incurred heavy legal expenses and have to pay the salaries of two headmasters for the period 7th July to 24th November. In addition to this, they have to provide lodgings for the new master, who is in the village and has earned the dislike of the greater number of parents of the scholars of his future school; it is likely that he will never be recognised as a member of the NUT and that possibly a new board will give him short shrift and reinstate Mr Jenkins.[24]

In the event Cleaton Davies did take over the headship.

Departure of 24th November 1897

In the days leading up to his departure, Dan approached the Llanfair School Board to ask if there was any interest in it buying any of his belongings located within the schoolhouse. Though he wrote to the secretary twice, the board did not respond. They were very uncommunicative and unhelpful to him, merely wanting him to serve his notice and leave. The NUT general secretary, J H Yoxall, wrote from Russell Square, London, to advise Dan to give up possession of the schoolhouse on 24th November. He also said that his last entry in the logbook should be as brief as possible. He suggested the following: 'November 24th. Gave up charge of this school. D Jenkins.'

The loss to Llanfair Clydogau

Dan Jenkins' longevity of service (1878–97) is impressive. The inspection reports confirm a good quality education being provided within the school. After he had left there were two short-lived headships: D R Cleaton Davies 1897–99 and R Satchwill 1899–1901, before a longer period of incumbency occurred with the arrival of Hugh Hughes who worked in Llanfair from 1901 to 1917.

The annual inspection report for 1898, after Dan had left, was very critical of the situation observed within the school stating as follows:

> This school has suffered during the year from changes in teacher and the consequent disorganisation of work. Both in elementary

> and class subjects there has been a falling off, though it is right to add that an improvement is also noticeable in some respects in some subjects (particularly in the English of the Upper Standards), since the present Master took charge. The staff is not strong.[25]

The one favourable comment about the English language would very much fit with the known view of HMI about the extreme importance of English and it is thought the new headteacher was of an English background. He resigned in April 1899 and left six weeks later to move to a school in Glamorgan. Miss Davies, assistant teacher also left in the April. Hence, Mr D R Cleaton Davies only lasted about 20 months. The legacy of the removal of Dan Jenkins is to be found in this staffing disruption and the lower quality of education received by the children which was found by the inspector.

Contribution to Llanfair Clydogau

Dan Jenkins' contribution to the school and parish of Llanfair was immense. The high esteem of the broad mass of the people towards him is unequivocally recognisable from the attempted defence of him by the population in both 1894 and 1897. The scale of rallying round him was considerable, but not enough to prevent his dismissal and departure from Llanfair. In its simplest sense, the explanation of his demise rests upon a three-to-two person division within the school board; a divide which was unshakeable and unable to be challenged by any of the rules of contract or employment law statutes of the time. Hence, the man who ran a very good school, serving a poor, rural area, who had good HMI reports, who introduced the Welsh language into the spoken and written curriculum and who had overseen stability of school operation for nearly twenty years, left the schoolhouse and moved back to Pentrefelin.

Socially and culturally he had done much for Llanfair and the surrounding area. His contribution to Capel Mair, singing, the inaugural St David's Day celebrations, parish-wide activities of an eisteddfod type, the parish council, political debate and his sheer enthusiasm could all be seen by those who chose to see. He had also demonstrated a strong commitment to the rights of the individual, whether it be tenant farmers' rights to be treated fairly, teachers' rights over their pay and conditions or childrens' rights to a quality education which reflected the rich culture of the Llanfair area. He thought landowners and employers had responsibilities and should exercise them fairly and reasonably.

Dan Jenkins left in 1897, but his image and legacy in the minds of the population was still prominent for many years. Two examples of this can be quoted. In 1926 there was published a *Jiwbili* (Jubilee) book[26] to commemorate the 100 years of Capel Mair (1825–1925) and it contained a chapter which he was asked to write about the parish. Demonstrating his research and detailed knowledge, he commented upon its history, heritage, origins, education and religion. Secondly, in 1955, some 57 years after Dan had left, at an evening performance of the Soar Drama Company from Lampeter in the church hall of Llanfair, Dan's son, Griffith Jenkins (of Blaen-waun-ganol, Llanwnnen), was invited to be chairman for the evening. The *Welsh Gazette* reported: "in his speech, which sparkled with originality, he recalled past times and friends. He mentioned that this was the first time he had fulfilled such a task, but he proved to be a master at work. In addition, much of the flair of his talented father, Daniel Jenkins, Pentrefelin, who had been a much-praised headteacher in the area, came across in his character."[27]

Effect on Government Policy

His actions in 1894, along with those of other witnesses before the Land Commission, helped highlight abuses in the tenancy system, as well as issues associated with the Witness Protection Act. His statements about Llanfair Clydogau would have made it more likely that devices inserted in tenancy agreements, designed to get around the act of 1875, were less likely. In addition, the Lord of the Manor had died in January 1897.

The brave testimony gave publicity and hence helped enhance understanding. In due course, in 1908, 1913, and 1923 and beyond, various improvements were made in the conditions attached to agricultural tenancies.

As far as the policy for education and schools was concerned, the failed attempt to dismiss Dan in 1894 and the successful action to remove him in 1897, helped add to the specific examples which the NUT compiled for its campaign work. This campaign aimed to improve salaries of rural school teachers, ensure a greater degree of security of tenure, introduce a pension scheme and see the ending of the parish-based school board system. Dan Jenkins' situation in Llanfair was not unique; the NUT had further cases which it had fought in other places, principally in England. These cases were usually played out in the media, with teachers urged to boycott the school post in question. In December 1898 the general secretary of the NUT wrote to ask the government to amend the school regulations "to prevent unjustifiable dismissals". The letter went on:

> The injury to a school when a teacher beloved of the scholars, respected by the parents and esteemed by the neighbourhood, has nevertheless to leave his post at the command of a board is almost incalculable. Many cases have occurred within the knowledge of the Executive, in which the good influence of a school, not only on the scholars, but upon the neighbourhood, has abruptly ceased as a result of a worthy teacher's dismissal; the parents being in revolt, but powerless, and the locality ceasing to esteem or support the institution affected.[28]

Much of the content of this quotation would sadly apply to Llanfair.

Some NUT successes occurred in 1898 when pension rights were recognised; from 1902, school boards were replaced by local education authorities and gradually greater security of tenure was introduced. For a place like Llanfair, it would no longer be possible for three people out of the five on the school board to determine policy on pay and conditions – instead Cardiganshire County Council became the responsible body.

CHAPTER FOUR

The Llanycrwys years (1898–1920)

DAN JENKINS CREATED at Llanycrwys School, which is located at Ffaldybrenin, near Ffarmers, Carmarthenshire, some of the most unusual features and practices of a school anywhere in Wales. These characteristics may well have been unique at the time. They broke new ground and were very much in the advance guard of educational developments at the beginning of the 20th century. They arose out of a movement, of which he was a very prominent member, to celebrate Welshness; to not succumb to the almost engulfing tide of Englishness; to use Welsh as an everyday means of spoken and written communication; to celebrate and record the culture and traditions of the country and to see to it that in schools within Wales, Welsh as a language, was not regarded, or institutionally classified by politicians, the public and employers, as second class to English. The above emblem is taken from Llanycrwys publications designed by Dan.

Llanycrwys parish and school

The spelling of the parish of Llanycrwys varies, sometimes with a 'y' in the middle and sometimes without. It is located on the eastern side of a range of upland which forms the boundary between Cardiganshire and Carmarthenshire which includes Llanfair mountain and Cellan common. The state publicly-funded school located at Ffaldybrenin, opened in 1878 as part of the wave of school building, like that at Cilcennin and Llanfair Clydogau following the 1870 Education Act. Before the school was constructed, such education as was available was hit-or-miss. It depended upon the interest and enthusiasm of some enterprising person in setting up a 'school' in their own home or public building, for those parents who both desired formal education for their children, and could afford to pay. Early schools in the parish were located at the parish church (1800–30), the old chapel (1830–46), chapel vestry (1846–78), Bryneithin School and Pantyresgair.

Llanycrwys School was designed to cater for all ages of children drawn from the predominantly scattered rural population in this area. Before the appointment of Dan Jenkins as headteacher, there was little leadership stability in operation at the school for some years, with nine incumbents of the position from 1878–98. There is a suggestion, based upon names and their next teaching destinations, that a number of these early headteachers were English. For instance, Mr J T Savage (1878–9), who had previously followed Dan Jenkins after his enforced departure from Cilcennin, moved on to Llanycrwys and eventually to Buxton in Derbyshire. J Williams (1879–80) left to go to Billingsgate, London. James Mildenhall (1894–5) went on to Kent. Thomas James (1895–8) moved to Longhope, Gloucestershire. In the middle of all these short-stay headteachers, the school did undergo a long period with Samuel Williams (1881–94). With the arrival of Dan in 1898, it did achieve an even longer period of stability in its leadership and much success. Some of this success was nationally acknowledged.

The appointment of Dan Jenkins

Following his departure from Llanfair Clydogau Board School in November 1897, Dan was out of teaching for several months. It is believed that he was located at his farm at Pentrefelin

Llanycrwys School and schoolhouse
Dan Jenkins' scrapbooks

at this time. His personal notes state that he started work at Llanycrwys on 18th April 1898. It is likely that he began initially in a temporary capacity, since the *Cambrian News* in July, in reporting a special meeting of the Llanycrwys School Board taking place earlier that week stated: "Mr Dan Jenkins received the permanent appointment of the mastership of the Llanycrwys Board School."[1]

Unfortunately, in 1981 the school logbook for Llanycrwys was destroyed in a fire. Joan Jones of Buarth-yr-oen, Ffarmers, told me that she could recall reading it when she was employed there as a teacher, some years after Dan had left following his retirement in 1920. Yet, in spite of the disappointment of the loss of this important source of information, we have quite a lot of detail available to us, in particular from newspapers and Dan Jenkins' scrapbooks, which allows us to report and comment on the work he undertook.

Early interest in Llanycrwys parish

The records he has left us show that either before he went to Llanycrwys, or once there, he collected written evidence about

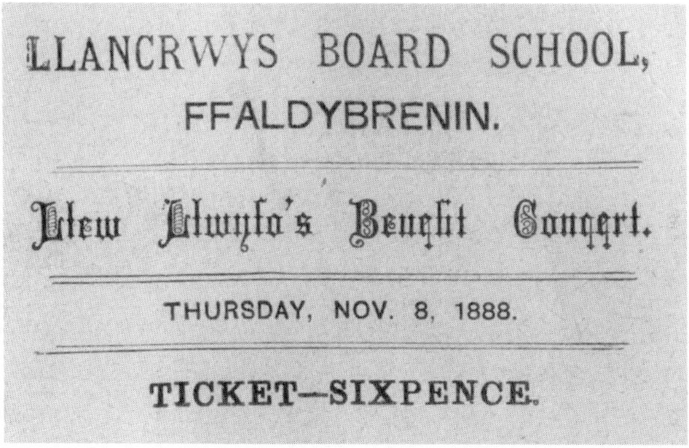

LLANCRWYS BOARD SCHOOL,
FFALDYBRENIN.

Llew Llwyfo's Benefit Concert.

THURSDAY, NOV. 8, 1888.

TICKET—SIXPENCE.

Concert 1888

Dan Jenkins' scrapbooks

the place. This demonstates his interest in its cultural activities. The exhibit above shows a ticket sold for a concert.

We already know that well before he left Llanfair Clydogau, Dan had visited Ffaldybrenin to sing, walking both ways over the mountain.

Living in Llanycrwys

Llanycrwys School was even further away from his home at Pentrefelin in the Aeron valley than Llanfair Clydogau. The distance by road can be measured at about 14 miles. During the period from 1898 until his retirement in 1920, Dan worked in Llanycrwys; living away from home during the week, but travelling back for the weekend. He lived at two different locations in the parish. The 1901 census shows him as a lodger at Wern Villa, with the head of the house, Rachel Jones (his older cousin) and a house servant Elizabeth Williams. By 1911, he was living at the schoolhouse, Brondderwen (built in 1903), near the school, with Rachel Jones still acting as housekeeper for him. Also in residence was the school's assistant teacher, Elizabeth Ross.

Accounts from a number of Dan's children refer to him having described to them travelling home each Friday night to Pentrefelin: by walking to Lampeter, then catching the

Aberaeron train to Tal-sarn halt, whereby he would either walk the rest of the way or be picked up by a pony and trap. However, this pattern could not have occurred until May 1911 at the earliest, since that was the date of the opening of the new Lampeter to Aberaeron railway. Before then, he presumably walked or sought a lift with someone.

There were probably many variations to his travel arrangements. One which can be identified from his scrapbooks involves assistance from the nearby rich and influential family of the Hills-Johnes, who lived on the large Dolaucothi estate. Dolaucothi was a large house and landholding in northern Carmarthenshire, in and around the valley of the river Cothi. It was owned by John Johnes in the 19th century. He was succeeded by his two daughters, Charlotte Anna Maria (1825–1911) and Elizabeth (–1927), wife of Sir James Hills-Johnes (1833–1919). Sir James adopted the name Johnes. In later years Sir James and his wife lived at Dolaucothi with Charlotte, after she was widowed. The estate covered a large area in Carmarthenshire and elsewhere, and received income not only from tithes, but also rents from tenants.

Sir James, who was born in India, had been a Lieutenant Colonel in the British army and saw action during the Indian Mutiny, the Abyssinian War and the second Anglo-Afghan War. He received the Victoria Cross in 1857 (during the siege of Delhi), the highest and most prestigious award for gallantry in the face of the enemy that can be awarded to British and Commonwealth forces. Though their backgrounds were very different, Dan had a good working relationship with the Hills-Johnes and a personal friendship with them. Elizabeth (Bertha), who spoke Welsh, was a major influence on social and cultural attitudes of the time, with an appreciation of music, literature, religion, folklore, the Welsh language and Welsh history. As such, she would have been of considerable interest to Dan, some of whose own interests overlapped. Sir James had a major involvement in local affairs and was elected member of the county council several times. So important to

Dan was this friendship with the Hills-Johnes that he retained several of the letters which he received from either Sir James or Elizabeth. Hence we know that, in terms of his complicated travel arrangements home to Pentrefelin, he received help from Sir James one Friday in 1916. A letter he received said:

> Sir,
> It will be alright on Friday for a seat in my motor to Lampeter and Felinfach. I don't think there will be any of my house guests going to Felinfach. Anyway the front seat will be available and David will be told to look out for you, and pick you up. He will leave Dolaucothi at 1.55 p.m.–2.00 p.m. and pick me up at Llanwrda station.
> Yours faithfully,
>
> J Hills-Johnes.[2]

Dolaucothi mansion and estate

The friendship which Dan established with the Hills-Johnes was important and long lasting. For instance, his scrapbooks contain a Parcel Post wrapper of a package that he received with a description of the contents as: "Pheasants one, to Mr

Dolaucothi

Dan Jenkins' scrapbooks

Sir James Hill-Johnes VC of Dolaucothi

Dan Jenkins' scrapbooks

Y'NGWLEDD FLYNYDDOL DOLAUCOTHY,

DYDD GWENER, AWST 19EG, 1904.

CENIR

GAN

Blant Ysgolion Cynghor Cwmtwrch, Farmers, Cwrtycadno, Caio, Crugybar, a Llanycrwys.

Alaw:—" Llwyn Onn."

Gogoniant i Gymru a'i glynoedd a'i bryniau,
  Mae nghalon yn caru pob dôl ynddi hi;
Ond nid oes yn llechu yn un o'i chilfachau
  Un llecyn fel Hen Ddolaucothy i mi;
Mae adsain yr awen a'r delyn yn canu
  Rhwng muriau y palas yn hanes y wlad,
A phlant y gym'dogaeth yn dal i folianu,
  Fod clod Dolaucothy o hyd mewn parhad.

Fy hen wlad fynyddig, mae anian yn urddo
  Pob mynydd a dyffryn, pob clogwyn a glyn;
Ac yspryd haelioni, a serch yn addurno,
  Pob aber ac afon, pob dôl a phob bryn;
Mae yspryd gwladgarwch a rhinwedd y'Nghymru
  Yn uchel ei fri, ac yn hen o ran oed,
A phlant y gym'dogaeth yn dal i folianu,
  Fod clod Dolaucothy mor fyw ag erioed!

Awst 8fed, 1904. WATCYN WYN.

Dolaucothi Annual Event

Dan Jenkins' scrapbooks

Jenkins at Llanycrwys School" dated 1904. He retained a letter from Sir James which stated: "Sir, The ladies and I were glad to learn that you were pleased with the pheasant and the almanac we sent you. J Hills-Johnes."[3]

Throughout his time at Llanycrwys, relations were good and the school children regularly went to Dolaucothi each year, where tea was provided and sports held. This importance was emphasised when on 17th February 1911, the school was closed on the occasion of the funeral of Charlotte of Dolaucothi. Once again on 10th January 1919, the school was closed for the funeral of Sir James Hills-Johnes.[4]

Welsh language

The evidence shows that Welsh was used and taught within the school, alongside English. A child's exercise book of 1910 shows writing taking place in both languages. To take part in the musical concerts which Dan introduced would have necessitated a good command of Welsh. The issue of if and how to utilise the two languages was a perennial one for any school in this isolated Welsh-speaking area. Something of this is conveyed in the logbook of the nearby Blaentwrch School which is located in the river Twrch valley, north of Ffarmers. The entry for September 1889 states: "25 children in school. Only 9 had been to school before. All the children are new, but very little English. Most of them could not understand a word of English."[5] Another logbook entry for the year 1895–6 states: "The general intelligence of the scholars would be greatly improved if the Mistress trained them to translate sentences from Welsh to English."

Pioneering St David's Day

Dan Jenkins took steps of an innovative type in order to try to bring before the children, a greater awareness of the Welsh language, along with Welsh culture and traditions. These included, as was the case at Llanfair Clydogau from 1894 to

1897, opportunities for singing, writing and reciting poetry and public speaking. However, the size and scale of his endeavours way exceeded those at Llanfair. He was probably aided by being older and more experienced.

He used as a vehicle for this, what he regarded as the insufficiently recognised St David's Day of 1st March. His creative talent extended not only to deciding to direct a whole evening's concert, but to plan the items and pay to have an official, well-designed programme or brochure for the event, professionally printed by a company in Llanbedr Pont Steffan (Lampeter). Events of this type were relatively rare at this time, and the size and scope of the Llanycrwys evening made it extremely unusual. However, what made it probably unique, was the decision by Dan, to contact a number of quite major literary figures across Wales, to ask if they would be prepared to write poetry or verses to apply to well-known pieces of music, especially for the evening, so that they would be personal and distinct to the concert he was planning. The fact that so many did, often using their bardic name, helped to give a real significance to the event in the minds of the children and the audience of parents and local notables and celebrities. His personal records and scrapbook cuttings show him regularly corresponding with a wide range of the literati of the country.

He clearly felt it was extremely important for him to do this. It was very personal, and almost part of an expression of his very being, to want to have the opportunity to develop and operate in this way. He wanted an outlet for the promotion of the Welsh language and culture across a wide audience. Hence, he was acting as an impressario, a producer, a director and creative artist all in one role. He also usually performed and conducted, as well as organised the publicity and tickets.

The St David's Day programmes which he had attractively printed, ran from 1901 to 1920 and later in 1934, he published in book format, *Cerddi Ysgol Llanycrwys* (Poems of Llanycrwys School).

An example of one of the eight-page programmes (the one

for 1908) is shown below. Pride of place on page one is given to the poem of Watcyn Wyn (Watcyn Hezekiah Williams, former coal miner, preacher, teacher and later headteacher of a school in the Ammanford area of Carmarthenshire). He was a very well-renowned bard across the country, who had won major awards at a number of the more important eisteddfodau from 1881 to 1893. According to his National Library of Wales biographical details he was "a well-known national figure".

The 18-item programme for 1908 shows singing by Dan Jenkins and the school's female teacher, Elsie Anne Davies, along with a range of pieces from the children and others.

Dan Jenkins collected people's written reactions to the annual programme whenever he could. Two responses to the 1908 programme are shown below: "The programme is extremely interesting. I like your plan of holding the celebration. May you have success in your labour of love to bring the literature and Welsh education closer together, Eifion Wyn." (Eliseus Williams; 1867–1926, Caernarfonshire, a bard.)

"Thank you very much for the St David's Day feast. There never was a better if not equal delicacies on the table. I'm envious of your patriotism. We here are dead in the injustice and sin of socialism. I remember chairing Michael Thomas, here in one of the Ffynnon Eisteddfodau, when he won his first chair somewhere in the south. Your obedient servant archdderwydd, Jones Mynydd-islwyn."[6]

Fame of the St David's Day concert

Dan was very good at circulating copies of the St David's Day programme to a wide circle of educational and literary people across Wales. He deliberately and systematically sought to show people that the Welsh language was alive and in daily use in this part of Carmarthenshire, as too, were Welsh traditions. He was also trying to encourage others to do the same, spread the word and show the example they could see occurring at Ffaldybrenin. He encouraged written responses. The content

GWYL DEWI, 1908.

Hen Gymru cryflon, dewrion, dwys,
Yn iawn eu cred yw gwyr Llancrwys;
Eu hawen hwynt a ymfwynha,
I gwnu dyn ag enw da;
O fewn y plwy', fe fyn y plant
O-hyd i son am Dewi Sant.
Watcyn Wyn.

CYNLLUNLEN SEITHFED

Cyngherdd Gwyl Dewi
Plant Ysgol Llancrwys

(NAWR A CHYNT).

Nos Wener, Chwefror 28ain, 1908.

Athraw—DAN JENKINS.

Athrawes—ELSIE ANNE DAVIES.

Cadeirydd ac Arweinydd—
DAVID EVAN DAVIES, GELLY.

Cyfeilyddion { ELSIE ANNE DAVIES ac
ETHEL PARRY, FROODVALE.

Dechreuir am 6.30 o'r gloch.
Tocynau—Blaenseddau, 2s.; Olseddau, 1s.

Yr Elw at gael Llyfrgell i'r Ysgol, yr hon fydd at wasanaeth y plwyf.

Trysorydd—
D. E. DAVIES.

Llywodraethwyr Lleol { T. DAVIES, Tycanol
W. MORGAN, Eithinduon

PRIS—DWY GEINIOG.

NODIAD.—Ni fu Cyngherdd yn 1905 am fod yr Ysgoldy dan adgyweiriad ar y pryd.

Argraffwyd gan D. R. Evans a'i Gyf., Heol-y-Bont, Llanbedr.

Llanycrwys programme
(source: Islwyn Walters)

Rhaglen Rhan Gyntaf.

1. Canu—"Duw Gadwo'r Brenin" .... Pawb.
2. Anerch .... Y Cadeirydd.
3. Canu—"Yr Ynys Wen" .... Y Plant.
4. Adrodd—"Hwian Gerddi" .... Y Babanod.
5. Canu—"Llangeitho Gynt" .... Yr Athraw.
6. Adrodd—"Robin y Sowldiwr" .... Ysgolor.
7. Canu—"Cymru yn y Nos" .... Yr Athrawes.
8. Adrodd—"Yr Yswain Mawr" (o "Storiau Cymru") .... Y Plant.
9. Canu—"Fy Iaith" .... Y Plant.
10. Adrodd—"Diarebion a Thrioedd Cymru Fu" .... Y Plant.
11. Canu—"Un o 'Ddyddiau Fu' Aberaeron" .... W. Lewis.
12. Adrodd—"Ymhoban a Goreuan Catwg Ddoeth" .... Y Plant.
13. Canu—"Sion y Go a Sian" .... Dosbarth 1af.
14. Adrodd—"Dysgu Saethu" (o "Dyddiau Ysgol") .... Ysgolor.
15. Canu—"Cerddi Cymru Fu" .... Yr Athrawes.
16. Adrodd—"Cotiau Coch Gogerddan" .... Y Plant.
17. Canu—"Shôl Fach Cymru Fu" .... Hen 'Sgolor.
18. Canu—"Hen Wlad fy Nhadau" .... Pawb.

of some of these help to place his initiative within the wider context of the position of the language and educational developments across the whole country. Some of the very complimentary letters he received (taken from *Cerddi Ysgol Llanycrwys*) were as follows:

In 1904: "Thank you very much for the programme. My heart warms thinking of the privileges Llanycrwys children have. Would that other schoolmasters would understand and appreciate the good efforts that concerts like yours have. As a collector of curios of this sort, I am glad to have a copy like this for years to years." (J H Davies, 21 Old Square, Lincoln's Inn, London WC)

In 1912: "Thank you very much for the programme, once more. It is excellent… Its contents seem to me to be quite equal to those of previous years. I am sure the neighbourhood quite appreciates what you do to foster a healthy national feeling in the minds of the rising generation. Welsh is now gradually making its way into our elementary and other schools –to you it is a distinction (and a privilege) that you are one of the small band of teachers who years ago brought Welsh into practical use in schools. I should like to see Welsh taught in every school in Wales so that all our young people would be able to read, write, recite and sing Welsh as well as English." (Owen Edwards)

In 1914: "Due to your usual generosity, I received the programme this year again. May you have great success in your efforts to elevate the old country." (John Thomas; Eifionydd)

In 1916: "Thank you very much for remembering me once again. I read every word of the programme. It is an excellent collection. You have been ahead of everybody. You indeed led the way to the national movement with regards to celebrating St David's Day in the school and Owen Edwards, myself and others followed you. You are keeping the standard and the standard of Llanycrwys very well." (L J Roberts; Aeron)

In 1917: "Thank you for remembering me again this year. It is a pity that every district in the country doesn't get the same chance as Ffaldybrenin district. You are a *pioneer* in the work. I congratulate you on your success in keeping the banner aloft so well, for such a long time. The poetry binds the past to the present and keeps in memory the thing that no nation should forget. You should publish the programmes in one book in order to instruct others in the work." (David Thomas – HMI for Cardiganshire)

An admirer called John wrote in 1917:

Tis from the bottom of my heart
I give thanks dear brother
For sending programmes all the time
To me, a poor pilgrim;
As usual the pieces
Are comical and clean
Whilst here I draw the pipe
And cough beside the fire.
Many remembrance,
As usual.

Daniel Davies from Ystrad, Rhondda said:

A hundred thanks I give you
For the St David's Day hymns;
The world's a sorry place, in trouble great
Tis only in Llanycrwys there's singing.

In 1919: "These concerts of yours must be very delightful to a Welshman aflame with the 'Cymru am byth' passion. You are building stalwarts by the series and I have had your programme now for years. I envy you the fame which is yearly accumulating, and when the Welsh language dies, if ever it does, there at Llanycrwys its last rites will take place. 'Dan, was da a ffyddlon' ['Dan, good and loyal servant'] must be your epitaph. You at any rate, keep the torch of the Welsh blazing bright." (Tom John)

Dan Jenkins' scrapbooks also show various individual letters which he received. For instance, a letter from Mr Nicholas, clerk to the Carmarthenshire County Council of

Llanycrwys School *c.* 1900
Dan Jenkins' scrapbooks

Llanycrwys Council School Field Day
Dan Jenkins' scrapbooks

Llanycrwys: school gardening
Dan Jenkins' scrapbooks

March 1914, thanking him for sending the St David's Day programme. He refers to item 11 as being the most amusing lines I have ever read: "Great credit and many thanks are due to you for your efforts, because I feel sure that the arranging of the concert is all due to you." An article in the *Carmarthen Journal* of 27th March 1913 congratulated Dan Jenkins for the actions he continued to take and "the ability to keep the old language on the tongues of the children".[7]

We cannot quantify the impact of the Llanycrwys St David's Day performances in terms of their influence on other schools. Knowledge of them was widespread, through both the immediate area and across Wales. Yet, not all schools were as bold, progressive or industrious as Llanycrwys. Nor did most school headteachers have the skills of a writer, publicist or campaigner as Dan Jenkins. For instance, according to the nearby Blaentwrch School's logbook, the first mention of St David's Day was in 1923, when the school was closed for a day in celebration.

Campaigns about individuals

Thomas Price of Wernfendigaid (1826–1910)

A campaign was launched in the Ffaldybrenin area of Carmarthenshire, to place a memorial tablet in the Congregational Chapel to the memory of Thomas Price of Wernfendigaid, in recognition of his services to the district, especially with regard to music. The funds for the tablet were raised by public subscription and the *Welshman* reported that these subscriptions were "collected chiefly by Daniel Jenkins, Llanycrwys, whose interest in the movement caused

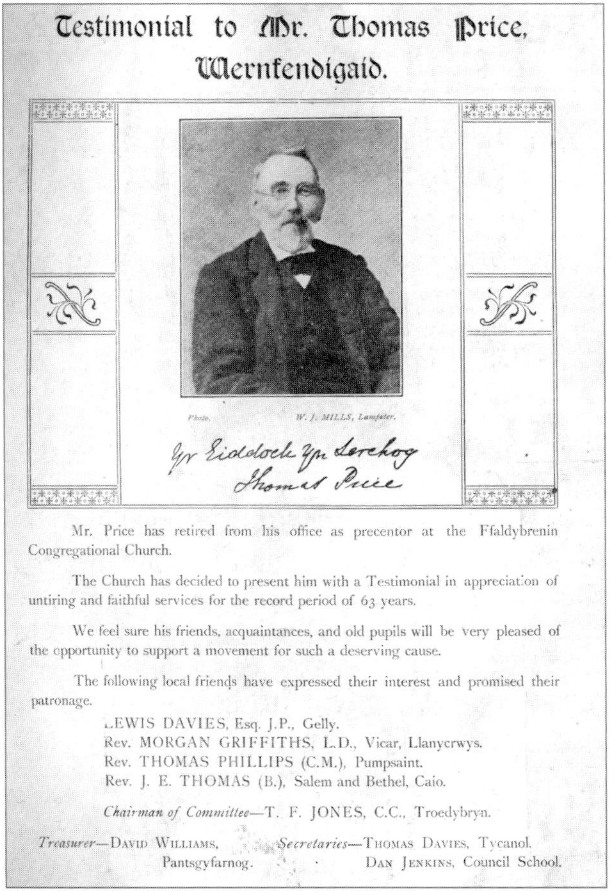

Testimonial to Mr. Thomas Price, Wernfendigaid.

Photo. *W. J. MILLS, Lampeter.*

Yr Eiddoch yn serchog
Thomas Price

Mr. Price has retired from his office as precentor at the Ffaldybrenin Congregational Church.

The Church has decided to present him with a Testimonial in appreciation of untiring and faithful services for the record period of 63 years.

We feel sure his friends, acquaintances, and old pupils will be very pleased of the opportunity to support a movement for such a deserving cause.

The following local friends have expressed their interest and promised their patronage.

LEWIS DAVIES, Esq. J.P., Gelly.
Rev. MORGAN GRIFFITHS, L.D., Vicar, Llanycrwys.
Rev. THOMAS PHILLIPS (C.M.), Pumpsaint.
Rev. J. E. THOMAS (B.), Salem and Bethel, Caio.

Chairman of Committee—T. F. JONES, C.C., Troedybryn.

Treasurer—DAVID WILLIAMS, Pantsgyfarnog.
Secretaries—THOMAS DAVIES, Tycanol. DAN JENKINS, Council School.

Testimonial

Dan Jenkins' scrapbooks

its complete success".[8] Once more, this is an example of the zeal and dedication of Dan to recognise and applaud the work of a man who did so much in developing and encouraging the singing tradition to which he (Dan) was so committed, and had throughout his life, devoted so much time to.

The tablet bears an inscription in Welsh and records Thomas' services as conductor and deacon of the chapel. It describes him as a man who had devoted the whole of his time and energy to the cultivation of congregational, as well as choral singing for 60 years. The newspaper reported that "his whole interest was centred in music, and he had the greatest regard for all lovers of music". Choirs trained by Thomas Price had for many years won prizes at local eisteddfodau, including Llanddewibrefi, Lampeter, Llansawel and Cwmdu. A large attendance at the chapel witnessed speeches about the choral and cultural contribution to the area of Thomas Price, including one from Dan Jenkins.

Granellian of Mydroilyn

The *Carmarthen Journal* reported in 1904, about a public meeting held to decide how to record the retirement, due to ill health of Granellian (Isaac Evans), headteacher of Mydroilyn Board School. A committee was set up, including Daniel Jenkins, to collect funds.[9] He was clearly a close friend of Granellian. This well-known Cardiganshire poet wrote pieces for the Llanycrwys St David's Day celebrations. He won the Chair at the Tal-sarn Eisteddfod in 1874.

Foundations for the modern Welsh school

People across a wide area of the country knew of Dan Jenkins and the work he did at Llanycrwys. It wasn't just the annual celebrations of St David's Day and the preparations leading up to the event, but the fact that the teaching within the school embraced both English and Welsh. The school had a liveliness about it – an interest which aided learning, since the effort being made was to make it relevant to the society and world in which the children lived. Hence, within the school building there were displays of information about local history and famous local people. The curriculum, too, had a place within it for gardening – a highly practical and useful activity, bearing in mind the number of children from homes which tried to produce as much of their own food as possible.

In 1911, Dr Timothy Richard, a famous missionary, visited and addressed the pupils. In 1913, Edward Owen, secretary of the Royal Commission on Ancient Monuments in Wales, visited the school. On 18th November 1918 it was closed for Armistice Day. Later that year a portrait of Lieutenant David Walters of Llwynglas was unveiled within the school. In 1919, Remembrance Day was observed with two minutes silence and the ringing of the school bell.[10]

Dan Jenkins' scrapbooks contain a copy of a song written for Llanycrwys School, by an 'old boy':

Learners are we, with books in hand,
Our task is but begun;
To earnest search we give ourselves,
Till we life's course have run.
In God's great plan of providence,
Whatever place we fill.
We all would take this lifelong now
'We would be learners still.'
Learners are we and scarce can read
The alphabet as yet;
But as we urge our onward way
We hope more light to get.

The value of truth is wondrous wide
But ransack it we will,
And if to us God's grace be given
'We will be learners still.'

Learners are we, and tardy too,
Our progress in God's school;

But line by line, and step by step,
We aim to reach the goal.
For on it lies – high up the path,
Along the rugged hill;
Yet we declare our stout resolve,
'We will be learners still.'

Learners we are, with buoyant heart,
Receptive is each mind;
We love the old, we love the new,
If in them good we find.
Learning we live, learning we die,
Harmonious with God's will,
And all throughout the Evermore,
'We will be learners still.'

(**David Thomas**, Cheshunt, Hertfordshire, 4th November 1907)

The school was fully involved with the community it served. For instance, the *Cambrian News*, on 20th October 1905, reported on: "Tea and sports at Rhosybedw when school children and their parents and all inhabitants of the parish were invited by Colonel and Miss Davies to join them in spending a jovial afternoon at Rhosybedw." Food was provided, games took place and prizes were given. Dan Jenkins supported the vicar in a vote of thanks.[11]

In August 1904, the *Carmarthen Journal* reported that there was held at Pumpsaint, a competitive concert and male voice competition in the Coronation Hall. The chairman was Sir James Hills-Johnes VC, of Dolaucothi and "Mr Dan Jenkins of Ffaldybrenin conducted in his usual able manner".[12]

Actions to help soldiers

The First World War raged from 1914–18. The scrapbooks show that Dan, like most citizens, did what he could to help the soldiers who were badly affected or injured by the conflict. In 1914 he organised the collection and sending

Llanycrwys School c.1917
Dan Jenkins' scrapbooks

of Aeron valley honey to wounded soldiers who were being nursed in Cardiff. In the Llanycrwys and Ffarmers area, he was a very active participant in the concerts of April 1918, in aid of the district soldiers' funds and January 1919, in aid of the district sailors and soldiers' fund, when he was involved in adjudicating.

National Union of Teachers

Dan continued his active membership of the NUT whilst at Llanycrwys. His scrapbooks show many newspaper cuttings about public educational discussions and the emergence of public policy on the school system. For instance, what was the role of the elementary school (all age) in the light of the emerging intermediate schools within Wales? What of teachers' salaries and conditions of service, how much discretion was to be left to the school boards and later county councils as overseers of the system? In 1899, he was at a large meeting at Felinfach, called by the Llanfihangel Ystrad School Board, but attended by board members and headteachers from a large area, to discuss the problem of pupil attendance at elementary schools. Mr Darlington, area HMI, spoke of confusion as to the school leaving age and attendance in general. He said:

> The fact has been too much ignored that the attendance in Welsh schools is considerably lower than it is in England. In the ultimate resort, everything depends upon the public mind – upon the enlightened cooperation of the public – and the difficulty in Wales is that public opinion is not sufficiently enlightened upon this subject.[13]

In 1900 the *Cambrian News* reported Dan's presence at a well-attended open meeting on the subject of elementary education in Lampeter, where the speaker was Ernest Gray MP. Dan seconded the vote of thanks to Mr Gray.[14]

Llanycrwys Parish Council membership

Once more, like at Llanfair Clydogau, Dan got involved directly in the work of the parish council. It was a small body of around seven members. Its minutes from 1894 show involvement with the adminstration of the poor law, the constuction of bridges over streams and a link with the board school. In 1910, Dan, of Brondderwen, was elected to the council, a role he performed for three years until 1913. In 1911, he was involved in a decision of the parish council to request the Carmarthenshire County Council to provide a training class on first aid in the village.

Retirement from Llanycrwys.

Dan Jenkins left his post as headteacher at Llanycrwys in July 1920. He had served for over 22 years. In the letter sent to him by the county council acknowledging his resignation, reference was made to his popularity and the high esteem in which he was held. It also described him as a very patriotic Welshman and well known throughout Wales.

For the 22 years that Dan Jenkins had worked at

Llanycrwys School, he had put into place his beliefs about education: a bilingual approach, local history, gardening, singing, combined with Welsh traditions and history. For 22 years he lived during the week at term time, in lodgings or in the schoolhouse. He had no car and there was no telephone. At home at Pentrefelin, were his wife and other members of his family. Yet in spite of his almost twin-track life, he managed to retain his strong commitment to his family, his interest in farming and rural pursuits, as well as pursuing a range of other activities across both the region and throughout Wales.

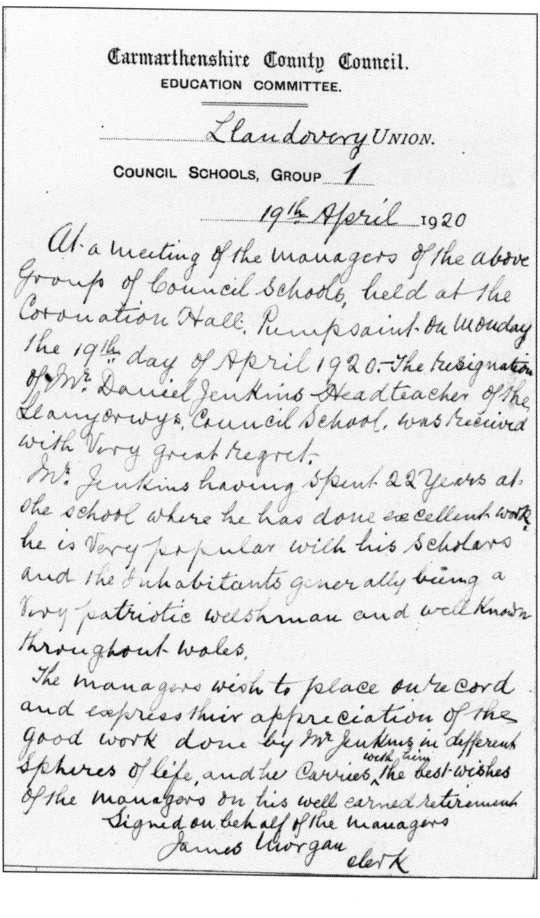

Carmarthenshire County Council.
EDUCATION COMMITTEE.

Llandovery UNION.

COUNCIL SCHOOLS, GROUP 1

19th April 1920

At a meeting of the managers of the above Group of Council Schools, held at the Coronation Hall, Pumpsaint on Monday the 19th day of April 1920. The resignation of Mr. Daniel Jenkins Headteacher of the Llanycrwys Council School, was received with very great regret.

Mr. Jenkins having spent 22 years at the school where he has done excellent work he is very popular with his scholars and the inhabitants generally being a very patriotic Welshman and well known throughout Wales.

The managers wish to place on record and express their appreciation of the good work done by Mr Jenkins in different spheres of life, and he carries with him the best wishes of the managers on his well earned retirement.

Signed on behalf of the managers
James Morgan
clerk

Retirement letter
Dan Jenkins' scrapbooks

Chapter Five

Cerddi Cerngoch

Dan Jenkins' personal notes and scrapbooks show evidence of his fascination with poetry and the lyrics of songs. He collected them from all around the country, mainly in Welsh, but sometimes English. He retained cuttings of all sorts and types of printed poems which had appeared in newspapers, or wrote out longhand those he came across on his travels or through his written exchanges with people.

He was exceptionally proud of the literary skills of his immediate Jenkins relatives and more distant ancestry. The local poet Cerngoch (1820–94), whose name was John Jenkins, an uncle of Dan, gave him particular pride, especially since he was extremely well known across west Wales. Perhaps his best poem or englyn was 'Y Morwr Colledig' (The Lost Sailor).

Cerngoch's poems were in many ways, a commentary on the social and literary life of late 19th century Cardiganshire: relatively physically isolated, and in terms of transport links, remote, undergoing severe population decline. From his earliest days, Dan was well aware of his uncle Cerngoch, his extremely gifted skill in terms of poetry composition, his ability to write verse about the local scenery and community in which he lived, and his personal esteem as well as the high regard with which he was held at eisteddfodau across Cardiganshire. As the 19th century progressed, Dan was becoming aware that a great deal of the folklore, poetry and songs of the region were being lost, as those who could recall an unwritten story or piece of verse from the past, had died. He wanted to see action taken to gather the material together and secure its recording and publication; an action which we will see later in the 20th century, involving him within the Cardiganshire Antiquarian Society and the Welsh Folk Song Society. Dan's interest had also seen him taking steps at Llanycrwys, through his annual St David's Day programme, to gather together poems and songs of distinction and to record in a published format, the material he had obtained.

The trigger for seeking to commemorate in some tangible way, the poetry of Cerngoch, was probably his uncle's death in 1894. Soon afterwards, an initial attempt to gather some of his poems together occurred, as part of a competition, held at the Llangybi (Cardiganshire) Eisteddfod of August 1895, with the prize being awarded by Dan Jenkins. The only submission was made by Thomas Davies of Dremddufawr, Silian.[1] Arising from this, the idea was developed of also collecting some poems written by three other family members, presumably to enable a suitably sized publication to be completed. This initiative took several years to evolve since Dan not only had to deal with the two attempts to dismiss him from his post at Llanfair Clydogau in 1894 and 1897, but also to find another job in Llanycrwys some months later, relocate himself and become established there. Therefore, he was a particularly busy man in coping with all these events. In the immediate three years leading up to the publication of the book, he was also very active in his other sphere of designing, writing and publishing, namely the St David's Day programmes for Llanycrwys School of 1901,

1902, and 1903. In 1902, he was also operating as the secretary of the Llangybi Eisteddfod committee, calling meetings and planning the next events.

With a range of poems written by the four Cardiganshire Jenkins family poets gathered together, he edited them, together with ap Ceredigion (David Lewis, cleric, poet and contributor to Welsh-language publications). Dan subsequently published a 234-page book entitled *Cerddi Cerngoch.* His co-editor, ap Ceredigion was born near Cilcennin and, although he was several years younger than Dan, their professional pathways probably crossed in the Lampeter area as he was educated at St David's College in the town. Apart from collaborating together on the publication of *Cerddi Cerngoch,* ap Ceredigion also worked to produce several pieces for the annual St David's Day programmes at Llanycrwys, for example in 1902, 1904, 1910 and 1915.

Cerddi Cerngoch was printed by Welsh church printers, Caxton Hall in Lampeter and sold for two shillings and sixpence. It is mostly in Welsh. For a regional publication, it sold well. Many people knew of Cerngoch through the informal social, cultural and religious networks of the time and hence there was a good degree of interest and curiosity amongst the public. At the time of its first edition in 1904, the book was well received by an appreciative audience in terms of its reviews. Dan's entrepreneurial drive, circulation of publicity literature and general enthusiasm for the project, ensured that there were 500 pre-publication subscribers. It was republished quite soon in 1904, and followed by a third edition in 1922. The binding of 1,000 copies for this last edition cost Dan £50 6s. 8d. (He kept the receipt in one of his scrapbooks.)

Apart from Cerngoch, the other three poets around whom the book concentrates are: Amnon II or Joseph Jenkins (Cerngoch's brother) of Trecefel, Tregaron; Aeronian (Cerngoch's son) otherwise Jenkin Aeronian Jenkins and Hywel, otherwise the Rev. John Davies, late vicar of Llandeloy and relation of Dan Jenkins' grandmother.

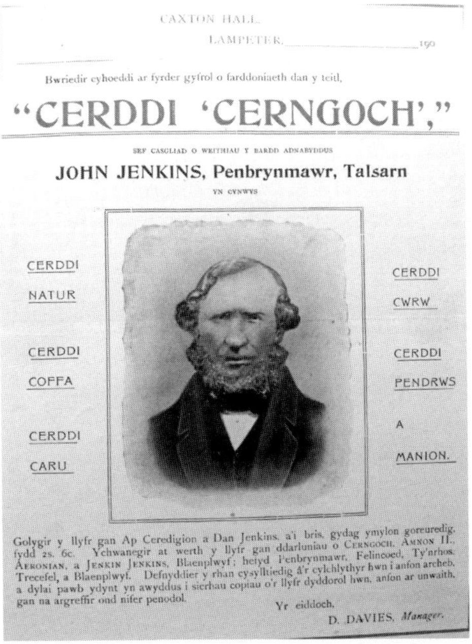

CAXTON HALL,

LAMPETER, ____________ 190

Bwriedir cyhoeddi ar fyrder gyfrol o farddoniaeth dan y teitl,

"CERDDI 'CERNGOCH',"

SEF CASGLIAD O WEITHIAU Y BARDD ADNABYDDUS

JOHN JENKINS, Penbrynmawr, Talsarn

YN CYNWYS

CERDDI NATUR

CERDDI COFFA

CERDDI CARU

CERDDI CWRW

CERDDI PENDRWS

A MANION.

Golygir y llyfr gan Ap Ceredigion a Dan Jenkins, a'i bris, gydag ymylon goreuredig, fydd 2s. 6c. Ychwanegir at werth y llyfr gan ddarluniau o CERNGOCH, AMNON II., AERONIAN, a JENKIN JENKINS, Blaenplwyf; hefyd Penbrynmawr, Felincoed, Ty'nrhos, Trecefel, a Blaenplwyf. Defnyddier y rhan cysylltiedig â'r cylchlythyr hwn i anfon archeb, a dylai pawb ydynt yn awyddus i sicrhau copiau o'r llyfr dyddorol hwn, anfon ar unwaith, gan na argreffir ond nifer penodol.

Yr eiddoch,

D. DAVIES, *Manager.*

Cerddi Cerngoch
Dan Jenkins' scrapbooks

The *Western Mail,* in reviewing the book wrote: "The whole, with biographical and descriptive sketches, making one of the cheapest and most handsome volumes ever issued from the Welsh press. The poets came from the same stock as the famous Davies of Castell Howel." Later Joseph Jenkins became better known through books recounting his life and detailing his diaries of his life as a 'swagman' in Australia.[2]

The *Western Mail* review went on to say:

> Mr Dan Jenkins seems to have been chiefly responsible for the introductory matter, though he received material help from a number of literary friends. This part of the volume is of permanent value, as it contains a description of life in that Welsh Arcadia – Cardiganshire – which can be found nowhere else. The photos, by different hands, also add to the value of the sketches. To a great extent, the poems, especially those of Cerngoch are reflections and echoes of Welsh life – life as it will never be lived again. Cerngoch like Burns, courted the muse and followed the plough, and his more spirited compositions, particularly his two well-known fox-hunting songs, are worthy of the author of 'Tam o'

> Shanter' himself. One, that of the Gwrtheyrn or Llanfair pack, though composed more than 50 years ago, is still on the lips of the peasantry in south Cardiland. Like Burns also, Cerngoch touched ever so many common subjects and invested them with fresh interest and even sacredness. A man of ready wit like him is ever in a rural district at the beck and call of his neighbours, and social functions, weddings especially afforded him a great opportunity to strike his lyre. The old institution of going in quest of a bride is in vogue in Cardiganshire, and Cerngoch provided the poetry on those occasions a hundred times. Biddings afforded a favourite theme for his prolific pen. His songs and englynion afforded his friends and neighbours unmixed delight for two generations, and now they are collected in book form they will ever remain an inexhaustible source of fun and pleasure for posterity. In his harp are many strings, and he strikes them all with equal ease and effect. It is not suggested that he soars high; it is the muse of ordinary flight the average man appreciates.
>
> Aeronian was a man of many gifts, a chip off the old block, but having had the advantages of education 25 and 30 years ago he won many a literary triumph at the eisteddfodic arena. Amnon II was a man of great originality and insight. He shows more refinement, but lacks the natural force of his brother Cerngoch. Hywel was a solicitor and a man of great culture, a happy combination of a county gentleman and a devine. The editors and printers have done their work well.[3]

The family tree of the Jenkins family was included within the book, in order to assist readers' understanding of relationships. Those to focus on would be: (a) Griffith Jenkins, son of the Blaenplwyf household, whose son was Daniel Jenkins; (b) Joseph Jenkins (Amnon II), son of the Blaenplwyf family; (c) John Jenkins, son of the Blaenplwyf family and (d) his son Jenkin Aeronian Jenkins (Aeronian).

Reviewing the book in September 1905, the *Herald of Wales* described Cerngoch as a country bard who was in his element singing to everybody and everything. "Poems and englynion would gush out of him – whatever took his fancy."

A *South Wales Daily News* review of August 1905 stated:

> As a book of poetry it cannot possess and does not claim equality with the works of some of our leading Welsh bards. The book however, contains some very interesting and pretty verses and a good many portraits of Cardiganshire worthies. The value of the book is in the short biographies it contains, which will nearly fill one half of the volume. These throw a flood of light upon the life of Cardiganshire farmers and the habits of the people. Cerngoch was a ready and prolific versifier and a good englynwr, and a tithe of his verses and stanzas would fill a decent volume, but the book now before us contains but a selection, showing the poet's perfect touch with human nature and that he was in harmony with his surroundings.[4]

In 1905, the Labour Party newspaper for Wales was complimentary about the book, but reminded readers that Cerngoch was essentially a 'country' and not eisteddfod bard.

When the third edition of *Cerddi Cerngoch* appeared in 1922 there was additional content, written by Dan Jenkins about Cerngoch. A newspaper review in the *Welshman* reminded the reader that the book contained a huge variety of poetry and song lyrics and that they were far away from the modern poetry of today. "The poems are natural; homely, on a wide variety of topics."

Prior to the book first appearing in 1904, Dan sent out marketing leaflets a year earlier to people he knew, drawing attention to its content and its published price of two shillings and sixpence. The leaflets were addressed as being from Dan Jenkins of Pentrefelin but with an address of "Llanycrwys Council School, Llanwrda".

Apart from the writings of the four poets, the two editors' biographical detail helped to draw attention to their Cardiganshire roots. The fact that three of the poets came directly from the Jenkins family at Blaenplwyf, helped not only to give them a status, but also to add something more to the character, esteem and importance of the family within the county and also throughout the region.

Cerngoch (John Jenkins)

Following his death at the age of 74, Cerngoch's obituary in the *Cambrian News* of the 30th of March 1894, described him as:

> ... never aspiring to any public position, was well known over a wide district as a man of strong intellect, keen observation and a jovial companion. Although comparatively uncultured, he was of a metaphysical turn of mind, and was never so happy as when he found himself in sympathetic company discussing the problems of man's destiny, influence of environments, drifting forces, the religion of humanity, etc. The incongruity of the subjects discussed and the surrounding circumstances were often grotesque. But it was in his capacity of bard that he is best known to most people.[5]

Upon hearing of his death, his brother Joseph wrote in his diary: "He was a genius and a ready poet. He could talk poetical all day on any subject."[6]

Most of the poetry within *Cerddi Cerngoch* is in Welsh, but a small number of pieces are in English. An example of a Cerngoch poem in his second language is as follows:

Autumn

To Thee the ever-bounteous Lord,
My soul, make all thy powers;
He calls, and at His voice come forth
The smiling harvest hours.

Well pleased, the toiling swains behold
The waving yellow crop;
With joy they bear the sheaves away,
And sow again in hope.

Thus teach me, gracious God, to sow
The seeds of righteousness;
Smile on my soul, and with thy beams
The ripening harvest bless.

Over 170 of his poems were included in the book.

Amnon II (Joseph Jenkins, the Swagman)

Amnon II died in 1898 at the age of 80. He was the elder brother of John Jenkins. Upon his marriage, he moved to farm at Trecefel, Tregaron. He was very active in the area in both farming and political circles, until he emigrated to Australia at the age of 51, leaving his family behind. He returned 25 years later. Incredibly, he kept a diary for 58 years, with entries in both Welsh and English.

This is the only English poem of his which was included in the book:

> O! Should my present crop be lost
> I cannot calculate its cost;
> But those who use the pick and spade
> Thank Peel and Cobden for 'Free Trade'.

Some 80 of his poems were contained in the publication. His diaries show him often writing poetry, including the more difficult englyn. We know that whilst living in Australia, he competed in the annual St David's Day eisteddfod on thirteen consecutive occasions and won the main prize for the best englyn each time.[7]

Joseph Jenkins
Cerddi Cerngoch

Aeronian (Jenkin Aeronian Jenkins)

In advance of the publication of the book, the *Western Mail* reported that Aeronian (Jenkin Aeronian Jenkins) was a very gifted man, and a perfect master of Welsh and English. It stated:

> Like many another Welsh bard, he seldom duplicated his poetical compositions, and many an excellent song has hopelessly been lost. Like those whom the gods love, he died young (in October 1892), but not before he served his generation well. He was at the time of his death a farmer, a miller, and a clerk to about half-a-dozen school boards. The Jenkinses of Penbryn and Blaenplwyf are descended from the same stock as the scholar-bard of Castell Hywel.[8]

He had over thirty of his poems published in *Cerddi Cerngoch*. He lived at Felin-coed with his wife and five daughters. The success of their daughters in becoming teachers and, in the case of at least three, headteachers, has been reported upon in a book describing the history of the parish of Nantcwnlle. They were Margaret Jenkins, who became headmistress of the County School, Cardiff and then Albany Road School, Cardiff (1908–30); Mary Jenkins a teacher in Roath Park, Cardiff (1904–30); Anne Jenkins, headteacher in Gabalfa (1911–26); Kate Jenkins, headteacher of Gabalfa (1926–30) and Gwladys Elizabeth Jenkins who taught in Wood Street School, Cardiff (1911–30).

Aeronian
Cerddi Cerngoch

David Davies or Davis / Dafis Castell Hywel

David Davies was an uncle of Dan's grandmother, Eleanor. He was a minister, poet and school master who was born in Llangybi in 1745. At Castell Hywel in the vale of Cletwr, he kept a school and had a superb reputation as a teacher. He died in 1827. He had the least number of poems included in this publication.

Without the drive, commitment, finance and enterprise of Dan Jenkins, the book *Cerddi Cerngoch* would not have been compiled and published. Hence it is likely that some of the poetry it contains would have been lost. Equally Dan and ap Ceredigion as editors, also gave the readers a real insight into a Cardiganshire society which existed in the second half of the 19th century. The fact that it was published twice in 1904 and again in 1922 is testament to the interest which surrounded the subject. On each occasion it was reviewed by the newspapers of Wales with accounts appearing in both Welsh and English. A review in 1922 commended the huge variety in the book which was far away from the modern poetry of the time.

Dafis Castell Hywel
Cerddi Cerngoch

Chapter Six

Cerddi Ysgol Llanycrwys

THIS BOOK WAS conceived by Dan Jenkins as a means of placing in one location, all of the St David's Day poems and songs from 1901–20, which had been especially written for the annual celebration and performance which he devised and masterminded.

Although he had retired from Llanycrwys in 1920, the book was not published until 1934, some 14 years after his retirement. The task of undertaking this work would have been demanding for a man in his late 70s, especially the research involved. Quite when he devised the concept for the book is unclear. As an idea it may well have had a long period of growth. A clue to its early development is provided by a report in the *Cambrian News* of 1926, about the importance of the bard Granellian, who had just died. The report reminded readers of his contribution to the St David's Day programme of Dan Jenkins of Pentrefelin and that: "the words thus collected were original verse which Dan Jenkins induced his many friends to send him." It went on: "These annual booklets put together would make a unique collection of rare flavour."[1]

The book was also a short history of the parish as well as

comments he wrote about some of the influences which had shaped his thinking. Amongst the detail listed is the bardic and real name of some 109 poets, together with their home locations. He chose to call locations in Cardiganshire by their ancient Welsh name Ceredigion, though the area did not acquire that as an official local government name until it became a district within Dyfed county in 1974. Hence, we learn that Granellian was Isaac Evans of Felin Blaenau, Llanwenog, Ceredigion; Isfoel was David Jones of Blaencelyn, Llangrannog, Ceredigion; Sarnicol was Thomas Jacob Thomas of Sarnicol, Capel Cynon, Ceredigion; and Watcyn Wyn was Watcyn Hezekiah Williams of Cwm Garw, Cwarter Bach, Carmarthenshire. The book was marketed by Dan Jenkins, with circulars sent out seeking to persuade people to order at four shillings or two shillings and sixpence. Printed by Gomer Press at Llandysul and published in June 1934, it is 163 pages long. Between 700 and 800 people subscribed to it pre-publication, including a number of his relatives, and all names are listed. He lobbied for and received the tacit support of the Carmarthenshire County Council for his publishing project. As a result he circulated all Carmarthenshire schools with the contents of a letter he had received from the council stating that: "the education committee are quite prepared to allow headteachers to include the book you refer to in their school requisitions, if they desire to do so."[2]

In a review of the book, the *Welshman* newspaper wrote:

> *Cerddi Ysgol Llanycrwys* is a mixture of songs and local lore and antiquities, mixed with biographical details and pictures, brought together by Dan Jenkins. Mr Jenkins is a retired school master and well-known eisteddfodwr. From 1898 until 1920 he was master of the village school of Llanycrwys, in Carmarthenshire, and to celebrate St David's Day, he had a school concert every year.
>
> Nothing very new in that you will say, but Mr Jenkins was not satisfied with the usual school concert. He had the verses to be sung written specially for him by a great number of Welsh poets, some of them well known, some of them obscure, and in this book he has gathered together the sheaves of those years, together with

> much about the history of the parish and locality. The result is curious and mixed, but interesting enough. Some of the ballads, whatever may be their poetic quality, enshrine a good deal of local lore about old customs, and emphasise the fact that poetry in Wales is still to a great extent a communal thing, the natural way of commenting on day-to-day life and happenings.
>
> There is a tabulated list of the poets who have contributed, with their dates and callings. It is interesting to note how many of them were or are farmers. The pictures are good.[3]

Dan was particularly skilled at publicising events in which he was playing a leading part. This book was no exception. He wrote to David Lloyd George and his scrapbooks show a letter from an aide in May 1932, thanking Dan for alerting the former prime minister, including four shillings to purchase a copy, when it was published.

In October 1936 the *Cambrian News,* in reporting upon Dan's fiftieth wedding anniversary, commented upon this book and reminded readers that "his Gŵyl Dewi entertainment was an outstanding event".[4]

An unnamed newspaper cutting in Dan's scrapbooks commented that he alone chose the annual topic and the tunes to which the words were composed. Further, that the book was beautifully produced with 96 people making contributions to the yearly St David's Day programmes. It went on to report that the *Daily Express* had published an article praising the venture.

The *Welshman* writing about Dan at the time of his sixtieth wedding anniversary in October 1946, said people gave him the title "Jenkins, Llanycrwys", and pointed out that he was best known as a Welsh patriot. It stated:

> While at Llanycrwys he did much to create a deeper interest in local folklore. He was one of the first in Wales to celebrate St David's Day in schools. Long before Welsh became a subject, he taught the children to sing Welsh songs and recite Welsh poems. He sent to renowned bards such as Watcyn Wyn, Pedrog, Dyfed and others for special verses for St David's Day. These he arranged

> in the form of programmes each year, and in 1934 he published them under the title *Cerddi Llanycrwys* which also included a history of the parish.[5]

One of the purchasers of the book was former pupil J P Walters, who was so enthusiastic about his friend Dan Jenkins as a man, and about Llanycrwys in general, that he attached the following note to his copy of the book on 4th June 1940.

> This is the history of my parish and the verses of songs sung by the pupils of my parish school along the years, before, during and after my time. It was produced by my school master and friend, (Mr Dan Jenkins). This will have value to those who understand Welsh and so please send it home, on my death.
>
> J P Walters (former pupil).[6]

Chapter Seven

The Language and Culture of Wales

The distinguished poet 'Sarnicol' wrote the following about Dan Jenkins in 1933:

- "He is not a bard or a great literary gentleman; but a collector and appreciator of literature";
- "He spent many years as a school teacher at Llanycrwys School, and he was one of the first to celebrate St David's Day in school;
- Long before Welsh became a subject taught in schools, Jenkins taught the children to recite poetry and sing Welsh folk songs. He wrote to poets such as Watcyn Wyn, Pedrog, Dyfed and others to ask for special poems for St David's Day;
- He has taught hundreds of children to appreciate the poets and literary people of their country. When I was at school I was taught to fear and tremble. I was not taught about Ceiriog or Mynyddog, or even about the daisies that grew on the hillside".

Western Mail 19th May 1933[1]

National Eisteddfod

Dan Jenkins had an enormous regard for the role and importance of all eisteddfodau, especially the National Eisteddfod. In the 19th century, eisteddfodau were held in very many small rural locations and provided an opportunity for people to gather together socially, provide entertainment for each other and hold competitions, for example in 1886 in Llanfair Clydogau.

Dan is described as an attender at a large number of local, county and national eisteddfodau throughout the years from 1864, when he was only eight years old. Over a very long time span he became a prominent eisteddfodwr.[2] When the National Eisteddfod began in something approximating to its present organisation, around the middle years of the 19th century, Dan Jenkins was a dedicated and enthusiastic attendee at its various locations across Wales, as it moved each year to different annual sites, alternating between north and south Wales. He derived a great satisfaction from his involvement and was a keen participant in the language and cultural activities which occurred. We do not have a precise record of how many National Eisteddfodau he actually attended, but know he first went in 1876 to Wrexham – at the time he was a student at Bangor College. His last was at Cardiff in 1938; an incredible 62 years later. It is clear that his involvement was a two-way thing, in that he made an important contribution to the evolution and trend of policy and thought on cultural and language matters, but also received an impetus from his individual personal conversations and exposure to the ideas of the literary people present, for the initiatives, which he was personally pursuing.

Dan's scrapbooks contain a number of examples of memorabilia connected with the eisteddfod: tickets for events, signatures of a number of the major artistic and literary figures of the time and photographs.

The scrapbooks provide evidence of his important position as a communicator, a facilitator and a liaisor with writers, politicians and opinion-formers across Wales. They also show that this relationship was not just functional, but personal and caring. For instance, one letter in February 1904 from Hwfa Môn (Rowland Williams) from Llys Hwfa, Rhyl, who won the national chair in 1862, crown in 1867, and in 1894 was elected archdruid, said: "Please excuse me as death has been hovering over me for many weeks and my spirit is too heavy to think about composing anything on such a topic. Yours sincerely, Hwfa Môn."

Hwfa Môn died the following year. There is also correspondence with Watcyn Wyn who died in 1905 and who won awards at many eisteddfodau in the period 1881–93. For instance, there is an englyn composed specifically for Dan in 1904, describing a new year's present he'd received from him, which consisted of a cockerel and a hen. It refers to the "splendid calennig I received; from a wealthy friend to a poor one". His extensive poetry had a lasting impression on Dan and, as recounted, he made much use of it at Llanycrwys School. Another letter from the scrapbooks (and reprinted in *Yr Ymofynnydd*), is from Je Aitsh (John Herbert Jones), who was editor of the weekly publication *Y Brython*. Writing from his home in Birkenhead in 1938, he said:

> My dear Dan, I am now free to disclose the secret that I get £100 of annual pension from the civil list for services to Welsh literature, according to the prime minister's letter. The programme began last year, the first £100 has arrived and future payments will be made, £25 every quarter. I know you will be happy to hear this. Word has arrived from Wrexham that they are so busy it will be the end of the month before *Gwin o'r Gorffennol* (Wine of the Past) comes from the press. Yours sincerely, if more untidy than usual, Je Aitsh.

Dan's scrapbooks also show evidence of his own writing to other national literary figures such as Wil Ifan (William Evans), who was a major writer in Welsh and English and won the crown three times at the National Eisteddfod.

Gorsedd Beirdd Ynys Prydain (Gorsedd of Bards of the Island of Britain)

The gorsedd is an important part of the National Eisteddfod. In 1907,[3] Dan became a member of this group, a body whose members consist of poets, teachers and people of significance in literature, science and art. He was exceptionally proud of his membership and retained a number of his tickets for individual eisteddfodau which he had attended, specifying his gorsedd membership. He stuck them into his scrapbooks.

A photograph of the gorsedd gathering at Birkenhead in 1917, also from his scrapbooks, shows him close to the front, with an arrow which he had drawn, showing his position. This was a very significant eisteddfod because it occurred at the height of the First World War at a time when casualties of the battles taking place in continental Europe were very high. The mood in society was very much affected by this. A study of the editions of the *Western Mail* on a daily basis shows reports of men who had been killed in action, often with a photograph of the individual and family detail. In Birkenhead, a special poignancy was attached to the Eisteddfod event because when it came to the award of the bardic Chair for a piece of poetry entitled 'Yr Arwr' (The Hero), the declared winner at the ceremony was not in attendance. Ellis Humphrey Evans from Yr Ysgwrn near Trawsfynydd, Merionethshire, had submitted the piece under the pseudonym, Fleur de Lys and when the archdruid asked him to announce himself at the ceremony, there was at first no answer. An observer explained what happened next:

> ... a gentleman appeared and made a communication with the archdruid, who announced that, the victor (who's bardic name was Hedd Wyn), had fallen in battle and lay in a silent grave in Belgium. This created a profound sensation in the great audience and instead of the usual chairing ceremony; the oak bardic chair was draped with black cloth. The audience rose in silence and stood while the archdruid and the bards of the gorsedd recited a series of in memorium stanzas.[4]

The detail is that Hedd Wyn was killed in action on 31st July 1917, near Pilckem in Flanders, on a day which saw over 4,000 other British troops die in the conflict. He was a member of the 15th battalion of the Royal Welsh Fusiliers. However, the officials at the eisteddfod had not known of his death. This sad

Y CYMRO, GORFFENNAF 4 1963 5

ORIAU OLAF BARDD Y GADAIR DDU

PRUN bynnag a fydd prifardd yn ei gadair ai peidio yn y Brifwyl eleni, ar ddydd Iau y bydd penllanw'r wyl i Mr. William Richardson, 75 oed, un o drigolion Llandudno. Neu ar y diwrnod hwnnw y bydd penllanw'r atgofion, beth bynnag.

A sôn am gadeirio'r bardd a Mr. Richardson yn ôl i'r dyddiau pan oedd yn aelod o'r Bymthegfed Fataliwn o'r R.W.F. i Ypres, bedair blynedd a deugain yn ôl, i Pilkem Ridge, ac i lecyn a elwid yn Iron Cross Road yn arbennig.

Yno, ar y dydd olaf o Orffennaf, 1917, yr oedd William Richardson yn un o'r rhai olaf a welodd Hedd Wyn yn fyw. Yr oedd yn un o'r pedwar a'i cariodd hanner canllath i gyrraedd y meddyg. Yr oedd yn y fan a'r lle pan fu farw'r bardd.

Adroddodd William Richardson yr hanes wrthyf yn ei gartref yng Nghraig y Don, Llandudno. Cofia'r olygfa fel pe bai'n ddoe, meddai. Cofia mai enw'r meddyg dewr oedd Dr. Day. Cofia mai dau o'r tri arall a gariai'r elor-wely oedd Eric Barnard a Charlie Lucas. Cofia'r archoll [illegible] [illegible] y milwr [illegible] ac fel y gwyddai pawb o'i gwmpas nad oedd gobaith iddo fyw.

Gorsedd yr Eisteddfod ym Mhenbedw yn 1917. Ar y Maen Llog saif yr Archdderwydd Dyfed, a rhwng y Maen Llog a'r delyn y mae telynores swyddogol yr wyl—Telynores Prydain, yn 17 oed.

Birkenhead Eisteddfod, 1917, gorsedd gathering (arrow shows Dan Jenkins)

Dan Jenkins' scrapbooks

AT NEATH EISTEDDFOD YESTERDAY.—Mr. Dan Jenkins, Glynfab, and Mr. Philip Thomas, fellow-students in Bangor Normal College in the early 'seventies, who attended their first Eisteddfod together at Wrexham in 1876. With few exceptions they have attended every "National" since then.

Neath Eisteddfod, 1918

Dan Jenkins' scrapbooks

Machynlleth Eisteddfod, 1937 (on the left is Dan Jenkins)

Dan Jenkins' scrapbooks

Dan Jenkins and a fellow member of the gorsedd

Dan Jenkins' scrapbooks

and moving event formed the basis for the Academy Award nominated film, *Hedd Wyn*.

Dan's scrapbooks show several newspaper cuttings about the war, but not the Hedd Wyn event. He was acutely aware of the enormous impact and personal turmoil caused by the war. As we have seen at Ffaldybrenin, Dan did what he could to raise funds for soldiers and sailors affected by the conflict.

Archdderwydd y Maes (archdruid of the field)

Dan Jenkins became popularly known as the 'archdruid of the field'. His acquisition of this title, according to the *Welsh Gazette* in 1936, owed much to Wil Ifan, who attached this description to him. It was not only a term of endearment or affection, but also a description of his importance. To speculate why it probably came about, it is necessary to consider his modus operandi over many years. He was a very reliable and regular attendee at the National Eisteddfod. He was extremely well known, knowledgeable on many matters of Welsh cultural significance and had a high level of awareness of the matters which the eisteddfod was seeking to promote. He networked and communicated with a large number and a wide range of people. He was a campaigner and a publicist. He was a very important figure, not only for his poetry, but also for his work on the Welsh language in schools, folk singing, eisteddfodau and St David's Day. The *Welshman* described him as: "an ardent Welshman, he has a special liking for Welsh music and literature. A fine raconteur, he is always an interesting figure on the eisteddfod field among a group of friends discussing literary topics."[5]

When he was 89, the *Cambrian News* described him as one of the "most interesting figures at the National Eisteddfod" and that "nothing delighted him more than to meet friends on the eisteddfod field and to discuss literary topics."

At the time of his golden wedding anniversary in 1936, the *Daily Mail* printed an article about him, as follows:

Druid's Pipe

> The gorsedd has its archdruid, but that integral part of the national festival known as 'Maes yr Eisteddfod' has its own special archdruid. His name is Dan Jenkins Llanycrwys. At every eisteddfod you will find him surrounded by bards, musicians and others, smoking his pipe and discussing the winning englyn, pryddest or awdl.
>
> He makes the 'pabell lên' his official headquarters. For 50 years Dan Jenkins was a village school master in Cardiganshire and Carmarthenshire. He might have stepped right out of 'The Deserted Village' of Goldsmith's to Llanycrwys.
>
> He is one of the few bearded bards still left at the gorsedd, and at 78 is more agile and active than many of those younger who use safety razors. He and Mrs Jenkins celebrate their golden wedding next week.[6]

Cardiganshire Antiquarian Society

Dan Jenkins was a member of the Cardiganshire Antiquarian Society. This organisation did much good work in trying to preserve ancient sites within Wales, such as Strata Florida and to collect and record material of an important historical nature. In 1929, one of the society's projects was to collect the folk songs which had been sung in Cardiganshire for centuries. These songs were gathered together and published in the form of a book. Dan attended the launch of this book, in November 1929, in Aberystwyth. He gave a solo, as did Mr J Ffos Davies of Felinfach and both "were enthusiastically applauded". The *Cambrian News* reported that:

> … the task of collecting these folk songs was undertaken when they were in peril of being lost for ever. In them are found echoes of the common life of the country in the 17th and 18th centuries. They include some of the most beautiful melodies recorded. 'Elisa Talysarn' is reckoned to be one of the most tuneful in any country… valuable work has also been done on the literary side by Cledlyn, the nationally chaired bard of 1919 and 1923. Mr J Ffos Davies, Felinfach had also done exceptional work in this direction. Mr D Thomas MA, late HMI, has also supported the movement

> since its inception about 30 years ago, and is perhaps the chief authority on Welsh folklore in the country.[7]

The folk song book which was produced was called *Forty Welsh Traditional Tunes*.

Dan Jenkins was reported in the same newspaper article as being a member of the executive committee of the society. Copies of this important body's notepaper, retained by Dan, showed its president as Colonel Davies Evans, its vice-presidents as Lord Ystwyth and the Earl of Lisburne, with David Thomas as secretary. A number of Dan's letters to David Thomas are to be found in the National Library of Wales. They show him corresponding regularly on antiquarian society matters. For instance, in 1928 he wrote about a campaign which was underway to raise money for a library and suggested that: "the literary society and women's society should form a special group for the collection of money for the NLW." In April, he wrote suggesting that every child in Cardiganshire should remember their part in the work of the NLW by singing gasgl geiniog (collect the pennies). In May of the same year, he described a meeting which was to be held in Cellan, Cardiganshire, but comments that: "I cannot attend because of my age, especially if it is in the evening." Another letter of the same month refers to him holding a meeting to collect money and that he had done his best to adapt a song re: Llanycrwys. In July 1929, he suggested the holding of a large meeting at Felinfach Memorial Hall and referred to the folk songs as "very valuable treasures for me". In another 1929 letter to David Thomas, he confided that "between the bees and the hay I am kept very busy". In August 1929 he wrote of his recent attendance at a Welsh festival in Liverpool where he came across a version of the song 'Elisa Talysarn' being sung. In September 1935 he wrote to David Thomas about the planning for a large meeting which was to take place in Tregaron, at which it was intended the speakers should be, in his words, "big guns".

This collection of letters often shows the close personal relationship between the two men with a reference in 1928, to David Thomas' sailing and Dan describing being ill for two weeks with bronchitis after attending a chapel meeting in Llangeitho in 1935. What is clear about the correspondence is the close alignment of ideas between them, towards furthering the NLW, antiquarianism in Cardiganshire and in particular, gathering the folk songs together. As part of this endeavour, David Thomas collected folk song details from all Cardiganshire schools in the period 1921–6.

Dan was an important member and campaigner for the work of the Cardiganshire Antiquarian Society over a number of years. He kept in his scrapbooks, newspaper cuttings referring to its work.

Welsh Folk Song Society

This society was founded in 1908 at a meeting held at Llangollen. Dan Jenkins was an early and active member. He appears on the membership list in the society's magazine of 1911.

In 1936, in an article within the Cardiganshire Antiquarian Society's *Transactions*,[8] Dan wrote a piece expressing concern at the death of the folk song. His scrapbooks also show a receipt for membership for the year 1937. He corresponded extensively on the subject of folk songs in an attempt to secure their retention for future generations. His scrapbooks show a copy of a letter he received in 1939 from David Thomas (referred to above as secretary of the Cardiganshire Antiquarian Society), not long before the latter's death saying: "we had an excellent meeting in Cardigan on Wednesday. But the best meeting the society had, was around 1929 when you and Ffos... [Jac Ffos Ddu, another teacher and a unique folk song singer] ... sang 'Elisa Talysarn' and some other old pieces. It was well worth being alive to hear that sort of singing."

Singing

Dan Jenkins was a keen and successful singer. He organised and participated in many events which occurred in schools, chapels, churches, village halls and eisteddfodau across a wide area. As a result, he was extremely well known. His own handwritten notes, largely contained within his many scrapbooks, show that he undertook research on important singers of the time and made summaries of their background and individual characteristics. In terms of his own public singing, a poster from 1884, lists Dan singing in both Welsh and English the following songs: 'Cân y Milwr', 'Arm, Arm, Ye Brave' and 'Awelon yr Eryri', with all proceeds going to Thomas Williams, tailor of Lampeter who had been ill for some time.

We know that in his teenage years, whilst staying with his aunt and uncle at Pant, Llanddewibrefi, he sang with the local choir. In other chapters of this book, reference has been made to his singing in Herefordshire, at Ffaldybrenin and in many other Cardiganshire locations.

Dan Jenkins and Jones Cantwr (Jones the singer)

In line with his interest and historic research activities, a few months before his ninetieth birthday, Dan published an account

John Jones
Dan Jenkins' scrapbooks

in the *Welsh Gazette*[9] of Jones Cantwr (Jones the singer). He had a very dear attachment to this old man and a report in the *Welshman* showed Dan attending his funeral in 1924, along with, amongst others, the Chief Constable and an unbelievably large number of eleven clergymen.

In his article he stated that during the 1850s, 60s and 70s, there wasn't a more famous person in Ceredigion and north Carmarthenshire than John Jones, bookseller of Aberaeron:

"The first name given to him that I heard from my mother was 'Jones bach y cantwr' (little Jones the singer). The 'bach' not only described his physique but was also a term of endearment across a wide area." He went on to say that he was born in 1832 at a cottage called Penbanc, just outside Tal-sarn in the parish of Trefilan, but the family then moved to Blaenwernlas, located between Abermeurig Chapel and Gartheli Church. He received some tuition from a music teacher who used to go to Abermeurig and Trefilan to teach old notation to two classes, but after a short time, ceased to attend, becoming self-taught after that.

After serving an apprenticeship as a tailor in Blaenpennal, he lived in Pontrhydfendigaid. During this time he began to teach music and conducted choirs. The account states that in 1856, he and his wife moved to live in the Aeron valley and he helped with singing and choirs at Gartheli, Abermeurig and Tynygwndwn. In 1859 they moved to Aberaeron and opened a bookshop. At the same time he was in charge of music at Trinity Church for 50 years. Dan wrote:

> He was conductor of the Lower-Aeron churches' singing festivals from the beginning. He was a valuable bookseller as he raised awareness of the best books being published at the time. He went from fair to fair with his stall, selling books, songs and anthems. He had an unequalled sound box and could switch to any one of the four voices. He benefited greatly from this as he had to teach his choir by ear the four voices separately… The first eisteddfod he attended was in Aberystwyth in 1856 with the choir from Abermeurig and was successful with 'Llawen floeddiwch i Dduw'. From then on until 1864, he conducted the

> Tynygwndwn, Ffaldybrenin, Cellan and Cwrtycadno united choirs in the Lampeter, Llandysul, Llanddewibrefi, Llangybi, Cwmdu and Llannarth eisteddfodau and as I understand, was successful in each one.

Dan goes on to relate the arrival of the tonic sol-fa system with Mr Jones being one of the first in Wales to promote and popularise the system. Tonic sol-fa is a form of musical notation and a system of teaching sight-singing, designed by John Curwen in mid 19th century England. Dan wrote:

> He held sol-fa classes in 60 chapels, 50 churches and many schools throughout Cardiganshire. Upon receiving an invitation from the boys of the Tal-sarn area at the cobbler's workshop, he came to Trefilan School where there were 30 to 40 present ranging in age from 10 to 50, males and females. Aeronian was the school master at the time and he was very supportive of the movement. He composed a poem of eight verses on the excellence/distinction of the sol-fa over the old notation.

He recounts how Mr Jones would often stay overnight after his classes and received accommodation at the Jenkins home at Pentrefelin many times:

> After he had chosen a meal – a basin of bread and milk, with a small lump of butter in it – he and my mother would reminisce about the Tynygwndwn choir at the eisteddfodau in Lampeter and Llandysul, and we, as children, would sit quietly and listen in wonder. He would leave early the following morning to go to his next class. His two feet were his train. On 28th November 1907 he was presented with a testimonial for his long, dedicated and unselfish service to music and literature.

The sol-fa system was important within the west Wales region. Dan wrote in 1946 about other significant people who promoted the movement in their own areas: Thomas Price of Wernfendigaid; Evan Davies, Gelli (headmaster of the Normal College, Swansea); William Thomas, Dryslwyn, Caio (the Minister of Bwlchnewydd); W T Samuel, Carmarthen and David Edwards of Llanddewibrefi.

Children's songbooks

It seems possible that Dan was involved in the production of several songbooks for children.[10] Support for this view is provided at the National Library in Aberystwyth which contains the following: *Caneuon i'r plant bach* and *Cloch yr ysgol a chaneoun eraill i'r plant*. The publications are both shown as authored by Dan Jenkins, though publication dates are after his death. The British Library holds other songbook publications in Welsh by a Dan Jenkins, entitled *Jerwsalem* (published 1957 in Swansea) and *Rhagom, filwyr Iesu* (Onward Christian Soldiers; published in Swansea in 1942). Some of these songbooks contain tonic sol-fa notation.

The Welsh language

We can see his interest and commitment to the Welsh language not only from the actions taken by Dan in his teaching career, but also through the content of his letters, involvement with both local and National Eisteddfodau and his general enthusiasm. In *Cerddi Ysgol Llanycrwys,* he refers to the fire and enthusiasm he felt for the language, and his commitment to do something to enable its use in schools, flowing from the meeting he attended at the Aberdare National Eisteddfod in 1885. As described in chapter three, this was a pivitol moment for the language and led to four headteachers (probably including Dan), starting to write teaching textbooks in anticipation of a change in the law in order to allow Welsh to be taught in elementary schools.

His newspaper cuttings in his scrapbooks give an insight into his interest in the subject. They include one of 19th September 1945 from the *Western Mail* entitled: 'We must make Welsh Language Fashionable' by Janet Evans. Her points include the following:

> Nothing can be so effective in preserving a nation as the constant and determined use of its own language. The danger lies in the ability of the Welsh people to speak English. If they were purely monoglot they would encourage the stranger to speak Welsh. Their

> versatility is a menace to the preservation of their native tongue, and moreover it deprives the stranger of the opportunity and incentive to become acquainted with the Welsh language.[11]

Much earlier than this at the turn of the 19th century, the *Cambrian News* regularly carried feature articles about the situation with the language and its position alongside English. A speech by a former HMI, the Rev. Shadrach Pryce in 1899, was recorded in some detail and shows an Establishment view of the time about the language:

> Taking Wales as a whole there were a great many people who clung to the old language of their fathers, though very many of them were equally conversant with English. The number of Welsh services in their churches and nonconformist chapels also showed the hold the Welsh language had upon the people. Welsh in these days was essentially the language not of commerce, but of the hearth and altar. Welsh was the language of religion, of poetry, and of descriptive writing.

Turning to the teaching of Welsh in schools, now that this was legally permitted, he said:

> The teaching of Welsh as an independent subject for its own sake was not in accordance with the general feeling and wishes of the Welsh people. The Welshman was shrewd enough to see that all commercial transactions were carried on in English, that the English daily newspaper had the latest and most trustworthy news and the latest markets, that modern works on all scientific subjects were published in English and that his child as soon as he crossed that narrow Welsh boundary must possess a fair knowledge of English.

As a result of this view amongst most Welsh people, he said that only 29 out of 1,410 schools had chosen to adopt Welsh as a subject – that is, as an independent subject in which reasonable proficiency could be expected. Apart from the reluctance of parents to encourage the teaching of Welsh in school, he cited another reason, "namely the difficulty masters experience in teaching it successfully". However, he emphasised that "Welsh should by no means be ignored by our schools, but that it should be made subservient to the children acquiring a more intelligent knowledge of English." Yet, in conclusion he said:

> ... you cannot galvanise an old language into a new existence, and no man or body can stem the steady advance of English into Wales. Though I yield to no man in love for my native language, though no man admires its force, its descriptive powers, its poetic beauty more than I do, yet from an educational point of view, and looking to the advance and prosperity of my countrymen, I cannot regret the steady progress English is making.[12]

It is perhaps not surprising that Welsh in schools was not very much in use in 1899, given such a view. Its position alongside English had not yet been determined by the teachers who were interested and had the capability to use it within the school system, even though it was, from 1891, permitted to be a taught subject within the elementary schools. For only 29 out of 1,410 schools to have adopted Welsh as a school subject is an indication of how difficult the position was. Yet, as we have seen in the 1890s, Dan Jenkins had introduced, and was using Welsh as a school subject at both Llanfair Clydogau School and later, at Llanycrwys School. He was at the forefront of the Welsh language movement.

The view of some government officials towards the language did not help to promote a positive attitude. An example well-publicised in the newspapers in the Lampeter area, related to a court case held at Lampeter County Court in June 1900. At the court hearing the judge treated Thomas Jones, vice-chairman of Cellan School Board, in a most rude and offensive manner as a result of his need and request to speak Welsh and not English in court. Upon Mr Jones entering the witness box, the *Cambrian News* reported that he: "at the outset, asked for an interpreter". In response the judge said: "A vice-chairman of a school board who cannot speak English! (Laughter.) Very well, if he is such an ignoramus as all that, he shall have an interpreter."[13]

Later the same year, the *Cambrian News* had a leader article entitled: 'Why Welsh cannot be taught in schools'. It pointed out that Welsh can only be satisfactorily taught by Welsh teachers and that many of the best and most patriotic Welsh teachers emigrated to England where pay levels were higher. This, the article stated, left Welsh elementary schools struggling to recruit and frequently having to engage "the less competent English teachers, who drift into lower salaried places in Wales". The newspaper went on to make a proposal:

> ... that a law should be passed, to compel every Welsh teacher, who is capable of teaching his native language, to return to the Principality and to accept whatever rates of remuneration may be tendered to him, and that in future, no Welsh teacher shall be allowed to attempt to improve his condition by leaving the country. If such a law were impossible, then the answer would lie with raising salary levels in order to make the Welsh schools more attractive.[14]

Dan Jenkins' scrapbooks contain a cutting of 1905, from the *South Wales Daily News* which states:

> HM Inspector of Schools for the Cardiganshire district reports that Welsh is not taught in the schools of that county, though practically all the children and their parents speak Welsh. Yet we have been taught to believe that Cardigan is one of the Welshest counties in the Principality with the exception of Merioneth. What a pity Welsh people fail to see the value of their language until they lose it.[15]

This kind of comment and the low level of use of Welsh in the county's schools was a source of concern to Dan, especially as he was doing all he could to use the language in school and show that it could and should be present and utilised, along with English. We see clear evidence of his analysis and view of the problem in his document written in 1916.

In a significant paper which he wrote and presented to a meeting of the Union of Welsh Societies (Dyfed area), he referred to his first attending a meeting of the union in 1885, at the Aberdare Eisteddfod when it was formed, to promote the adoption of Welsh in schools. He wrote:

> I was inspired in the meeting by the fervour of the late Dan Isaac Davies, who died far too young. The flame that was lit in me at that time still burns in my heart. It is a long time since I was a pupil in school myself, but I remember well the first copybook I had, and in it a line of handwriting I had to copy. My teacher was William Davies from Trefilan. This is the line: 'Always keep good company'. I have never forgotten it, even though it was in English. It is sad that there is no encouragement for the use of Welsh in Dyfed, the land of the archdruid Daniel Ddu. It is important to remember that it is in the home that the use of the Welsh language should be instilled; then school is there to support it and introduce the children to the classics in literature, nursery rhymes and poetry. Then college should develop them further.

Outlining his opinion of what should occur, and the role of chapel and church, Dan went on:

> But it is in the pulpit that we expect to hear the language in all its wealth and refinement. It is more important for the gospel to be simple and understood than for the preacher to be dressed in a silk hat and gown. It is simply pride and vanity to use complex language that no one understands, in the house of God. The ministers and teachers are more sinful than all the people of Wales, as they are the ones that speak English to their children on their hearth at home. Some schoolmasters are totally responsible for the anglicising of small villages in Dyfed, and all over Wales.

Explaining his views on how the language should be developed he wrote:

> After learning to speak its native language, the child moves to elementary school. To start with, Welsh should be the first language in the school, enabling the children to understand English better. There would also be the employment of bilingual officials and teachers. This would answer the needs. We should all, without asking permission from anybody, do all we can to keep our language alive, in the house, in school, in college, in our churches and chapels.

He emphasised four key numbered points:

1 It is a help to learn English and other languages.
2 It is necessary to learn to read Welsh books and magazines, and newspapers, and to learn about Wales.
3 It is not a country without a language and a person is not a Welshman if he cannot speak the language.
4 We will keep our language alive for (a) yr Esgob Morgan, Pantycelyn, Mynddog, Ceiriog, Islwyn, Watcyn Wyn and the Eisteddfod; (b) our nursery rhymes and folk songs; (c) its dialect and cultures; (d) its hymns, its beautiful poems with its rhymes, cynghanedd and englynion.

Dan saw a key role for the chapel in the position of the language. He wrote:

> The chapel is the theatre of the Welsh – the pulpit is the place of the imagination. It is here that the Welshman experiences – humour, sadness and danger. The Englishman goes to the theatre for excitement; the Welshman to his chapel, at least in the days of Dr T C Edwards, Mathews Ewenny, Hiraethog, Penry Evans, Ceinewydd a Herber. Isn't this the reason why the English have snatched our teachers in recent years? Maybe it's because the drama has disappeared from the pulpit that you now find it on the stage in our eisteddfodau. The minister should be our example in speaking, writing and the reading of Welsh. Dare I say why he is not? Well, follow his pattern of training – first the County School. After doing all we can at elementary school to set him on the right path, it's heartbreaking to think that the attention it deserves is not given to Welsh in our middle schools, and especially in my dear Ceredigion, where Welsh is ignored in the entrance examination for County Schools, and gets little attention, if any, during the whole course, unless there happens to be a S M Powell, S O James or Sarnicol on the list of teachers. In our colleges, Welsh is not on the agenda. Also, the students are not allowed to choose Welsh in their final course: Special or Honours. I could give an example of one student who was expelled because he chose Welsh for his Honours course, instead of the old traditional Greek.

Looking towards a sad, but nevertheless possible future for the language, at this time, Dan wrote: "If Welsh is to die in our country and the Cardi is the last to speak it, it will live on in the National Library, and it will stand as witness against all the people who destroyed it."[16]

It is important to recognise that the campaign initiated at Aberdare in 1885 was also a reaction to the horror felt throughout Wales at what was regarded as the treason of the 'Blue Books' of 1847, (a government report on education in the country).

St David's Day

As recorded, Dan did much to spread the idea that St David's Day should be recognised and indeed celebrated by people and groups within the country. He wrote that it was his association with Llanddewibrefi and the village's connection with St David which was a major influence in helping to motivate him, through his stays with his relatives at Pant and his later work as a student teacher at the village school there. He recalled his meetings in the cobbler's workshop and how they discussed St David's message, and the two men from Llanddewi who became bishops.[17]

Hence, combining the concept of 'the national day' with his singing skills and personal organisational drive, he began to work out how to hold a St David's Day concert in a school. As we have seen, this was a tremendous success at Llanfair Clydogau and Llanycrwys and he received much praise, with other schools gradually following the practice of beginning to recognise and celebrate the day.

The *Welshman* of March 1913 applauded this approach. The paper commented: "There are many excellent patriots all over Wales, collecting together with their amazing skills to keep the children speaking their mother tongue and to preserve the culture."[18]

The article went on to praise the Llanycrwys School St

David's Day programme and concluded as follows: "Our grateful thanks go out to the teacher, Dan Jenkins and his helpers, for planting the seeds of Welsh culture deep in the soil of Wales. The Llanycrwys way is the right way."

Celebrating the life of Benjamin Morris (Ben Morus)

We see a perfect example of Dan's high regard for individuals who had contributed to the Welsh-language movement, in the detail of his relationship with Ben Morris. Ben was born in Llanfair Clydogau in 1880 and was taught by Dan at Llanfair Board School. After finishing his schooling, he served his time as a compositor in Lampeter and later worked in Aberdare as a printer, before joining the National Library of Wales as a librarian. He became a very well-known Welsh-language writer who contributed many times to *Cymru* and other publications, as well as writing *Enwogion Aberdâr* (The worthies of Aberdare). Upon his early death from consumption at the age of 32 in 1913, Dan became the secretary of a committee of fellow Welsh literary figures, aiming to erect a memorial to him at his grave in the cemetery at Llanddewibrefi. Literature was sent from Llanycrwys inviting people who wanted to "promote the movement" to make a donation. Unfortunately, the campaign failed. In frustration Dan wrote a confidential note stating: "His mother adamantly refused to allow us to donate a 'Llanddewi Stone' according to his wishes, and our taste, as a committee. I had collected about £10 – sufficient for the business – and had started to organise the holding of an unveiling ceremony at Llanddewibrefi. It's strange how ignorance kills beneficial movements."[19]

Ben Morris had written special pieces for Dan and the St David's Day programme at Llanycrwys. At his funeral, a short address was given at the graveside by Dan, in which the *Aberdare Leader* reported him saying: "that Ben was one of the six best young Welsh writers in the Principality."[20]

Chapter Eight

Countryside activities

Dan Jenkins with his bees
(source: Ifor Lloyd)

DAN JENKINS WAS involved in an almost unparalleled range of countryside activities during his long and eventful life. That he managed to do this, in spite of spending over 40 years of his adult life working as a headteacher, is both unusual and remarkable.

His formative years were essentially shaped by his early life and experiences within the environs of the picturesque Aeron valley. These experiences were added to by his visits to, and life as a headteacher in, both the Teifi valley of Cardiganshire and the Twrch and Cothi valley areas of Carmarthenshire. He enjoyed the countryside and marvelled at its changes of colour and texture; he appreciated the weather and the range of produce which could be obtained from the land. From his birth in 1856, until his death 90 years later in 1946, central to his life was his family home of Pentrefelin. It was here that he, with his wife Elizabeth, farmed, experimented with good agrarian practices and made his own unique and highly personal contribution to an understanding and development of the Welsh countryside and its customs and practices. He participated in all Welsh country pursuits: horse riding, hunting, shooting, fishing, as well as rearing farm animals for sale, growing apples and keeping bees. He was also an avid participant in farm shows, with the competition and personal socialising which accompanied them.

Lampeter Agricultural Society

The Lampeter Agricultural Society was an important body within Cardiganshire in the late 19th century, staging an annual show each summer in Lampeter. Dan Jenkins was an active member, amongst an extensive group of farmers drawn from a large geographical area. In 1896 the *Cambrian News* wrote:

> The general success of the society is to a large extent secured by the interest both landlords and tenants take in the business and to the satisfactory arrangements made. As in Merioneth, the landlords get the honour without the money, and the prizes of the society are open to tenant farmers and freeholders possessing incomes not exceeding £250 per annum on subscribing 2s. 6d. to £1 according to the value of their holdings; freeholders holding land under £50 rateable values have to subscribe 7s. 6d. and of £50 and upwards £1, while cottagers, labourers and servants are allowed to compete without subscribing anything.[1]

In 1896, the society committee included Dan Jenkins (described as, of Pentrefelin), along with about 40 others, including a number of important local landowners such as the Earl of Lisburne, Mr J C Harford of Falcondale, M Vaughan Davies MP, William Jones of Glandenys, W Inglis-Jones of Derry Ormond, Col. Evans of Highmead and Major Lewis of Tyglyn Aeron. The newspaper report of the 1896 annual general meeting[2] shows Dan as a major speaker and activist. He moved a motion that stewards, as a rule, be selected from the members, and another that the date of a future show should be 30th September 1897.

He also moved a motion thanking various members of the committee: Mrs Vaughan Davies, Tanybwlch; Mr J C Harford; J M Davies of Froodvale; W Cotterell, Derry Ormond; John Davies, Maespwll and William Jones, Penllwyn for the special prizes they had given.

At the 1898 annual show on a Wednesday in September, Dan was reported in the *Cambrian News* as being the steward for coloured cattle. At the annual show luncheon, with the Earl of Lisburne presiding, the report states that Dan was in attendance, along with his uncle, Jenkin Jenkins of Blaenplwyf.[3]

The newspaper accounts quoted above, show Dan Jenkins mixing easily with not only the major farmers of the Lampeter area, but also with some of the richest and most powerful Establishment figures. These included his protagonist over tenants' rights from the 1894 Welsh Land Commission tussle, William Jones of Glandenys and J C Harford who, as a magistrate, was involved in hearing the case over his eviction in 1897. We know that Dan was still a member of the society in 1936 when, in a newspaper article to celebrate his and Elizabeth's 50 years of marriage, he was described as its oldest

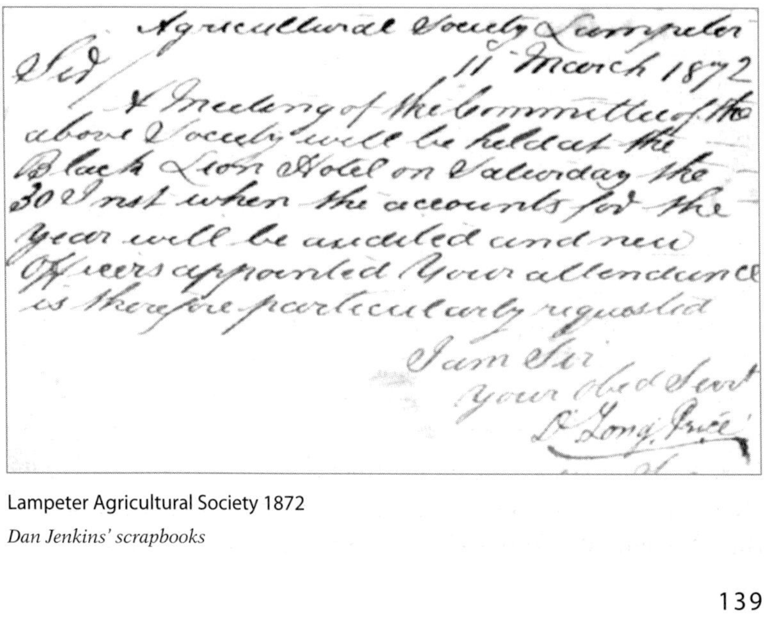
Agricultural Society Lampeter
Sir
11 March 1872
A Meeting of the Committee of the above Society will be held at the Black Lion Hotel on Saturday the 30 Inst when the accounts for the year will be audited and new Officers appointed Your attendance is therefore particularly requested
I am Sir
your obed Servt
D Long Price

Lampeter Agricultural Society 1872

Dan Jenkins' scrapbooks

Dan Jenkins leading the cob with Dafydd Gwarallt, 1908
(source: Ifor Lloyd)

member. Ten years later, another article written to record the couple's 60 years of marriage in 1946, referred to him as the 'father' of the Lampeter Agricultural Show society. This period of membership is but one of many examples of his longevity in relation to organisations and campaign groups. His interest in collecting historic documents and placing them in his scrapbooks is once more seen, in this case, with his possession of an 1876 letter inviting members to a meeting of the society.

'King of the Beekeepers' (*Welsh Gazette*, 1945)

There was a family interest and very active participation in the keeping of bees from Dan's earliest years. The *Welsh Gazette* of 1945 referred to him seeing his first beehive when he was with his grandmother, Eleanor Jenkins at Blaenplwyf in 1866, when he was 10 years old. At that time they made a honey sandwich at Blaenplwyf. This early experience clearly had a formative impact on the young man since, later in life, when he had his own children, he made use of the delicacy of a honey sandwich with them. His daughter Elin "often spoke of this special sandwich which they ate as children. She also took honey in her tea, every morning of her life."[4]

Dan Jenkins with bees
(source: Ifor Lloyd)

In 1936, Dan was the chairman of the Lampeter Beekeepers' Association. He was very active in keeping bees right up to the end of his life. During the Second World War, under the 'Food Rationing Orders' of the Ministry of Food, it was necessary to complete an official form to make an 'application for a permit to obtain supplies of sugar for the purpose of feeding bees'. His scrapbooks show that on 7th September 1945, he received permission from the ministry to purchase from Messrs E Hughes & Son of Dihewyd, Lampeter, 90 lbs of sugar for feeding to his nine colonies of bees at Pentrefelin.

A list of members of the Lampeter Beekeepers' Association for 1945 shows Dan as one of some 47 who had paid their subscription for that year. Among the other members was his son Ivor of Brynaeron, Felinfach. That same year, the association held a special meeting at Felinfach Memorial Hall in order to honour him. The *Cambrian News* reported him: "as the 'Grand Old Man', not just of beekeeping in the vale of Aeron, but of the two allied and inter-dependent crafts of fruit culture and agriculture."

There was a large gathering of members and friends present. Dan was referred to by speakers as the 'King of the Beekeepers' and presented with a medal consisting of a queen

Beekeeping lecture
Dan Jenkins' scrapbooks

Christmas Cheer for Soldiers

Splendid Patriotism of Welsh People

Honey for the Wounded at Cardiff

A splendid instance of the all round patriotism of the Welsh people has just come to light in Cardiff, where a parcel of about 20lb of honey, collected from the Mid-Aeron apiaries, has been received at the Albany Road Section of the 3rd Western Military Hospital as Christmas cheer for the wounded soldiers in that section. The parcel was forwarded by Mr. Dan Jenkins, Headmaster of the Llanycrwys Council School (one of the best known educationalists in Cardiganshire) to Miss Jenkins, Headmistress of the Albany Road Infants' Department, who has delivered this most acceptable gift from Cardiland to the soldiers who now desire to thank their Cardiganshire friends for their thoughtful action.[5]

bee as a pendant. The pendant was made by an anonymous donor who was an expert craftsman and medallist. Praise was also given to the prominent part played by Elizabeth Jenkins in the beekeeping activities of her husband.

The careful blending of Welsh traditions and culture within this social evening can be seen from the fact that "Mr Gwilym Jones, county horticulturalist and secretary of the association, read englynion to him as a beekeeper, which had been composed by a local bard". In addition, "Mr Soarian Evans, a veteran beekeeper, read an ode" to Dan and also "some humorous verses". There was also a short programme of music. The *Cambrian News* reported that Dan: "entertained those present for about half an hour with amusing reminiscences about his career as a beekeeper. The clues to success in beekeeping were patience, calmness, perseverance and assiduity,"[6] he said. The *Welsh Gazette* also reported upon the same presentational event and recounted Dan taking bees to the heather on Trichrug (the three hills above Tal-sarn), by horse and cart when a hive opened accidentally, the bees were released and everyone scattered, with the mare up to her waist in the lake and those helping in the transport nursing stings. "Many a poem was written about this event, including one by Granellian,"[7] the *Welsh Gazette* stated. Dan Jenkins often recounted this story to his family and it is often recalled today.

He also told the 1945 audience of an occasion back in 1917, when he travelled to Arthog in north Wales in order to give a lecture on beekeeping. On route he saw a poster stating: 'Dan Jenkins of the University College of Wales, Aberystwyth, will lecture, etc.' However, he pointed out that he was not from the university but instead, operating on its behalf. He was, in fact, on approved leave of absence from his teaching post at Llanycrwys for one week to enable him to work for the university on giving instruction on the rearing of bees. He was clearly recognised by the university for his expertise in this field and this was used to help others.

Ivor Jenkins (Dan's son), continued with the beekeeping

tradition. Between the two of them, beekeeping was an important activity within the family for over a hundred years.

Mid Aeron Bull Club

Dan Jenkins was always at the forefront of farming developments, especially those focused on improving animal husbandry. Hence in 1898, he was a founder member of the Mid Aeron Bull Club. A newspaper report described the actions to be taken as follows:

> It is satisfactory to find that the proposed bull club is progressing well. On Tuesday Mr Jenkin Jenkins and Mr Dan Jenkins, Pentrefelin, proceeded to north Wales where they met Mr Evan Jonathan of Tynygwndwn and inspected a number of first-class Welsh pedigree bulls. They will report the results of their visit to a meeting at Trefilan next Saturday evening. Other members are proceeding to a Birmingham sale to buy shorthorn bulls.[8]

Welsh Pony and Cob Society

Dan was one of the very early members of the Welsh Pony and Cob Society at the beginning of the 20th century. So too, was his uncle, Jenkin. The studbook records of the society show Dan's name against a number of registered horses. For instance studbook 1 shows a horse called Lock, which foaled in 1877 and another called Polly which foaled in 1895. In studbook 3 his horse Quito Fach foaled in 1901 and another Aeron (which became Dan's prefix), also foaled in 1901. Betty was a chestnut which foaled in 1898, whilst a further example, Aeron Menna is listed in studbook 8.

Dan's scrapbooks show correspondence with the society. His 1903–4 subscription was five shillings. He has also retained a copy of the society's notepaper, with a letter of 8th June 1906 which shows the patron as HRH the Prince of Wales.

Dan's daughter Elin, married Roscoe Lloyd and he too was an enthusiastic participant in the owning and breeding of Welsh cobs. Today Dan's grandson, Ifor Lloyd of Derwen

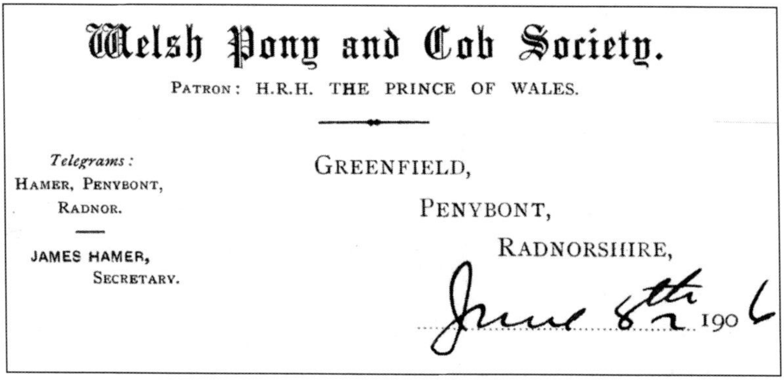

Welsh Pony and Cob Society.

PATRON: H.R.H. THE PRINCE OF WALES.

Telegrams:
HAMER, PENYBONT,
RADNOR.

JAMES HAMER,
SECRETARY.

GREENFIELD,
PENYBONT,
RADNORSHIRE,

June 8th 1906

Welsh Pony and Cob Society notepaper
Dan Jenkins' scrapbooks

Stud, Pennant in Ceredigion, carries on this tradition in that he runs, with his wife Myfanwy, this very well known and highly successful stud. Ifor Lloyd has written: "It has always been our aim to produce animals of good temperament with the ability to do a job of work, in line with the traditions of our forefathers. During the years we have competed at all the major shows in the United Kingdom, and in 1986, we won the championship for Welsh cobs at the International at Achen, with a mare called Derwen Tawela." Eight different Welsh cobs from the Derwen Stud have won the Prince of Wales' Cup at the Royal Welsh Show, an amazing thirteen times. In addition to his excellence as a breeder of cobs, Ifor is a well-known singer, having won the Blue Riband at the National Eisteddfod, as well as Singer of the Year at the Llangollen International Eisteddfod.

Ifor Lloyd started and named Lloyd Motors 45 years ago in Aberaeron and was later joined by his brother Evan Lloyd, who still runs the business today. Ifor negotiated the Volvo franchise in 1971, following a visit to the Motor Show as a correspondent for Welsh television. The brand is still sold from the garage in the centre of the town.

Dan's interest in horses, especially those bred and raised in the Cardiganshire area must have started at an early age. As a young man he collected publicity leaflets (retained in

Ifor Lloyd

his scrapbooks), which were prepared by horse breeders to try to attract custom for their stallions. One he had, was for 1869 relating to "that fine bred sire Tom Steel", owned by Mr D Williams of Llwyncolfa, near Tregaron, with a publicity statement that "colts got by Tom Steel have very often been sold at from 70 to 200 guineas each". Others of which he held promotional literature were: Trotting Comet in 1860, "a splendid bay horse"; Wippo-Wil (owned by Dan's uncle, Jenkin Jenkins of Blaenplwyf), in 1879 at £1 for each mare; and Major General in 1871 (also owned by Jenkin Jenkins).

Hunting

An important part of country life was the operation of the various hunts across the county. Dan was a comfortable and important member of many Welsh rural organisations and the hunt was no exception. In this photograph he is shown wearing the trilby and riding his mare Bess of Pentrefelin.

The importance of the activity is highlighted in Dan's scrapbook records. One of his books contains an undated story from the *Carmarthen Journal* entitled: 'A day with the Neuaddfawr Hounds'. It names the riders and looks like a list of many of the important members of local society since it contains: "Colonel, Mrs and Cadet Lewis, Col. and Mrs Douglas,

Hounds of the Neuaddfawr Hunt, Llanwnnen
(source: Ifor Lloyd)

Mr and Mrs Lewis of Tyglyn, Mr, Mrs and Misses Price of Ty-mawr, Major Harford and Commodore Raikes of Falcondale, Mr Lloyd of Trefilan Court… Davies of Talfan and Jenkins of Pentrefelin." The report states: "As we passed through Tal-sarn, the villagers were all agog to hail and welcome the Master and her beautiful pack." Collecting these newspaper cuttings about the hunt is indicative of his interest in retaining evidence of not only his own involvement, but also of its importance within local society.

Shooting

Shooting was another important country pursuit which was very popular. Dan also had some involvement. His correspondence shows a letter he received in 1904 from his uncle, Jenkin Jenkins of Blaenplwyf, which stated: "Dear nephew, Please come here next Saturday. Rabbits sporting if weather permitting. Yours truly, Jenkin Jenkins."[9]

Fishing

Information from Dan's scrapbooks suggests that he had a keen interest in fishing. He retained a copy there of his licence to fish for trout and charr within the Towy Fishery District of Carmarthenshire, dated 18th March 1912, which shows his address as Bronydderwen, Llanycrwys. Another, of 22nd March 1920, also shows his address as Bronydderwen. He also retained two other receipts for a fishing licence. They were for September 1935 covering the Aeron Fishery District and April 1936 covering the Teifi and Aeron Fishery Board.

Royal Welsh Agricultural Society

Dan Jenkins was a member of the society for a number of years. It was established in 1904 with the aim of improving the breeding of stock and encouragement of agriculture across Wales. Its first show was held in Aberystwyth in 1904, under the presidency of the Earl of Powys. During the first part of the century, the annual show was held in a variety of 37 different locations. Since 1963 it has been located at its present

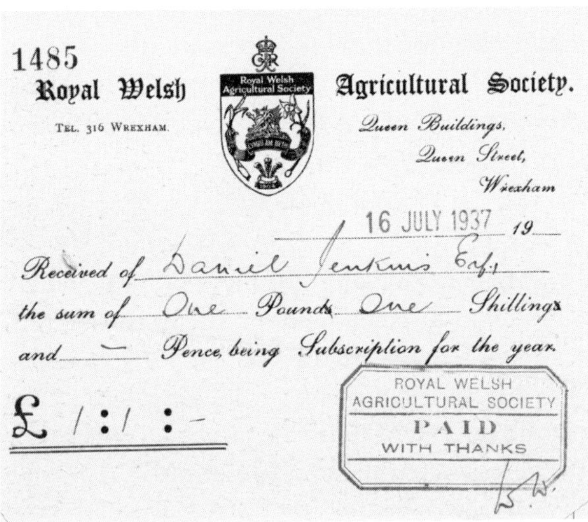
1485
Royal Welsh Agricultural Society.
Tel. 316 Wrexham.
Queen Buildings,
Queen Street,
Wrexham
16 JULY 1937 19
Received of Daniel Jenkins Esq.
the sum of One Pounds One Shillings
and — Pence, being Subscription for the year.
£ 1 : 1 : -
ROYAL WELSH AGRICULTURAL SOCIETY
PAID
WITH THANKS

Royal Welsh Agricultural Society receipt
Dan Jenkins' scrapbooks

permanent location at Llanelwedd, Builth Wells. The show, under the auspices of the society, has become a major event in the summer calendar of Wales.

Tal-sarn Show and Fair

In August 1897, in the middle of his dispute with Llanfair School Board, Dan Jenkins managed to serve as secretary of the Tal-sarn fair. A record from his scrapbooks shows him writing to inform people that the Tal-sarn Horse Fair would in future, be held in connection with other popular and well-known fairs. He wrote: "The fairs will be convenient and advantageous to farmers and merchants of horses, and I earnestly invite them to give support."[10]

The long-term positive involvement of Dan Jenkins in local Tal-sarn affairs and events can be seen from the tone of a letter he received, dated 25th August 1945, from the secretary of the show and races committee, asking for his "patronage and support" and referring to their awareness of "your intense interest in all worthy causes". The letter went on to state that "the committee will feel highly honoured by your attendance and support".[11]

Tal-sarn show, 1920

(source: Ifor Lloyd)

Farming at Pentrefelin

In January 1944, at the height of the Second World War, all Cardiganshire farms were given an order on how much farmland they should cultivate under the Cultivation of Lands Order, 1939. A copy of the order was retained by Dan in his scrapbooks and shows him being instructed to grow not less than 3 acres of potatoes, 7 acres of bread grain, an acre of kale or cabbage, and 3.3 acres of rape and the rest grassland or stubble.

All his scrapbooks show the strong flavour of life at Pentrefelin. For instance, an invoice of August 1925, from a man called Daniel Jenkins of Abermeurig, smith and general ironmonger, for £3 11s. 1d. details nails, horse shoes and repairs to the harrow, plough and pig trough.

He retained in his scrapbooks, hundreds of letters, invoices, and newspaper cuttings which show life in the Aeron valley from his earliest days, through to the last year of his life. They are a superb record; they show his considerable range of interests and direct involvement in so many of the rural activities of the time. They demonstrate him participating, sometimes leading, especially in his earlier life, and supporting. They also show his interest in collecting mementos of the past and trying to see that these activities succeeded and flourished.

CHAPTER NINE

Published writings

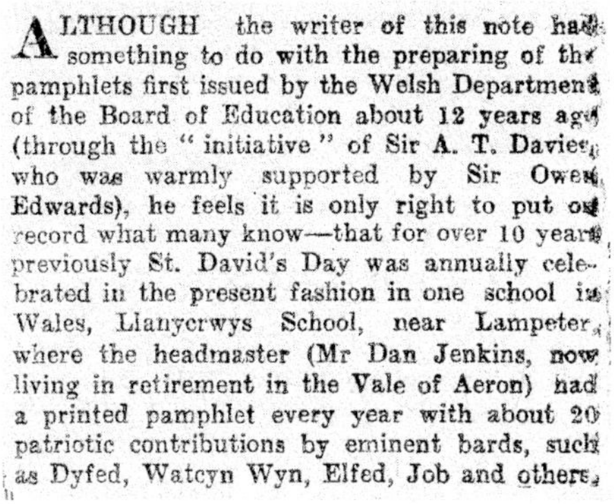

ALTHOUGH the writer of this note had something to do with the preparing of the pamphlets first issued by the Welsh Department of the Board of Education about 12 years ago (through the "initiative" of Sir A. T. Davies, who was warmly supported by Sir Owen Edwards), he feels it is only right to put on record what many know—that for over 10 years previously St. David's Day was annually celebrated in the present fashion in one school in Wales, Llanycrwys School, near Lampeter, where the headmaster (Mr Dan Jenkins, now living in retirement in the Vale of Aeron) had a printed pamphlet every year with about 20 patriotic contributions by eminent bards, such as Dyfed, Watcyn Wyn, Elfed, Job and others.

Dan Jenkins' scrapbooks

DAN JENKINS HAD a love of language and its application to describe and explain people, places, circumstances and history. Sarnicol (T J Thomas), writing in the *Cambrian News* in the 1930s, described Dan as "a collector and appreciator of literature". He collected a large number of newspaper cuttings from the 1860s, until his death in 1946, on a wide range of subjects, such as Jenkins family members, people he knew from school or Bangor College, eisteddfodau, schools, societies, the Welsh language, the First and Second World War and farming. As well as collecting, he wrote and published a number of newspaper articles.

Discovering the full extent of this is not straightforward, since various pieces which he wrote and published appeared unnamed in the newspapers at the time.

The Journalist

We believe that he did publish a number of unattributable newspaper articles, from several documents which he retained in his scrapbooks, along with newspaper cuttings kept by him and other family members. The earliest clue is a letter of December 1897, written just after he had ceased work at Llanfair Clydogau School. This letter was written to Ralph Bland, the Carmarthen-based reporter for the *South Wales Daily News, South Wales Weekly News* and *South Wales Echo,* offering to supply news for publication. In exchange for "supplying me often with Welsh gossip you will be supplied with a 'News' daily if you will give me an assurance you will [also] send news regularly," replied the reporter. In January 1898 the Cardiff office of the same newspapers wrote to Dan at Pentrefelin, emphasising the arrangement of a free copy of the *Daily News* regularly by post, in exchange for "all news of general interest arising in your district" and items for the "Welsh gossip" section. He was also sent some envelopes for posting to them, and telegraph passes. After Dan started at Llanycrwys School, he wrote on 14th June 1898 to the Cardiff office to confirm a continuation of the arrangement and received the following day a letter confirming that the intention was still that he received a free paper in exchange for his "sending us all matters of interest coming under your observation".[1]

The front piece of an envelope (page 153) shows an item sent by Dan from Pumpsaint post office, a few miles from Llanycrwys School, to the *South Wales Daily News*. The envelope contained "news intelligence".

He didn't just produce news for the local Welsh media, but also the national UK press which reported on educational matters. In June 1898 he wrote to the editor of the NUT's *Schoolmaster,* a weekly paper with quite a large readership, which was circulated to schools throughout England and Wales. He offered to send in "comments" for publication.[2] As far as can be ascertained, this offer was taken up, since Dan's scrapbooks contain a large number of cuttings taken from the *Schoolmaster,* but all, in common with the general policy of the newspaper for correspondents, are unnamed. The articles, upon which these *Schoolmaster* cuttings focus, are all small biographical pieces about the life and background of specifically named headteachers of rural country schools.

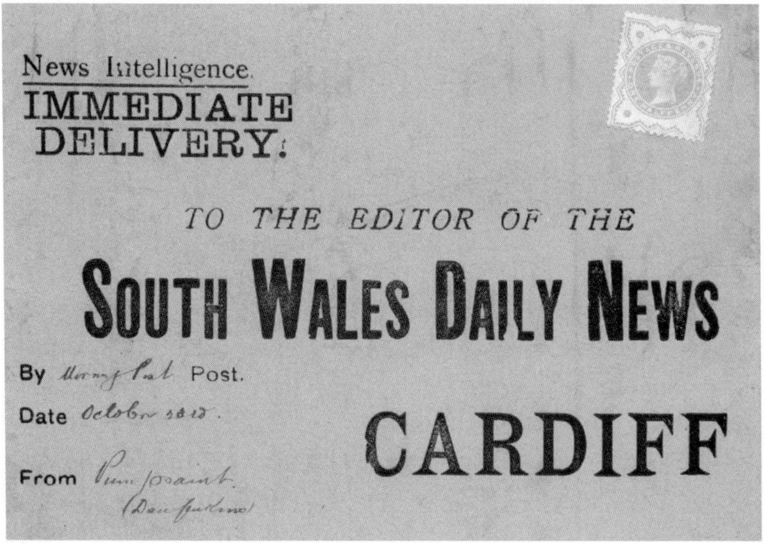

News envelope
Dan Jenkins' scrapbooks

Credence is added to the belief that Dan did produce some of these biographical pieces, in the fact that his own notes, in his scrapbooks, show in many places, long handwritten jottings about people and places; almost as if he was both recording and gathering information in anticipation of an eventual publication. His scrapbooks show him always recording facts, ideas and historical pieces about some one or some place.

Under his own name, there was a long article in the *Cambrian News* in 1905, about his friend William Davies of Myrtle Hill, Llanwnnen and formerly of Caeronnen, Cellan. He described him as a member of the 'inner circle', known as 'Ashfield'. At a guess, this is a reference to some sort of literary grouping. Dan said "he was an opponent of hypocrisy and pomp", who he had known as a member of the county council representing Llanwnnen, for three years.[3]

In addition, his scrapbooks and newspaper cuttings show literally hundreds of stories which he had saved, usually dated by hand, but which contain no authorship identification.

His efforts at historical research, along with his determination to try to publish interesting features of the past, went on throughout his life. Well into his ninetieth year, Dan's correspondence records in his scrapbooks show his receipt of a letter from the editor of the *Welsh Gazette,*[4] thanking him for the article which he had recently submitted for publication.

Articles and books

As already recorded, Dan Jenkins wrote, produced or contributed to, a number of documents and books. In summary the list includes: 'Cynnydd a gwelliant Llanbedr Pont Steffan yn ystod y 15 mlynedd diwethaf (1863–1878)' in Welsh; 'Dyffryn Aeron' (vale of Aeron), 7 pages in Welsh in *Cardiganshire Antiquarian Society* Vol. XI 1936; *Cerddi Cerngoch,* mainly in Welsh, published in 1904; *Cerddi Ysgol Llanycrwys,* mainly in Welsh, published in 1934; a chapter in *Capel Mair Cyfrol y Jiwbili,* in Welsh, in 1926.

Radio broadcast

On the 6th December 1937, Dan and two other people broadcast live on BBC radio in a programme entitled 'Awen Aeron' (poetic gifts of the Aeron valley). It was a programme about writers who were poets and concentrated on his favourite geographical area. The programme, in the relatively early days of the wireless, was transmitted from the Corporation's Aberystwyth studio and aired between 8.30 p.m. and 9.00 p.m., with a rehearsal taking place in the hour and a half prior to broadcast. In the contract offered to Dan, which he retained in his scrapbooks, it refers to his fee being £3 3s.

Following the radio broadcast, he received a number of letters. One from D Davies of Lampeter, commented that the broadcast came through perfectly clear. He wrote: "... the whole was very realistic and I could well imagine myself on the Pentrefelin hearth in front of a blazing log fire, and I could almost hear you telling Dai Williams not to burn his fingers when he was dealing with the kettle."[5]

A niece, Gwladys (Davies) in Cardiff, also wrote to congratulate him. She said that her family gathered around the wireless and hoped it would work. She said: "We loved the discussion and oh, uncle, you were so natural."[6]

Recording of poems and sayings

Dan's scrapbooks contain hundreds of entries placed there over many years. They show correspondence with many people, official bodies, autographs and unusual features of life, not only as it was in the recent past, but also as it was at that time. There are dozens and dozens of pages of beautifully handwritten poems, sayings, quotations or memorable pieces of prose which he had come across. The written pieces are in both Welsh and English. In order to give a flavour of his interest in this field of work, several of those which he recorded in English are shown below. They show his curiosity about words and the expression of language.

There's so much bad in the best of us,
And so much good in the worst of us;
That it ill behoves the best of us
To find fault with the rest of us.

(Recited by Dan Jenkins' cousin, Anna Jenkins of Bangor, Wisconsin, USA, during a visit in 1926.)

God's minute

I have only just a minute,
Only sixty seconds in it;
Forced upon me, can't refuse it,
Didn't seek it, didn't choose it;
But it's up to me to use it,
I must suffer if I lose it,
Give account if I abuse it;
Just a tiny little minute –
But eternity is in it.

(Quotation sent to Dan Jenkins from his aunt, M J Jenkins of Rockland, Wisconsin, USA in 1927.)

Maggie

O Maggie, I am eager – yet again,
My sweet girl to linger,
And to tame, if naught deter,
Your heaving heart for ever.

The Harp

Wake sweet harp, why warp in woe? Why linger
And languish in sorrow?
Let no rough and bluff wind blow
Thy wailings on the willow.

The War 1914 – Lord Robert's message

From the pocket Gospel of St John, I ask you to put your trust in God. He will watch over you and strengthen you. You will find in this little book guidance when you are in health, comfort when you are in sickness and strength when you are in adversity.

Hours of sleep

Nature requires five
Custom gives seven
Laziness takes nine
Wickedness eleven.

New Year Resolution

Speak a shade more kindly
Than the year before;
Pray a little oftener,
Love a little more.

Recording the past: researching history

One example of Dan's fascination with Cardiganshire and Welsh history is quoted here. In 1935, he wrote to W R Hall of Leytonstone, London, asking for recollections of 'Cardiganshire traditions'. As a result, he received a long, handwritten letter detailing a number of examples from W R Hall's knowledge and recollections of life as it was. One paragraph on Welsh cobs is reproduced below:

> Before nonconformist ministers were college trained and became attached to certain chapels, many godly men were itinerant preachers on Sundays, and engaged in business or farming during the week. One excellent preacher in the Tregaron district was a breeder of famous Welsh cobs and in the northern part of the county an itinerant farmer-preacher who bred fine thoroughbred horses which fetched a high figure.
>
> When he went on his preaching visits, though it meant a journey of 40 miles, he got up early on Sunday morning and rode one of his fine horses to his various chapels. The tradition says that when he went to the horse loving town of Tregaron, he had a larger congregation in the stable looking at his horse than he had in the chapel listening to his sermon![7]

Dan was a keen observer of people and places. He had a fascination with history, political events, the use of language and the press. He liked to write in order to record both the past and present. He collected interesting and sometimes unusual facts. As recorded, this extended throughout his life, in that he was writing for a competition in Lampeter whilst in his teens and was still crafting pieces of prose for publication in his ninetieth year.

Chapter Ten

The Pentrefelin years (1856–1946)

Elin Jenkins (Lloyd) with Dan and Elizabeth
(source: Ifor Lloyd)

THE YEARS INVOLVING Dan Jenkins at Pentrefelin run from his birth at the farm on the day of Tal-sarn fair in November 1856, until his death in 1946. This enormous period of over 90 years encompassed huge social and economic changes in Wales, with none more so than those in Cardiganshire, plus the Boer War and both the First and Second World Wars. We have already examined a number of segments and spheres of his life, with some, such as his involvement in Welsh countryside matters, being very much focused upon Pentrefelin. This chapter looks at the farm as a central point in both his personal and family life, a place where he was very pleased to be, to work on agricultural pursuits, to collect and assimilate literary papers, to write and from which to campaign on matters which concerned him. We can divide his life into the following segments:

- 1856–77: living at Pentrefelin and receiving his education at various schools and Bangor College.
- 1877–97: headteacher at Cilcennin School and then Llanfair Clydogau School; took over the farm tenancy in 1882, after his marriage in 1886; Elizabeth Jenkins ran Pentrefelin during the week.
- November 1897 – April 1898: living at Pentrefelin.
- April 1898 – July 1920: headteacher at Llanycrwys School; Elizabeth Jenkins ran Pentrefelin during the week.
- August 1920 – November 1946, living at Pentrefelin.

Taking possession of Pentrefelin

Chapter three describes how Dan came to take possession of Pentrefelin in 1882 as a tenant farmer. It had been first taken by a family member in 1837, when his father Griffith acquired it on the basis of an annual rental. Written notes in Dan's scrapbooks show that the Blaenplwyf estate was sold off in 1893 and that of the 28 premises owned, Pentrefelin went for the highest price of £910; his notes imply there was a further payment in the period 1915–17.

Inscription in the wall of Pentrefelin (2010)

Twin issues of the Crown Estate and Tithes

Dan's scrapbooks allow us to see that he was clearly aware of the impact on the rural community, of annual payments to the monarchy for property which formed part of the Crown

Estate. Petrefelin was part of the Crown Estate of Mabwnion. A document collected and retained in the scrapbooks shows that on 8th December 1886, the collector acting for OHMS (On Her Majesty's Service) signified: "received this day the sum of 1s. 2d. chief rent for Pentrefelin, due last Michaelmas".

Another historic document which he kept was a letter dated January 1885, describing the tithe payments for the farm. It stated: "One year's payment was £8 12s. 1/2d. The tithes are due to the vicar and Christ College, Brecon."

Another old memento is dated 13th Oct 1939, demonstrating the continuing presence of the Crown. It is a receipt for "rental number 226 re: Land Revenues in the Principality of Wales and County of Monmouth for 7s. 6d., being one year's rent due to the Crown for sporting over land in the parish of Mabwnion". Hence, we know that he was fully aware of the difficult and contentious issue of tithes and of the anger these payments caused in Cardiganshire. His scrapbooks confirm this, in that they contain a newspaper article from the *Cambrian News* of June 1913, under the authorship of 'J' (possibly Dan Jenkins), recounting the death of Mr W J Lloyd (cousin of Dan), and the eldest son of Mr Daniel Lloyd of Pant, Llanddewibrefi. It states:

> During the 1880s he resided with his widowed mother at Trefynor. It was during those years that the anti-tithe movement flourished in Wales. Mr Lloyd took a prominent part in that movement and became one of its most prominent leaders in Cardiganshire. The tithe sales and riots at Trefynor in the presence of 50 constables must be reckoned amongst the most striking incidents of that great campaign. He was well read, especially in contemporary politics, social movements and agricultural science.[1]

Election to Cardiganshire County Council

During the period between his positions as headteacher at Llanfair Clydogau and at Llanycrwys, Dan stood for election to the Cardiganshire County Council for the Nantcwnlle ward, in which Pentrefelin was located in March 1898. It was a contested election between two men whom the *Cambrian News* described as farmers. Dan received 122 votes against the 109 cast for his rival, John Jones of Gwastod farm. There was no specified party political label attached to candidates across the county at this time, though people were known to be radicals or unionists and Dan was the former.

The minutes of the county council and accounts of debates recorded in the *Cambrian News,* allow us to trace his six years as a councillor. He attended his first meeting in March 1898. His uncle, Jenkin Jenkins of Blaenplwyf, was already a well-established councillor. Dan served on the technical instruction committee, the finance and general purposes committee and the roads, bridges and public buildings committee (north). A number of the important landowners, farmers and employers within the county were councillors, including Mr J C Harford of Falcondale, Lampeter. As we have seen, several of the members were already known to him since he shared membership of the Lampeter Agricultural Show committee with them. He also knew others from his attendance at the hunt of the Neuaddfawr Hounds. For a new councillor, he progressed rapidly up the political ladder. By 1900, he was operating as the chairman of the important finance and general purposes committee and in May of that year, moved, at the full council meeting, acceptance of the budget for the year, and replied to points made in debate. Some of his replies were witty and displayed an easy spontaneous use of interesting responses which was reported as producing "loud laughter" from the assembled councillors.[2] The minutes show him as a very active and energetic participant, moving and seconding resolutions. In the technical instruction committee, which in 1904 became the education committee, debates surrounded the award of scholarships, promotion of the dairy industry, the teaching of cookery at the new intermediate schools at Tregaron, Aberystwyth and Aberaeron, plus rural crafts and industries in general.

In 1904, after six years, he ceased to be a member when he chose not to stand for election. During the three years prior to his departure, the county council had an overwhelming majority of radical members as the newspapers called them. Right through to the end, he played an important role in debates and his amusing, disarming manner was well thought of. At the council meeting in February 1904, the clerk read out a Board of Agriculture circular about the 'Legs of a Horse'. He said: "the board were anxious that farmers in cases where horses showed a tendency to swell in their legs should give notice at once. Mr Daniel Jenkins: 'Do they promise to send a vet down!' (Laughter.)"

It must have been exceedingly hard for him to find the time and to organise his travel in order to undertake his county council activities. Daytime meetings would have meant that he needed the agreement of his employer (Llanycrwys School Board), for leave of absence. This work within the county council would have added to the complexity of his personal, political, professional and family life, at a time before the motor car, good roads and the telephone.

Cardiganshire Liberal Party

We know that Dan was politically described as a radical during his days at Llanfair Clydogau, and that it was leading members of the Liberal party who came to support him in 1897. At this time, the party was less formally constituted in terms of its membership than today, and its structure less well defined. Hence, both during his membership of the Cardiganshire County Council from 1898–1904 and Llanycrwys Parish Council from 1910–13, he, like others, had no specific Liberal party label affiliation. His scrapbooks show his interest in politics in general. They also show his retention of election literature in relation to his uncle Jenkin Jenkins and of some general election campaigns. The Cardiganshire constituency returned a Liberal Member of Parliament continuously from

1880–1966. However, during the 1920s there was a split within the county between the coalition Liberals and the independent Liberals, with candidates from both groups contesting the seat in a by-election in 1921 and the general elections of 1922 and 1923. From 1923 to 1932 the county was represented by an independent Liberal. The minute book of the independent Liberals shows Dan's involvement with this group. The book dates from 1923 and first shows his attendance and membership of the executive committee of the county association in 1930, when he represented the Tregaron Union area. Also on the executive, was his cousin Mr J Lloyd of Pant, Llanddewibrefi. At this meeting Hopkin Morris MP spoke about the problem of unemployment and the efforts being made to introduce protectionism. After his speech, Dan Jenkins was the seconder of a vote of thanks. The minutes continued to show his membership of the executive through until October 1943. Sometimes the meetings of the association's Annual General Meeting (AGM) attracted attendances of over 250 people. At the time of his last recorded meeting, Dan had become a representative from the Aberaeron Union. At the December 1946 AGM, soon after his death, the minutes show a reference to the death of "stalwart Liberal Dan Jenkins of Pentrefelin".[3]

Promoting local activities

Some of Dan's local activities operated from Pentrefelin are recorded here. Others have already been included within some of the earlier chapters, such as his work at the National Eisteddfod, campaigns about the Welsh language, farm tenants' rights, St David's Day and many more. The items quoted are indicative of the large range of innovative and creative activities within which he was involved, extending over a large area, not only of west and mid Wales, but also further afield. Frequently we see him as, not only an active and energetic participant, but also as the driver, initiator or conduit for the action or change which is being considered and undertaken.

For instance, Christmas Day in 1900 saw a concert taking place at Felinfach Board School. Dan Jenkins was the adjudicator for singing, whilst others dealt with the spoken word. Competitive areas included soprano, literary pieces, solo for children, tenor solo, male voice, answering questions, wit, baritone solo, impromptu speech.[4]

A newspaper report of 1901 about Tal-sarn stated:

> By the efforts of Mr Daniel Jenkins, county councillor, the travelling dairy school of the county council, under the superintendence of Miss Thomas, UCW Aberystwyth, has visited this place and is available for the parishioners of Trefilan, Nantcwnlle and Gartheli. The school will be here for a fortnight, during which time lectures and demonstrations in butter making will be given. The pupils take great interest in their work and are making satisfactory progress. Fifty persons sent in their names to the committee, but only twelve could be accepted – six the first week and six the second.[5]

This activity would have arisen as a direct result of Dan's activity on the technical instruction committee of the county council.

In 1902, the *Cambrian News* reported Dan as the secretary of the Llangybi Eisteddfod committee and his holding a meeting of the 1895 Llangybi Eisteddfod committee at Llangybi Board School. It stated:

> He said that a sum of £15 was in the hands of the treasurer, and he had called them together to take steps for having the hearse as was first decided. After some discussion the secretary was directed to communicate with the parish councils of Llanfair Clydogau, Betws, Cellan and Gartheli, asking each to contribute a sum equal to a penny tax. A meeting is to be held next year. [6]

The precise nature and outcome of this initiative concerning the hearse is unknown.

In 1938 Dan, having researched the subject, gave a lecture on Kilsby to the Cymrodion Society in Aberystwyth. His retained newspaper cutting is shown below:

Also in 1938, long after his retirement, the people

CYMRODORION. — Mr. Dan Jenkins, Pentrefeiin addressed the Cymrodorion Society at Shiloh Schoolroom on Friday on "Kilsby." The lecture was most interesting and was one of the best delivered to the Society. Mr. J. O. Reese presided, and a vote of thanks was proposed by Mr. D. Evans, J.P., "Llanio," North-road, seconded by the Rev. John Evans, Cae'rgog.

Felinfach Dramatic Society
(source: Ifor Lloyd)

of the Twrch valley (Cwm Twrch), north of Ffarmers in Carmarthenshire, invited Dan as one of their speakers at the centenary celebrations for Saron Chapel (1838–1938).

The scrapbooks also show some involvement with the Felinfach Dramatic Society.

The *Cambrian News,* reporting the meeting of the Gartheli Parish Council on 13th May 1910, detailed discussion about drainage problems in the area and the need for a new wooden bridge over the river Meurig near the schoolroom. Under the heading 'Sarcastic' it went on to say:

> The following letter was read from Mr Daniel Jenkins, Pentrefelin, Felinfach, addressed to the Tregaron Sanitary Authority (if any!): 'I beg to call your immediate attention to a nuisance on the roadside between Maesyfelin and Llundenfach. It has been here for a month and is dangerous to public health. I do not question your officers' attention to duty, but I have my scruples as to the efficiency of a public body which has authority, but has not the courage to enforce it.' (Laughter.) The medical officer said the question had been under consideration before. There was a difficulty as to the disposal of the refuse owing to the blockage of the outlets. The county council denied liability for the pipes which had been laid down. The matter was deferred for further information.[7]

Connections with the Dolaucothi estate and mansion

After he had retired and left Llanycrwys, Dan continued to maintain his contact and friendship with the Dolaucothi family through Lady Elizabeth, the remaining Hills-Johnes (who celebrated her ninetieth birthday in April 1919). Dolaucothi mansion was a very large house by comparison with most in the north Carmarthenshire area. It had 26 rooms and in 1911 employed seven live-in house servants, plus numerous others on the estate as gamekeepers and coachmen. Sadly the building has now been demolished, though the estate is owned by the National Trust.

Dan retained a letter which she wrote to him in 1922. The letter indicates a formally correct, but easy, personal relationship, which also includes a reference to his family at Pentrefelin:

> Dear Mr Jenkins,
>
> Only a hurried line, to show you that I have not forgotten you. I was asked by little lady for the enclosed the same time as your friend Mr Evans. So when you feel the need for a bit of sport [shooting] pop over to DC [Dolaucothi], Mr Ross is here till the 22nd and Lady Evans [her husband's sister] and Miss Bertha [her husband's niece]. Our precious little lady is better but frail and the

weather is against her. When the weather will be kind enough to oblige us by turning a bit warmer, there will be more hope for her to pick up again.

How is all your dear ones, keeping fairly and yourself, I hope. All at DC are well and if they knew I was writing, there would be all kind of messages sent to Mr Jenkins and always a warm welcome from my dear servant and kind little lady down to the kitchen maid.

With kind regards,

Always,

your little friend Elizabeth.[8]

Clearly all the estate staff knew him and had a warm and kindly regard towards him. Lady Elizabeth was 92 or 93 years of age when she wrote the letter. Her "little lady" could well have been the elder of her two lady's maids, Anne Margaretta Down, a single woman of 63 in 1911. Apart from visiting, it seems likely that Dan did travel to Dolaucothi to stay for a while during the summer time and use the extensive library the family possessed.

A newspaper cutting in one of Dan's scrapbooks refers to an article which he wrote for the newspaper *Cymru,* about Dolaucothi and Lady Hills-Johnes.

Farming at Pentrefelin

Pentrefelin was a key part of Dan's life. Its importance cannot be overstated, even though until his retirement in 1920, his presence was discontinuous. The farm was regarded by visitors and general observers as a model of good practice.

After leaving teaching, Dan planted apple orchards and extended his beekeeping activities. He also experimented with new forms of grass seed. He developed it according to the most modern information.[9] In March 1922, correspondence shows him communicating with the Welsh Plant Breeding Station at Aberystwyth, with regard to a seeds mixture experiment which they, and he, were conducting.[10] In older age Dan and Elizabeth were supported on the farm by their son Jonathan (Jack).

Family and friends
Dan Jenkins' scrapbooks

'The Bag of the Saints'

Yr Ymofynnydd (The Inquirer), the monthly magazine of the South Wales Unitarian Society, carried an article in 1963 by D Jacob Davies, minister at Alltyblaca, which focused on Dan's scrapbooks or, 'Bag of Saints' as he called them. He wrote: "These books contained a near endless collection of interesting information, old letters, autographs of famous people, stamps, local verses of poetry, as well as all kinds of trivia and local anecdotes."

I confirm the existence of the 'Bag of Saints'. They are a superb repository of detail of Dan's extensive range of interests: farming, education, politics, society, language, newspapers and family. The pieces he kept and stuck into his scrapbooks fall into four main types: press cuttings from the *Cambrian News, Welshman, Welsh Gazette, Carmarthen Journal, South Wales Daily News, Daily Mail* and *Schoolmaster*. Secondly, letters; thirdly: handwritten words of poetry, songs and sayings; and fourthly: historic notices publicising an event or activity. Some items are in Welsh and others in English.

A lot of the press cuttings are articles relating to him, or campaigns in which he was involved, such as widening the use of the Welsh language and recording the poetry and songs of the 19th century before they were lost. Some are pieces which he almost certainly wrote and had published, but because these did not carry an author's name, we cannot be sure which he did pen and which he did not. He also retained an extensive

Pentrefelin family c.1910

Dan Jenkins' scrapbooks

Jack Jenkins, crossing the river Aeron

(source: Aeron Jenkins)

range of newspaper articles dealing with the Second World War, including many of the leading cartoons of the time. As the *Ymofynnydd* reported:

> His list of autographs included nearly all the nation's greats of his period and include: Llewelyn Williams, Towyn Jones MP, Dr Joseph Parry, Tom John MP, Eos Morlais, Watcyn Wyn, and one of D Emlyn Evans' tunes in his own handwriting has been pasted into a volume. There is a letter shedding light on how one of our oldest folk songs was discovered – 'Elisa Talysarn'. The author of the letter is David Thomas. All sorts of useful things were placed in the Saints' Bag when he went on a pilgrimage and it is obvious that the old saint of a teacher believed in the custom of keeping all sorts of equipment and tools.[11]

Chapel attendance

Dan was a deacon at Tynygwndwn chapel, just south of Talsarn; he and Elizabeth would travel there by pony and trap on a Sunday.

Fiftieth Wedding Anniversary

Family photograph

Dan Jenkins' scrapbooks

The *Welsh Gazette* reported on the golden wedding anniversary of Dan and Elizabeth in October 1936 stating:

> The event has aroused much interest in the district, as Mr and Mrs Jenkins have spent all their married life in the locality and are firmly established in the hearts of their neighbours.

On a personal note, the paper reported that since his retirement, Dan Jenkins still slept in the room where he was born. The *Gazette* stated:

> While Mrs Jenkins has applied herself with all the diligence of a good wife and mother to matters of the home, Mr Jenkins has taken a keen and practical interest in the public and social life. An ardent Welshman, he has a special liking for Welsh music and literature. A fine raconteur, he is always an interesting figure on the National Eisteddfod field among a group of friends, discussing literary topics.[12]

Such was the importance of the couple in Welsh-language and cultural circles that the poet Wil Ifan composed and sent them a special poem.

The anniversary event drew a large attendance at Pentrefelin. Dan kept a visitor's book to record the day. Some 138 people from all over Wales, and some family members from England, signed the book.

Visits to Pentrefelin

Over the 26 years following Dan's retirement, many people who were involved in the world of politics, culture, the arts, farming or education, visited Pentrefelin and signed what has been described as an impressive, but now unfortunately missing visitor's book. Some wrote news pieces about their visit.

Tramps were regular callers at the farm seeking refreshment and work. Daughter Elin has written on the back of the photograph shown below: "Dic Baxter (cutting trees), gentleman of the road as father used to refer to tramps when they signed the visitor's book. Father and a friend looking on."

Dic Baxter and friend with Dan Jenkins
(source: Ifor Lloyd)

At a time when Dan was unwell in 1939, a journalist wrote following a visit:

> I called to see Dan Jenkins, Pentrefelin; he had had an attack and had not been well, but is now a little better:
>
> This is another world,
> World of the eisteddfod,
> World of the singing,
> World of the Llanycrwys school concerts,
> World of the Welsh magazines,
> World of the gardens and bees,
> World of the old things.
> The attack could not steal his blush or his spirit.[13]

In the year prior to being unwell, when he was for a time transported around the farm site by Elizabeth in a wheelchair, he had spent some time taking the waters at the health spa of Llanwrtyd Wells in Breconshire. His scrapbooks show receipts for 20th September 1938 and 26th September 1938, for board and lodging and a weekly ticket for the pump house.

Family links

The Jenkins family was large, with seven adult children (after the death of daughter Anne 1887–1915), many grandchildren and a multiplicity of cousins, nephews and nieces, plus family members of the Williams and Richards families from Llanfair Clydogau. There was a strong tradition of the use of the names of older family members when christening a child. For instance, the *Cambrian News* of September 1945 reported the arrival home from Germany of "Captain Daniel Jenkins Davies, son of Mr D Edwards Davies of Highgate, London and grandson of Mr and Mrs Daniel Jenkins of Pentrefelin. He has been engaged in some of the fiercest battles of the war and has been mentioned in despatches several times."[14]

Another important family link for Dan was with his American cousins. As described, two of his father's brothers had emigrated to the United States and Dan's scrapbooks and newspaper cuttings show his frequent correspondence with their families. He retained a large number of the envelopes of the post he received from the USA, including the stamps. Letters which he retained in the scrapbooks came from Blanche Chamberlain, Bangor, Wisconsin and Anna M Jenkins, supervising teacher of rural schools, Bangor, Wisconsin, Thomas E Jenkins, Daniel E Morgan of Cleveland, Ohio, and Mrs M J Jenkins of Rockland, Wisconsin. The *Bangor Independent* reported in 1937 that Dan had undertaken a long correspondence with Mrs Blanche Chamberlain and an Auntie Jenkins (his cousin), and that it was recently his fiftieth wedding anniversary. It stated: "relatives met at the home in goodly numbers. The couple received 53 telegrams and 84 letters of congratulation." The article reported that the editor was to send a copy of the *Bangor Independent* to "Dan Jenkins and his good wife who have kept the matrimonial ship right side up for many years".[15]

A letter from Auntie Mary Jenkins of Bangor, Wisconsin, in March 1907, shows Dan corresponding with her about not only the Cerngoch book, but also the death of his uncle, who was her brother-in-law, Jenkin Jenkins. She asks him "Who is ap Ceredigion whose picture is in the book?" She recounts her memories of life at Blaenplwyf: "The gatherings around the wide old fireplace were very enjoyable and brother Jenkin was always genial with a good vein of wit and good common sense which drew out the best that was in people. I felt a high respect for him."[16]

Another letter within Dan's scrapbooks is from April 1937, from Daniel E Morgan, Law Office, Cleveland, Ohio. He enclosed a press cutting from the *Oak Hill,* Ohio's newspaper, with an article showing how St David's Day was celebrated at a dinner in the town, by Welsh settlers from the Llangeitho area of Cardiganshire: "Nearly all the early settlers from Sir Aberteifi in and around Oak Hill, Ohio, were known generally, not by their surnames but by the farms from which they emigrated – this still continues to a considerable degree."[17]

Family recollections

Daniel Davies (grandson)

"When I was a boy living with my parents in London, I had a constant longing to return one day to Cardiganshire where I spent many happy times on my grandparents' farm in the vale of Aeron. As soon as the school holidays arrived, my father and mother, and my two sisters and I, would pack into the car and drive out of London at the crack of dawn, bound for the land we adored.

"I used to laugh when the local people said that the vale of Aeron vied with the vale of Clwyd as the most beautiful valley in Wales. But it was. In summer it was indeed a paradise for us grandchildren staying with our grandparents. I would spend days fishing in the river Aeron with my cousins in this valley which also had orchards and apple trees laden with fruit and honey bees gathering honey for our tea.

"In this lovely place beauty blended with poetry and legend. This was the land of Cerngoch, the Robbie Burns of

Cardiganshire; Idwal Jones, the dramatist and humorist; Nans o'r Glyn, the fabulous racehorse; not forgetting also the sojourn of Dylan Thomas during the war."[18]

(Written in 1975 by Daniel Davies, formerly employed by the Ministry of Agriculture.)

Mary Davies, née Hughes (granddaughter)

Mary was born in Southall, London in 1922 and the family later returned to Wales. After completing her education in Carmarthen, she trained and became a children's nurse. Mary now lives in Nantwich, Cheshire. She recalls going to Pentrefelin with her parents in their Humber car every other Sunday and spending time with her grandparents. She told me: "He was much taller than his wife. He had a real presence about him. At the meal table the grace was always said: 'for what we are about to receive'." She recalled him being keen on peace and respect for the Lord's Day, reminding the children that it was Sunday. "The parlour was his office and you were not allowed to touch anything; there were documents and papers in abundance. He was always writing." She remembers that her grandparents were lovely, good-living people. Her grandmother ran the farm which had a number of milking cows; she also made butter. "At 4.00 p.m. every day, Dan would go out to collect the eggs. He did not have a car but instead drove a pony and trap."

Mary Davies, granddaughter of Dan Jenkins (2010)

Evan Lloyd (grandson)

Evan remembers going to the farm and the welcoming nature of his grandparents. He also recalls his grandfather's enthusiasm for writing and the advice he gave his grandson to "always keep a dictionary near at hand". Evan Lloyd's photograph is taken from his time as an international concert singer who has had appearances on S4C, as well as BBC television and radio. He was born in London of a very musical family. He won a number of important awards at major eisteddfodau and other musical festivals. He also won the prestigious Blue Riband at the National Eisteddfod and was then accepted by Covent Garden. Today, he runs Lloyd's Motors in Aberaeron, Ceredigion.

Evan Lloyd (grandson)

Sixtieth Wedding Anniversary

Dan and Elizabeth Jenkins celebrated their diamond wedding anniversary on 29th October 1946, a short time before Dan's ninetieth birthday on 7th November. They held a large celebratory event for family and friends at Pentrefelin. The *Welsh Gazette* reported on both the events. Dan was described as "tall and upright, his hair, moustache and beard naturally white". His wife was described as "like her husband, she is very active, attending to household duties daily". As a teacher, "at all the schools he proved himself to be the ideal schoolmaster,

Diamond Wedding Anniversary
Dan Jenkins' scrapbooks

beloved by parents and children alike. Sincere, original, with a high sense of duty, he instilled into the children a love for knowledge, and there are many in responsible positions throughout the country who owe much to his thorough training."

The *Gazette* continued:

> It can be truly said that there is no one in Cardiganshire, exactly like Dan Jenkins, Pentrefelin and to quote Sarnicol who wrote in 1933, 'Wales should be grateful for such sons as the one born on Tal-sarn fair night... more of his calibre are wanted in Wales'. The anniversary day was a busy one. The newspaper stated: "numerous relatives and friends were entertained to tea, and conspicuous on the table was an iced cake inscribed '1886–1946' made by Mrs Olwen Evans, their daughter. About 50 telegrams of congratulation were received and a shoal of letters. Among the telegrams was one sent by the monarch's private secretary, which read: 'The King and Queen send you heartiest congratulations and good wishes on your diamond wedding day'. Gwladys Evans, a granddaughter, wired from Cairo. From Frankfurt, Dilys wired 'Congratulations and love. Many more years together.'[19]

Death of Dan Jenkins

Sadly, the hope of more years together was not fulfilled. Dan enjoyed his ninetieth birthday on 7th November and appeared well. The poet Isfoel wrote him a special birthday poem:

> God will not take Dan Jenkins to heaven –
> from amongst his bees and hives;
> Until he dies let him stay
> With his honey and his apple trees.[20]

However, he died a few days later on the 18th of the month. His death certificate describes the cause of death as "acute heart failure". The *Cambrian News* referred to his horse-drawn gambo, lined with green, taking his mortal remains to be laid to rest in Abermeurig cemetery. "He was a well-known figure with a large circle of friends in every sphere of Welsh life."[21]

The inscription on the grave, which is in Abermeurig Methodist Chapel cemetery, reads as:

> Teacher he was, and through his day
> a straight line was his religion
> She, likewise, their renown
> sincerity shall live, blessed pair.

Cledlyn

Dan Jenkins' funeral cortège
(source: Aeron Jenkins)

Mrs. Dan Jenkins and Family

are profoundly grateful for all the comforting messages which have reached them in their bereavement, caused by the loss of one so greatly loved and admired by all who knew him.

Pentrefelin
Llundainfach
Lampeter

November, 1946

Acknowledgement card from the family

Ceredigion Archives

Grave at Abermeurig Cemetery

(source: Aeron Jenkins)

Obituary

Following his death, the *Welsh Gazette* published quite a long obituary about Dan:

> Mr Jenkins was one of the best known men in mid Cardiganshire and west Carmarthenshire, having been school master in turn in Cilcennin, Llanfair Clydogau and Llanycrwys, and having many interests outside his school environment. Of a farming stock, he retained his connection with agriculture throughout his life.
>
> In the spheres within which he lived and worked, Mr Jenkins did much to create and deepen interest in folklore. His old scholars may forget the things they learned at school, but the love of Welsh culture and the Welsh way of life, which he planted in them, is likely to remain with them as long as they live. Their penmanship should also be faultless for Mr Jenkins' own handwriting was a model to admire, even at the age of 90. He had not been seen in the National Eisteddfod and the gorsedd circle for some years. Now organisations and movements nearer home will miss him – his chapel at Tynygwndwn, where he was a deacon, the Beekeepers' Association, the Welsh Cob and Pony Society, Lampeter Agricultural Society etc. Articles from Mr Jenkins' pen appeared in the *Welsh Gazette* from time to time and were read with much pleasure.[22]

After his death, Pentrefelin passed to his wife Elizabeth and his son Jonathan.

Chapter Eleven

Elizabeth Jenkins

Elizabeth Williams, *c.*1877 in London
(source: Gwyneth Jones)

IT WOULD BE unfair to produce a biography of Dan Jenkins without researching, analysing and commenting upon his matrimonial partner of 60 years. What was she like and how much did she contribute to the life and character of her husband? How much of the story attributable to him, is, in fact due in part to Elizabeth Jenkins?

The account in chapter three describes much of her early life in Llanfair Clydogau and the skills she acquired in terms of household and farm management. The 1881 census shows her as the eldest daughter of William Williams, in a farmhouse in which there lived seven other adults and teenagers.

Judgements about her life, especially those aspects to do with her public position and known social prominence, need to be set against the legal and societal circumstances for women in the latter years of the 19th and early 20th century. It was a period of great change, none more so than in relation to the role and position of women within United Kingdom society. Yet, though change was underway, women were only just beginning to move from a position of being totally subservient to men, to one in which they acquired rights. For instance, it wasn't until 1870, as a result of the Married Women's Property Act, that married women were allowed to keep money which they had earned. It wasn't until 1891, that women could not be forced to live with a husband unless they wished to. In an essay, 'The Subjection of Women', the renowned philosopher John Stuart Mill, described the position of women in Britain in the following terms: "We are continually told that Christianity has restored to the woman her just right. Meanwhile the wife is the actual bondservant of her husband; no less so, as far as the legal obligation goes, than slaves so called."[1]

Women also had no recognised position within the representative or political process. They had no right to vote until 1918, when every man over the age of 21 and every woman over the age of 30 was given this right. In 1928, the legal right to vote was given to every woman over the age of 21. Occupationally, women primarily worked in the home or as paid domestic servants.

As a consequence of these limitations upon women, we don't see Elizabeth working outside the home or read reported accounts of her engaging in public speaking, leading campaigns or writing to the press. Yet, her role was vital in co-running the family farm and supporting her husband with his multifarious activities.

Elizabeth was small in stature, certainly when alongside Dan. She made a tremendous contribution to the marriage. She spent over 34 years living apart from her husband for five days and nights each week during the school term. Hence, for a majority of that long period of time, she managed and operated the 80-acre Pentrefelin farm, of which he was initially the recognised tenant, and then later, the owner. Its success would to a large extent, be dependent upon her skills and enterprise. In the event, it flourished. In addition to all this, Elizabeth gave birth to ten children and had the joy of seeing eight of them survive through to adulthood.

She also supported her husband with his work as a headteacher in both Llanfair and Llanycrwys. The *Cambrian News* reported her helping with the provision and serving of refreshments at a pupils' tea party in Llanfair in 1894.[2] She was also an enthusiastic supporter of Dan's multiplicity of agricultural, social, cultural and political activities, whether they were being operated from Pentrefelin, from his lodgings in Llanfair or later, from his lodgings in Ffaldybrenin. He would not have been able to succeed in the way he did, or operate on the local, regional and national stage to the extent he did, without her active involvement, support and commitment.

A good overall description of part of her life is provided by one of the newspaper accounts of her and Dan's life which stated that the young girl "took on the challenge of responsibility at such a young age, with so much determination that her father was heard to say how well she attended to her duties in the home, organising the food, clothes and comforts for the family, as well as attending to the other duties on the farm". An unidentified newspaper article, after her death in 1951, wrote that at Pentrefelin:

> ... she soon showed that she had the knowledge, and was able to put into practice, all duties relating to the farm – inside and out – and was able to do so with much skill, punctuality and to a high standard. She had the ability to get her children and the servants to co-operate with her, as they believed that her way was the best. She was renowned for her organising and how she carried out her plans with ease. She hated waste and untidiness and as a result she kept Pentrefelin in such a way that was admired by all who called in... She brought up her children according to God's philosophy and education, emphasising the things that count in life. As a neighbour, she was respected by everyone and was noted for her readiness to help others; there was no end to her sympathy for those in need.

Elizabeth Williams c.1881
(source: Gwyneth Jones)

A newspaper report in *Y Cymro*[3] reporting her diamond wedding anniversary said: "on their first day of marriage, they agreed to continue with their own occupations. That is, the wife would farm at Pentrefelin, work she did with skill and success, and the husband would continue as a school master – Llanfair Clydogau and Llanycrwys (the latter for over 20 years) before retiring much respected."

There must have been an amicable division of labour. On Saturdays, he would organise and supervise the farm work, the orchard and the apiary. He was well before his time as an orchard owner and a beekeeper.

A real time insight into life at the farm is provided by the *Welsh Gazette*[4] in 1936, which published a major article entitled, 'A visit to Pentrefelin' which focused upon the farm and the different roles of Elizabeth and Dan. It stated:

> One only has to stand the other side of the river Aeron – on the Abermeurig side – to see that the place looks as if it has been placed neatly and in an organised fashion in the middle of the pretty valley. Not only does the land show signs of good use of manure, but the neat hedges, the well kept shrubs and the cluster of trees, planted here and there, symbolise the artist. It is probable that the artist was Dan Jenkins, but I secretly believe that Mrs Jenkins looked after the land and the farm. It is one thing to be an artist but another to breed store cattle for the market at Ystrad. Yes, it is one matter to plant trees and dahlias along the cowshed walls, but it is another to feed and milk the cows.

The article went on that the different actions of the two of them indicated that there was:

> Mrs Jenkins buying and selling [animals] and the husband in his literature, planting trees, building walls, organising the yard and painting gates, and his son [Jack] tending to the land. And there we have the three: merchant, thinker and cultivator. 'Archdruid of the Field' as the poet Wil Ifan calls him at the Eisteddfod, but the 'supervisor of the field' at Pentrefelin is his wife.

The author of this article (D J Morgan) went on:

> It is not required this evening to make the link between the old Ffaldybrenin headmaster and his literary work, nor that time I played the part of Twm Siôn Cati, on his school stage years ago. No, he must stand in front of me this evening only as a farmer, as the man of the potatoes, mangolds, hay and animals, and he must bow to the shrewd, busy little lady by his side. They have been together 50 years and even though the two of them are remarkably lively and agile, I think I would back her 2:1 for the 'hundred yards' today.

The writer goes on to make the distinction between the school and the farm:

> To help you understand it all, Dan Jenkins was a headmaster. That is what is responsible for the trees, the flowers, the bees, the gates, the vegetable patch, the cluster of trees and the square dunghill. What (rather than who) is responsible for the stock, the green grass and the hay, the sow and her piglets? Oh, Mrs Jenkins, and of the children raised there. One at school and the other on the farm;

> and the school and the farm are evident at Pentrefelin, the artist and the farmer. In the house, we find a kitchen and a study – a crock and a book.

Over a time span of 21 years, Elizabeth gave birth to her ten children. Sadly in 1894, Gwilym died aged 11 months, followed a year later by the death of Dilys aged 14 months. As recounted, the children were: Anne, Griffith, Kitty, Gwilym, Dilys, Anna, Ivor, Olwen, Jonathan (Jack) and Elin. Seven of the children saw their parents' golden and diamond wedding anniversaries and the death of first their father and then later their mother.

An unnamed friend sent a memorial poem in Welsh to Elizabeth and Dan upon the death of their son Gwilym Gwallter Jenkins in 1894. A translation of the first part of a long piece which refers to the sadness of the child's death, heaven and an idle harp is shown below:

The Idle Harp

Amidst the blessed choirs
High in the paradise of the land of song,
There was an idle harp
That no one could play.
Despite the excellence of angels
When playing 'For Him',
They couldn't play the harp
Sitting idle in heaven.

It was necessary to call one home
From the families on earth,
To play the idle harp
In front of the large throne,
A blessed angel was summoned
Down to our land,
To look for a harpist
To play its beloved strings.

(translated by Gwyneth Jones) (ref 2)

Her children were a joy to her and she took a great pride in their growth and progress through life. Her two youngest daughters are shown overleaf in about 1908.

Olwen and Elin
Dan Jenkins' scrapbooks

Dan's scrapbooks contain a poem written by Elizabeth upon the marriage of a grandchild:

Matrimonial congratulations to Mr and Mrs Peter Stanne by their grandma Mrs E Jenkins, Pentrefelin:

For Mr and for Mrs Stanne
I wish you all the best I can –
Long life, and health, let be your share,
Without a sorrow to impair.

Your grandma wishes you happy life –
Without a quarrel, grief, or strife:
Place wisdom daily on its throne,
And love to keep affairs in tone.

May fortune daily to you bring
Some pleasant cause for you to sing:
May the Almighty daily pour
On you his blessings in galore.

The hospitality at Pentrefelin was of a high order. Visiting was encouraged and people were made very welcome. In addition, for more than 60 years it was home, both to the children she

Dan and Elizabeth Jenkins
(source: Aeron Jenkins)

raised, and to the numerous grandchildren who returned for family calls or children's holidays. The *Cambrian News* reported:

> Pentrefelin is home from home for their friends when on visits. A courteous welcome is extended to all who call, rich and poor alike, as provided by the visitor's book kept by Mr Jenkins. Among the 2,000 entries are: Elfed, Crwys, Eurig, Prof. W J Griffiths MP and Sir D O Evans. None the less welcome are the casuals who call for food and shelter, which is never refused. Among them was Robert Ball, who, when asked to put his address after his name on the visitor's book, wrote 'On the Road'. Another, Robert Williams wrote: 'On Tramp'.[5]

Elizabeth was a widow for just over four years. She died of broncho-pneumonia, on 12th January 1951, at the age of 88, whilst staying with her daughter Anna Hughes and family at Inglenook, Flecknoe near Rugby, Warwickshire. At this time Pentrefelin was run by her son Jonathan (Jack).

Following his death in 1976, the farm became the home of his son Aeron, who married Glenys in 1980. It continues today

Aeron Jenkins outside Pentrefelin, 2010

Elizabeth Jenkins with Jackie Armitage husband of her granddaughter Myfanwy

Dan Jenkins' scrapbooks

to be the largest dairy farm in the Aeron valley. Aeron and Glenys have four sons: Eurig, Irfon, Elfed and Rhys, with the two eldest sons, working on the farm. The Pentrefelin Jenkins family's male line remains strongly to the fore in that Dan's great-grandson Eurig also has two sons Hedd and Arawn. Recently another great-grandson, Elfed has become a father to a son called Dion.

Pentrefelin with all its memories was the home base for Dan Jenkins. The importance of the farm to him, and he to it, is seen by the two inscriptions containing his name on the walls of the buildings. It is a place steeped in history, with direct line male members of the Jenkins family in residence for almost 200 years. It is the place where the scrapbooks which were assembled to record and describe Cardiganshire and Welsh society were compiled. It is the place where Dan welcomed, entertained and offered hospitality to visitors. It is the place where he read, researched and wrote as part of his many interests and communications. It is the place which helped provide his very foundation, but also which gave him a secure base for his long, successful and innovative life.

Notes

Chapter 1

1 Bethan Phillips: *Pity the Swagman*, p.8, Cymdeithas Lyfrau Ceredigion, 2002.
2 Bethan Phillips op cit.
3 William Evans: *Diary of a Welsh Swagman 1869–1894.*
4 *Welsh Gazette* newspaper.
5 Myfanwy Armitage, granddaughter of Dan Jenkins, unpublished paper on family history.

Chapter 2

1 *Welshman* newspaper, 1936.
2 Holt Academy documents, MSS NLW.
3 *Cerddi Ysgol Llanycrwys*, 1934.
4 Alan Leech: *Llanfair Clydogau: History of a Cardiganshire Parish*, 2008.
5 Bangor University Archives, email from archivist 2010.
6 Myfanwy Armitage, op cit.
7 *Cynnydd Llanbedr Pont Steffan*, ap Tulas, MSS NLW.
8 Ben A Jones: *Y Byd o Ben Trichrug,* 1959, p.82.
9 *Cilcennin School Centenary Publication,* Ceredigion Archives.
10 Ben A Jones.
11 Myfanwy Armitage, op cit.
12 Cilcennin, op cit.
13 *Cambrian News,* 22/10/1936.
14 Ieuan Gwynedd Jones in *Transactions of the Cardiganshire Antiquarian Society* Vol. 5, 1967.
15 Ieuan Gwynedd Jones, op cit.

Chapter 3

1 Capel Mair: Cyfrol y Jiwbili, 1926.
2 *Cyfrol y Jiwbili* op cit.
3 Llanfair Clydogau School logbook, Ceredigion Archives.
4 Myfanwy Armitage, op cit.
5 Myfanwy Armitage, op. cit.

6 *Cambrian News*, November 1886.
7 *Cardiganshire in Modern Times,* Vol. 3, p.553.
8 *Cerddi Ysgol Llanycrwys*, 1934.
9 logbook, op cit.
10 *Cyfrol y Jiwbili,* op cit.
11 Islwyn Walters, conversation, June 2010.
12 *Cyfrol y Jiwbili,* op cit.
13 *Cambrian News*, March 1894.
14 Alan and Sally Leech: *Struggle for survival in the Cardiganshire Hills*, 2009.
15 *Cambrian News*, September 1894.
16 Jenkins family, recollections.
17 *Cambrian News*, May 1894.
18 *Cambrian News*, August 1894.
19 *Cambrian News,* 5/3/1897.
20 Dan Jenkins' scrapbooks.
21 *Cambrian News*, August 1897.
22 *Cambrian News,* 23/8/1897.
23 *Welsh Gazette*, 25/8/1897.
24 *The Schoolmaster*, 4/9/1897.
25 School logbook, op cit.
26 *Cyfrol y Jiwbili,* op. cit.
27 *Welsh Gazette*, 26/1/1955.
28 *The Schoolmaster,* December 1898.

Chapter 4

1 *Cambrian News*, 1/7/1898.
2 Letter to Dan Jenkins, 16/2/1916.
3 Letter to Dan Jenkins, 7/2/1904.
4 Joan Stacey, *History of Neuadd Bro Fana and the Community of Ffarmers and Ffaldybrenin,* (2007).
5 Elfyn Davies, *History of Neuadd Bro Fana*, op cit.
6 *Cerddi Ysgol Llanycrwys,* op cit.
7 *Carmarthen Journal*, 19/2/1904.
8 *The Welshman,* 1910.
9 *Carmarthen Journal*, 1904.
10 *History of Neuadd Bro Fana*, op cit.

11 *Cambrian News,* 20/10/1905.
12 *Carmarthen Journal,* August 1904.
13 *Cambrian News,* 28/12/1899.
14 *Cambrian News,* 16/2/1900.

Chapter 5

1 D Islwyn Edwards, *Cerddi Cerngoch,* 1994.
2 Bethan Phillips, op cit.
3 *Western Mail,* June 1904.
4 *South Wales Daily News,* August 1905.
5 *Cambrian News,* 30/3/1894.
6 William Evans, op cit.
7 William Evans, op cit.
8 *Western Mail,* October 1892.

Chapter 6

1 *Cambrian News,* 1926.
2 Carmarthenshire County Council, 15/1/1934.
3 *The Welshman,* June 1934.
4 *Cambrian News,* October 1936.
5 *The Welshman,* October 1946.
6 Islwyn Walters provided the letter in 2010.

Chapter 7

1 *Western Mail,* 19/5/1933.
2 W W Price: Biographical Index, NLW.
3 *Ibid.*
4 Jeffrey and Jeffrey 1918, *Souvenier of the Welsh Division.*
5 *Welshman* newspaper, October 1936.
6 *Daily Mail,* October 1936.
7 *Cambrian News,* November 1929.
8 *Transactions of the Cardiganshire Antiquarian Society,* Vol. XI, 1936.
9 *Welsh Gazette,* 18/7/1946.
10 Dylan Williams, Gomer Publishers, letter of 2010 to the author.
11 *Western Mail,* 19/9/1945.
12 *Cambrian News,* 20/10/1899.
13 *Cambrian News,* 8/6/1900.

14 *Cambrian News*, 3/8/1900.
15 *South Wales Daily News*, 26/8/1905.
16 *The Welshman*, 7/9/1916.
17 *Cerddi Ysgol Llanycrwys*, p.145.
18 *The Welshman*, March 1913.
19 NLW Manuscript.
20 *Aberdare Leader*, 1/2/1913.

Chapter 8

1 *Cambrian News*, 21/2/1896.
2 *Ibid.*
3 *Cambrian News*, September 1898.
4 Myfanwy Lloyd recollection, July 2010.
5 *Western Mail*, 18/12/1914.
6 *Cambrian News*, 5/1/1945.
7 *The Welshman*, January 1945.
8 *Cambrian News*, 4/3/1898.
9 Jenkin Jenkins letter, 9/3/1904.
10 Dan Jenkins' scrapbooks, unknown source.
11 Dan Jenkins' scrapbooks, letter, 25 August 1945

Chapter 9

1 Letters to Dan Jenkins taken from his scrapbooks.
2 Letter to Dan Jenkins from NUT, 30 June 1898.
3 *Cambrian News*, unknown date, 1905.
4 Letter from editor of *Welsh Gazette*, 17 July 1946.
5 Letter to Dan Jenkins, scrapbooks, 6 December 1937.
6 Dan Jenkins' scrapbooks.
7 Letter from W R Hall to Dan Jenkins, 18 June 1935, MSS NLW.

Chapter 10

1 *Cambrian News*, June 1913.
2 *Cambrian News*, summer 1900.
3 MSS in NLW.
4 *Cambrian News*, 28/12/1900.
5 *Cambrian News*, 2/8/1901.
6 *Cambrian News*, 10/1/1902.

7 *Cambrian News*, May 1910.

8 Letter from Elizabeth Hills-Johnes, 5 April 1922, Dan Jenkins' scrapbook.

9 *Yr Ymofynnydd*, August 1963.

10 Dan Jenkins' scrapbooks.

11 *Yr Ymofynnydd*, August 1963.

12 *Welsh Gazette*, October 1936.

13 Dan Jenkins' scrapbooks, unknown source.

14 *Cambrian News*, September 1945.

15 Dan Jenkins' scrapbooks.

16 Dan Jenkins' scrapbooks.

17 Dan Jenkins' scrapbooks.

18 Notes held by Eleri Davies.

19 *Welsh Gazette*, October 1946.

20 Dan Jenkins' scrapbooks.

21 *Cambrian News*, November 1946.

22 *Welsh Gazette*, 21/11/1946.

Chapter 11

1 John Stuart Mill essay: 'The Subjection of Women' (1869).

2 *Cambrian News*, September 1894.

3 *Y Cymro*, 8/11/1946.

4 *Welsh Gazette*, 5/11/1936.

5 *Cambrian News*, October 1946.

Poems in the original Welsh

Ref 1
Pa beth yw'r gallu hwnw
Sy'n gwneuthur dau yn un
Gerbren yr hwn y gwelir myrdd
O gewri'n plygu glin?
Mae'n fflamio yn y llygad
Gwna'r wyneb prudd yn llon
Mae'n chwareu ar y wefus fwyn
Ymwea trwy y fron?

Pwy draetha pa beth ydyw?
Mae fel rhyw drydan byw, –
Ateba Dan a Lizzie 'nawr
Mai gallu cariad yw;
Pwy all roi gwell esboniad
Ar air mor llawn o dân?
Mae'r ddau'n awdurdod ar y pwnc,
Mae'r ddau'n teilyngu cân.

O fown i fodrwy cariad,
Y gwelaf fab a merch,
A'u calon yn glymedig gan
Arianaidd rwymau serch;
Gall Dan roi solo heddyw
Mewn cywair llon i gyd,
Gorchfygodd gyda rhian dlos,
Enillodd sedd ei bryd.

Meddianed mwy ei chalon,
A hithau'i galon ef,
A'r undeb fyddo'n undeb dan
Fendithiol wenau'r nef;
llwyddianus fyddo'ch gyrfa,
A hono'n yrfa faith,
A'r nefoedd – cartref cariad pur –

Gorono ben eich taith.
Gwyn-wenau a byd gwanwynol – lanwo
Arluniau'ch dyfodol,
A seiriau heulwen siriol, – fyddo rhi
I Dan a'i Lizzie hyd Eden Iwysol.

Carolan

Ref 2

Y Delyn Segur

Ym mhlith y côrau dedwydd
Fry ngwynfa gwlad y gân
Roedd yno Delyn segur
Nas medrai neb ei chân
Er gwyched yw'r angylion
Am chwareu 'Iddo Ef'
Nis medrent ganu'r Delyn
Oedd segur yn y nef.

Rhaid ydoedd cael un adref
O deulu llwch y llawr
I chwareu'r Delyn segur
O flaen yr orsedd fawr
Ac angel gwyn a wysiwyd
I lawr i'n daear ni
I chwilio am delynydd
I chwareu'i Nhannau Cu.

Index

H

I

J

K

L

M

N

O

P

R

S

T

U

V

W

Other books by Alan Leech:

Llanfair Clydogau:
History of a Cardiganshire Parish (2008)

Struggle for Survival in the Cardiganshire Hills (2009)
(co-written with his wife, Sally)

Also from Y Lolfa:

£8.95

y Lolfa
A Very Small Corner of
Paradise
The Story of Llanllŷr: a Garden in Wales
Loveday Lewes Gee

£6.95

y Lolfa

TALYBONT CEREDIGION CYMRU SY24 5HE
e-mail ylolfa@ylolfa.com
website www.ylolfa.com
phone (01970) 832 304
fax 832 782